STAN LEE

AND THE RISE AND FALL
OF THE AMERICAN COMIC BOOK

STAN LEE

AND THE RISE AND FALL
OF THE AMERICAN COMIC BOOK

BY
JORDAN RAPHAEL
AND
TOM SPURGEON

CHICAGO
REVIEW
PRESS

Library of Congress Cataloging-in-Publication Data

Raphael, Jordan.
Stan Lee and the rise and fall of the American comic book / by
Jordan Raphael and Tom Spurgeon.
       p.   cm.
    ISBN 1-55652-541-9 (paperback)
     1. Lee, Stan.   2. Cartoonists—United States—
Biography   I. Spurgeon, Tom, 1968–   II. Title.

   PN6727.L39Z88   2003
   741.5'092—dc21   2003004378

Cover art: Jeff Wong
Cover design: Todd Petersen
Interior design: Pamela Juárez

Published by Chicago Review Press, Incorporated
814 North Franklin Street
Chicago, Illinois 60610
ISBN 1-55652-541-9
Printed in the United States of America
5 4 3 2 1

For Stan

CONTENTS

INTRODUCTION AND ACKNOWLEDGMENTS

Stan Lee is one of the most important figures in American popular culture. He is also one of the least understood. To the general public, Lee is the face of Marvel Comics, the creator of Spider-Man, the X-Men, the Fantastic Four, and hundreds of other colorful heroes. To comic-book aficionados, he is a notable player in the history of comics whose artistic legacy is the subject of a furious and long-running debate. Lee is renowned variously as a dazzling writer, a skilled editor, a prodigious talent, a relentless self-promoter, a credit hog, and a huckster—a man equal parts P. T. Barnum and Walt Disney.

Here is the truth about Stan Lee: he didn't create Spider-Man or any of Marvel's most famous characters. He *cocreated* them. The distinction matters, because in that distinction lies the essence of his considerable accomplishments. Contrary to his media image, Lee's greatest achievement wasn't in superhero invention but in his clever revamping of an outdated genre. Working with a team of virtuoso illustrators, many of them idiosyncratic square pegs in the round holes of a simpleminded children's entertainment medium, Lee unleashed a legion of characters that rank among the most enduring fantasy icons in a cultural landscape soaked with imaginative contenders. Three generations of young people read Marvel comics under bedroom covers, traded them with friends, and stored them in plastic. Now, four decades since its humble beginnings, Marvel is hitting its stride as a wellspring for motion pictures, TV shows, and major licensing efforts. Big-budget movies spawned from Lee's cocreations crowd the cineplexes; 2003 alone saw the release of *X2: X-Men United*, *The Hulk*, and *Daredevil*. The sequel to the box-office smash *Spider-Man* was released in 2004.

Stan Lee is one of the central characters in the history of the American comic book. Lee was there near the beginning, when comics exploded onto newsstands with a burst of garish costumes and crudely drawn supermen and -women. He stuck around during the postwar boom years, toiling as a journeyman writer and editor, and, in the 1960s, helped revitalize the medium after it had grown stale. Even today, in his eighties, Lee remains a figure of consequence in what remains of the comic-book industry, if only on the sidelines—a Grand Old Man to a marginal art form.

Stan Lee became a public figure at age thirty-eight and never stepped away from his place in the spotlight. He is certainly the most famous person ever to have worked the majority of his life in comic books. But a satisfactory account of his life and artistic career has been sorely missing. This book is our attempt to remedy the problem. Through exclusive interviews with Lee and many of his former associates, an examination of rare archival material, including unpublished private letters and Hollywood scripts, and analysis of his comics oeuvre, *Stan Lee and the Rise and Fall of the American Comic Book* aims to set the record straight. It is at once a professional history, an appreciation, and a critical exploration of Stan "The Man" Lee and his contributions to popular culture.

A project like this one owes many debts to many people. The authors would like to thank all of the artists, writers, and friends of Stan Lee who agreed to be interviewed for the book. Your reminiscences and insights were invaluable, and we hope we did them justice. Special thanks are due to: Jim Amash, Dr. Michael J. Vassallo, Blake Bell, Robert Beerbohm, Eileen O'Farrell, Randy Scott, Mike Kelly, Denis Kitchen, Gus Mastrapa, Harvey Botwin, Andrei Molotiu, and Bob Levin for research assistance; the fine folks at the University of Wyoming's American Heritage Center for their patience and help digging into the Stan Lee Archives; illustrator Jeff Wong for the exceptional cover art; John Miller at *Comics Buyer's Guide*; and Gary Groth, Mike Dean, and Milo George at *The Comics Journal*. We would also like to thank our agent, Jim Fitzgerald, and editor, Yuval Taylor, for making this book happen. And, finally, to our friends and family—Michele, Michael, Courtney, Raymond, Sally, Whit, Dan, and Sunny—an extra big thank-you for your love and support.

PROLOGUE

On a Sunday afternoon in April 2002, one month before *Spider-Man* was set to open in nearly 4,000 movie theaters nationwide, Stan Lee sat on the edge of a stage in the Los Angeles Shrine Auditorium. The venue for several Academy Awards shows, the white, Moorish-style building on that day played host to a comic-book convention, a gathering of science fiction and superhero fans flushed from their one-bedroom apartments and suburban bungalows by the lure of panel discussions and a dealer's room full of collectibles. Lee, the man popularly known as Spider-Man's creator, was the convention's guest of honor and most awaited speaker. For this event, like so many others in the last forty years, the fans were out in force to meet "Stan the Man."

Dressed in black jeans and a black shirt opened two buttons down, his thinning gray-white hair combed back, Lee gently leaned forward and watched a large projection television. More than 2,000 fans—some sitting in $8-per-head seats, the rest standing—watched with him. Onscreen, a cartoon version of Lee was terrorizing a comic-book store in faraway fictional Springfield in an excerpt from *The Simpsons*. The long-running TV satire had finally gotten around to caricaturing the comic-book legend, in an episode that would air later that month. Lee, following the tradition of the show's previous guest stars, had provided the voice-over for his animated doppelgänger.

In the episode, the cartoon Stan Lee appears at the comics shop where Bart Simpson tries to sell copies of his self-published comic book *Angry Dad*. "The creator of Marvel Comics!" Bart exclaims upon spying the loosely drawn septuagenarian. When a nerdy kid picks up an action figure of Batman, a hero owned by DC Comics, Marvel's main rival, Lee enters the scene, bellowing, "Hold it, son! Wouldn't you rather have an exciting action figure?"

"Ahh . . . " the kid stutters, "but only Batman fits in my Bat-mobile."

"Are you nuts? The Thing fits in there perfectly." Lee wedges the orange-skinned Marvel superhero into the Dark Knight's ride, shoving his legs through the floor. "Look, he's fitting right now."

The Shrine audience laughed knowingly at the lampoon: Stan Lee, in his trademark tinted glasses, shilling ceaselessly and unabashedly for Marvel and its cast of characters. It's a role that Lee has played for more than four decades—first as Marvel's chief writer and editor, later as its publisher, and all along in college lectures and media interviews as its public front man.

It's an image that evokes mixed responses from habitués of comics and pop culture. Fans soak it up with warm, admiring recognition, happy for any adult who loves to talk up the objects of their affection. Critics denounce it, deriding Lee as a shameless huckster and hopeless company man who greedily stole credit from Jack Kirby, Steve Ditko, and the other artists who cocreated the Fantastic Four, the X-Men, Spider-Man, and the rest of the Marvel Universe.

Good and bad, it's an image that Stan Lee has learned to accept and occasionally use to his advantage. Still on stage, observing his animated alter ego, the flesh-and-blood Lee smiled. It's the smile—broad, cheerful, guileless—that lets the fans know Stan's in on every joke, even the ones at his expense.

The lights went up and a line formed for the question-and-answer session. Lee parked himself on a folding metal chair behind a long wooden table. A teenager with a Spider-Man mask pulled up high on his forehead said, "I feel like I'm talking to Jesus here." The crowd whooped in appreciation. The teen asked Lee if he had a favorite Marvel character. "The one I was working on at the moment, whichever one I was doing," Lee responded, ever the cheerleader. "I loved them all."

Another fan stepped forward and inquired about the status of Stan Lee Media, Lee's shaky Internet venture that only two years earlier had enjoyed a stock market capitalization exceeding $300 million. Without pausing, Lee said, "It is dead, defunct, finito. Unfortunately, it was one of the most successful Internet companies in the world. My partner was less than totally honest. He's now in prison in Brazil, and that's the way it is." Somehow, Lee, enunciating his words with gravelly earnestness, made even the worst defeat of his career sound lofty.

More questions: What does Lee's famous catchphrase "Excelsior!" mean? Why do comic books cost so much? What happened to the original Spider-Man story that Jack Kirby drew for *Amazing Fantasy* #15? In his long career as Marvel's pitchman, Lee has answered queries like these hundreds of times. These are the kinds of esoteric tidbits that the denizens of the dwindling subculture known as comics fandom have sought since its nascent days in the early 1960s, when Marvel aficionados met in clubhouses and university gatherings and communicated via mimeographed fanzines.

E-mail, on-line bulletin boards, and the World Wide Web have changed the dynamics of fandom—and the comics industry as well—but Lee remains a figure of universal interest. After all, he was there near the beginning, when Superman and Batman and Captain America roused a nation from the throes of the Great Depression with four-color tales of superheroism and adventure. And he was there in 1961, perhaps dejected and weary and desperate for a hit, but with enough on the ball to pull one final big concept out of his dusty carnival-barker's hat. Hastily assembled and thrown at the public, *The Fantastic Four* #1 inaugurated the Marvel Age of comics, turning a medium on its ear and reinvigorating a company that would eventually dominate the comic-book industry and boast several billion-dollar properties.

Later, when juvenile interests turned to television, video games, and the Internet, and comics began their long, slow decline, Lee stayed visible, a pop-culture icon aging alongside the medium that made him famous. Comic books were no longer culturally relevant, but somehow Stan Lee still was. Why? For one thing, he answered questions—sometimes truthfully, other times cagily, but always congenially. Lee was charming, quick with a joke, and, like a politician, keenly attuned to his audience, whether it was a lifelong comic-book devotee or a television reporter skeptical of a grown man's enthusiasm for a cosmic-powered space alien who roams the space-ways on a sleek, silver-coated surfboard.

The Shrine interrogation continued. About *Spider-Man*: Did Lee have veto power over the comic-book title after he stopped writing it? "No, I didn't have any power. You see, I always felt with great power comes great responsibility," Lee quipped. The crowd cheered. Soberly, he continued, "Once I was no longer doing the books, it wouldn't have been right for me to tell other people how to do them." Another question: What was Lee's involvement in the production of the movie? Not much, Lee responded cheerfully. "I'm just like you guys. I see the trailer, I love it, I can't wait to see the whole thing." More applause. It was his room.

Soon it was time for autographs. The crowd pressed forward, hundreds of boys and men, a few women, clutching comic books, posters, and action figures that, once anointed with Lee's signature, would find their way into keepsake boxes hidden under beds or comics-shop display cases or, more likely, onto eBay. Since time was short, the autographs were limited to one item per person. Lee gamely inscribed everything put before him with a felt-tip pen, doling out a minute or so of merriment to each fan.

Thirty minutes later, he was gone.

A few weeks after the Shrine convention, Lee strode along the red carpet at the *Spider-Man* film premiere, rubbing shoulders with the likes of Hollywood actors Adam Sandler and Will Smith and music stars Steven Tyler and Macy Gray. The seventy-nine-year-old Marvel VIP dined with the glitterati under a web-like tent pitched in an upscale L.A. neighborhood with acrobats performing overhead and red cosmopolitans served out of ice-sculpted martini bars. Kirsten Dunst, the pretty young actress who plays Mary Jane Watson in the film, posed with him for a photograph that was later distributed by the Reuters news agency.

Spider-Man took in a record-breaking $114 million in its open-ing weekend and went on to become one of the top-grossing movies of all time. It even outpaced *Episode II Attack of the Clones*, the fifth installment of George Lucas's *Star Wars* series, once the Tiffany standard of popular imagination. During the summer of "Spider-Mania," Lee was commemorated in dozens of newspaper and magazine articles as the originator of the arachnid magic spilling into the nation's multiplexes and toy stores. The wave of mainstream appreciation for the Grand Old Man of comics rolled through the culture like a gentle wave, evoking bouts of cozy nostalgia in the hearts of middle-aged men who had long ago stopped wishing for superpowers and funky space machines.

For Lee, who once dreamed of being an actor, the web slinger's big-screen success represented a long-delayed affirmation from a movie industry that has drawn heavily from the wellspring of Marvel Comics' creativity without ever granting its exuberant coauthor an all-access pass. After twenty years in Hollywood and dozens of scrapped or fouled-up movie projects, new opportunities materialized for Lee. Bruce Willis's production company signed a first-look deal with Lee's POW! Entertainment, and Lee announced a pact with former *Baywatch* star Pamela Anderson to create *Stripperella*, a TV cartoon series.

It was another good summer to be Stan Lee.

Once upon a time, a young comic-book writer named Stanley Lieber invented a pseudonym by splitting his first name. Dissatisfied and embarrassed by the kiddie material he felt forced to produce, the writer wanted to reserve his given name for the cover of the Great American Novel he hoped to write one day. Decades later, the nom de plume had become his legal name, the kiddie material his artistic legacy. The story of Stan Lee is the story of a man who reinvented himself into what he'd been all along, and of the uniquely American art form that never failed to provide him a platform.

PART I

"FROM HUMBLE BEGINNINGS . . ."

STANLEY LIEBER

All superheroes require a secret origin. That's the first rule of the long-underwear league. Whether your powers are of the pyrotechnic variety or you merely possess superstrength, you need a story that explains how you came to acquire your awesome gifts and why you're using them to battle crime instead of, say, exploiting them for profit. In his long career as a comics writer, Stan Lee has dashed off hundreds of origin stories. To the Hulk, he gave a gamma-ray bomb, to Spider-Man, a murdered uncle. Daredevil gained supernatural senses from a radioactive spill, and the Silver Surfer sacrificed himself to save his planet. The only secret origin Stan Lee has had trouble keeping straight is his own. He readily admits that he has a bad memory. It's no surprise, then, that in personal interviews, in media profiles, and even in his autobiography, many of the details of his life vary. Some are shaded by the passage of time, possibly embellished to fit a neater version of the past. Others are unverifiable, with no public records or living witnesses to back them up. Yet somewhere in this hazy morass of recollection is the true story of how Stanley Lieber became Stan Lee.

Stanley Martin Lieber was born on December 28, 1922, over a decade before the dawn of the American comic book. He would miss out on the medium's formative years but arrive in time to help steer it through puberty. Like many of the second-generation immi-

3

grant kids who grew up to form comics' pioneering vanguard, including his future collaborator Jack Kirby, Stanley's early life was marked by grinding poverty.

His parents, Jack and Celia Lieber, were Jewish-Romanian immigrants who lived in New York City, near the corner of 98th Street and West End Avenue. Jack Lieber worked as a dress cutter in the city's garment district until the Great Depression left him jobless. Celia tended the home. To save money, the Liebers moved to a tiny apartment in the Bronx, an ethnically diverse borough with a large Jewish population. Stanley slept in the living room. Much to his dismay, the new Lieber household stared onto the side of another building, making it impossible to see the neighborhood kids at play. "My dream was to one day be rich enough to have an apartment that faced the street," he recalls.

When Stanley was eight years old, his brother, Larry, was born. Because of their age gap, the Lieber boys weren't very close, but later in life they would work together on comic books and the "Spider-Man" newspaper comic strip. Money was scarce in the Lieber home, and the family often accepted financial help from Celia's sisters, who were better off. Stanley's parents quarreled constantly. Jack was intelligent, but difficult and demanding, recalls Jean Goodman, a close relative. "He was exacting with his boys—brush your teeth a certain way, wash your tongue, and so on." Celia, on the other hand, was warm and nurturing to the point of self-sacrifice. "The demanding father and the persecuted mother, that made the atmosphere difficult," Goodman says.

Stanley sought refuge in pulp novels and the books of Sir Arthur Conan Doyle, Edgar Rice Burroughs, and Mark Twain. He frequented the movies as often as he could afford the 25¢ admission, wrapping himself in the celluloid adventures of Charlie Chan, Roy Rogers, Errol Flynn, and other swashbucklers of the day. He took particular interest in the works of William Shakespeare, which he started reading before the age of ten. "I didn't understand a lot of it in those days," he later recalled, "but I loved the words. I loved the rhythms of the words." His passion for Shakespeare would resurface in his 1960s work at Marvel Comics, from the ponderous philosophical pronouncements of the Silver Surfer to the exaggerated Elizabethan dialogue of the Mighty Thor.

Stanley also read newspaper comic strips, although not with the dedicated interest of someone who hoped to one day write them. Among his favorites were George Herriman's surrealist comic drama "Krazy Kat" and Jimmy Hatlo's quirky one-panel feature "They'll Do It Every Time." He was a voracious reader of books, magazines, pulps, cereal boxes—whatever he could lay his hands on. Comic strips were just something else to read. One of his early role models was animator Walt Disney. "I admired him so when I was a kid," Lee says. "I probably created many more characters, but he created an empire. I'm not an empire creator."

Sunday night at the Lieber home was family night. For dinner, Celia would serve hot dogs and beans, and on the rare occasions when money was flowing, a helping of sauerkraut. The family gathered around the radio set to listen to ventriloquist Edgar Bergen and his dummy Charlie McCarthy, comedians Fred Allen and Jack Benny, and other stars of the early broadcast era. "All the chairs were arranged in a semicircle facing the radio, and we would sit and watch the radio as if it were a television set," Lee told an interviewer on National Public Radio.

The Liebers were Jewish, and so were most of their neighbors and friends. At Jack's insistence, Stanley had a bar mitzvah when he turned thirteen. ("There were about two people in the temple at the time," he quips. "We were very poor.") But Judaism didn't leave much of an impression on Stanley, and it faded from his life when he reached adulthood. "I never believed in religion. I don't mean the Jewish religion—I mean in religion," he says. "To me, faith is the opposite of intelligence, because faith means believing something blindly. I don't know why God—if there is a God—gave us these brains if we're going to believe things blindly."

Jack's chronic unemployment persisted through Stanley's teens. Demand for dress cutters was low, and Jack spent most of his time reading the want ads or trolling the city for jobs, trying to earn enough money to keep his family nourished and off the streets. "I always felt tremendous pity for him, because it must be a terrible feeling to be a man and to not be bringing in the money that's needed for your family," Lee said in the NPR interview. In high school, Stanley pitched in by taking on a number of part-time jobs. He delivered sandwiches to office workers and ushered at the Rivoli Theater on Broadway. His father's bleak resume taught him the importance of bringing home a regular paycheck. Throughout most of his career as a writer and editor, Lee would hold staff positions, steering clear of the freelance arrangements that were common in the comics industry.

Lee is fond of telling the story of how he became interested in writing. As he related in his autobiography and in countless interviews, the pivotal event was an essay competition for high schoolers sponsored by the *New York Herald Tribune*. Begun in the spring semester of 1936, the Biggest News of the Week contest invited students to write, in 250 words or fewer, what they considered to be the most significant news development of the week. The top seven entries each week were awarded cash prizes. When he was fifteen years old, Lee recounted, he entered the contest three weeks in a row. He won first prize, which paid $20, all three times. His domination of the competitive field, which included thousands of kids, prompted an editor at the paper to contact Stanley to ask him to please give other aspiring scribes a chance. Sensing talent in the skinny teenager, the editor then advised him to consider professional writing as a career. With such wise counsel offered from on high to one so lowly as he, how could young Stanley refuse his newfound destiny? He never looked back.

It's a nice story, gilded with classic themes—the archetypal father figure, a wide-eyed youngling who finally recognizes his burgeoning talents. But it's also false. At best, it's vastly distorted. Stan Lee never won the *New York Herald Tribune*'s Biggest News of the Week contest. An exhaustive search of the paper's archives turned up no first prizes for Stanley Lieber, only a seventh-place finish on May 7, 1938, for which he netted $2.50. The following week, Stanley didn't place. But, on May 21, his essay won an honorable mention, one of 100 such awards handed out that week. He snagged a second honorable mention a week later, and then disappeared from the standings.

While winning seventh prize in a contest with thousands of entries is undoubtedly a praiseworthy achievement, that distinction added to two honorable mentions hardly seems likely to have attracted the attention and advisement of a busy newspaper editor. Perhaps, in his misty memory, Lee has confused the editor with a teacher or some other authority figure. And maybe, after so many decades, a seventh-place finish and a pair of near-misses have acquired the nostalgic sheen of three first prizes. Or maybe his imagined teenage glory provided the convenient details he needed to polish the tale of his secret origin. Lee may not be an intentional liar, but he has been known to massage the truth on occasion. Not that most people seem to mind. His enthusiastic amiability usually gets him off with some good-natured chiding—"Oh, that's just Stan." After all, Lee is a storyteller, and his account of the *Herald Tribune* essay contest certainly made for a good story, even if it's untrue.

The story continues with a few novice writing gigs. Stanley's first stop was a news service, where he compiled advance obituaries of famous people in anticipation of their demise. He quit that job, he says, because it was too depressing. He also wrote publicity material for a Jewish hospital in Denver. At one point, he joined a local company of the WPA Federal Theater, the national public-works project founded to provide jobs for unemployed theater professionals. After working on a few plays, he left to seek more profitable climes. But that experience instilled in him a love of acting, and in later years he would return to performing of sorts on the college lecture circuit and in Hollywood cameos.

Stanley attended DeWitt Clinton High School, an overcrowded Bronx institution that housed 10,000 students from all parts of the city: Irish kids, Italian kids, Jewish kids—even some African-American kids—many of them children of immigrants or immigrants themselves. His schoolmates included future author James Baldwin and eventual TV and film writer Sidney "Paddy" Chayefsky. The all-boys school had previously graduated two other New York Jews destined for comic-book stardom—Batman cocreators Bob Kane (class of 1934) and Bill Finger (class of 1932).

Stanley was active in extracurricular activities, joining the law society, the chess club, the Ping-Pong club, the French club, and the public-speaking club. In his yearbook entry, Stanley M. Lieber, nicknamed "Gabby," wrote that his life's ambition was to "Reach the Top—and STAY There," with the parting quote, "Join the navy, so the world can see me!" Bob Wendlinger, a high-school friend, remembers Stanley as a good-looking, extroverted "charmer" who was clearly destined for great things. "You always knew that he was going to be successful. It was a given," says Wendlinger, a retired writer.

The school published a student literary magazine called the *Magpie*. Every semester, a group of artistic-minded students holed up in their office in an area of the school known as "the tower" to pull together a collection of poems, articles, short stories, drawings, and photographs. "Stan Lieber" was listed as a member of the *Magpie*'s business staff in its June 1939 edition. He apparently never wrote anything for the magazine, serving instead as a publicity director. But while he may not have made a literary mark during his time at the *Magpie*, he did make history of a different sort. One day, he arrived at the magazine's office to find a ladder leading up to the room's high ceiling. The ladder had been placed there by a painter, who was gone for lunch. Seizing the opportunity for mischief, Stanley scrambled to the top and inscribed four fateful words on the ceiling—"Stan Lee is God." That was the first known use of his famous pseudonym. Recently, Lee admitted that he can't remember exactly when he invented the pen name "Stan Lee," but it was certainly his preferred alias by the time he started writing comics a few years later.

In 1939 Stanley graduated high school. Because he had to help support his family, he couldn't attend college—a fact that he views now with some regret. "I think I would have enjoyed going to college," he says. "Like you see in the movies—living on campus, having beer parties, getting laid every night. It would have been nice." At the time, though, he accepted the reality of his situation with the resigned practicality required by those economically depressed times. Later, he would sign up for night school at the City College of New York in order to spend time with a girl he was dating. "I don't remember what I studied or what course I took, but I enrolled just so I could be with her," Lee recalls. When they broke up six months later, he quit.

The last port of call on his voyage of miserable yet character-building jobs was a trouser manufacturer. Stanley ran errands for salesmen on the shop floor, frantically jumping to attention every time someone yelled "Boy!" The work was difficult and humiliating, and when the company fired him after a few weeks, it was almost a relief.

Now Stan Lee's secret origin nears its climax. Stanley Martin Lieber, seventeen years old and unemployed, is adrift. He harbors soft-boiled notions of being a writer, but he doesn't know how to make that happen. Then Robbie Solomon, his mother's brother, has an idea. Timely Publications, the publishing company where Solomon works, might have an opening. It so happens that Timely is owned by Martin Goodman, another relative.

On a morning in late 1940, Stanley hikes over to the Timely offices in the McGraw-Hill Building on West 42nd Street, a thirty-three-story skyscraper layered with swatches of blue-green terra cotta. Timely, it turns out, publishes comic books, including a hot new title called *Captain America Comics*. Stanley is familiar with comic strips, which are a popular feature of New York City newspapers, but these comic books, vulgar and boisterous, are strange. They lack the cleverness and visual elegance of their crisply drawn forebears.

The firm's editor, Joe Simon, who is tall and slim and has a booming voice, interviews Stanley and shows him around. Joe introduces him to the art director, a short, compact man named Jack Kirby. Sales for Timely's comics are soaring, and Simon and Kirby's workload has increased proportionately. They need an assistant, a gofer, someone to fetch sandwiches or to erase stray pencil marks on finished artwork—and maybe, down the road, to do a little writing. Stanley accepts.

The job pays eight dollars a week. It isn't much of a job, but it's a job.

It's a start.

MARTIN'S COUSIN-IN-LAW

The comic-book industry that Stanley Lieber joined in late 1940 was young, formless, and chaotic—the ideal place for a teenager looking for some easy writing experience and, perhaps, to make a mark. Like most lively arts, the American comic book began as a hybrid of previous cultural forms. The early comic books, with their simple illustrated storylines and garish, titillating cover art, borrowed heavily from the form, content, and economics of at least two older commercialized creative endeavors: newspaper comic strips and pulp magazines.

Comic strips had been creeping into the American consciousness since the 1895 debut of Richard F. Outcault's "The Yellow Kid" in Joseph Pulitzer's *New York World*. Outcault's character—a bald, obnoxious slum kid whose immense popularity earned him a slot in the paper's Sunday color supplement—was the original cartoon-licensing franchise. Eighty years before "Garfield" became a billion-dollar merchandising behemoth, the Kid appeared in plays and his image adorned key chains and collectible cards. The Yellow Kid's success inspired dozens of strips, among them Rudolph Dirks's "The Katzenjammer Kids," James Swinnerton's "Little Jimmy," and Winsor McCay's "Little Nemo in Slumberland." And later, "Boob McNutt," "Barney Google," and "Toonerville Folks"—oddly titled features rendered in stark black and white on weekdays and in glorious full color in the weekend editions.

Fresh genres soon invaded the comics page, with jungle stories butting up against topical yarns and tales of science fiction. In the pre-television age, newspaper strips were a cheap, accessible form of entertainment that inspired large followings. For example, "Wash Tubbs," an adventure strip by Roy Crane about a pair of itinerant swashbucklers, hooked readers with a fast-moving plot that was worthy of the best serial movies. The most popular cartoonists became minor celebrities. Some, like George Herriman of "Krazy Kat," flirted with modern art movements, such as dadaism and surrealism.

Meanwhile, pulp magazines had been making their own inroads with racy tales of crime, fantasy, and romance. In the years after World War I, hundreds of titles poured forth onto newsstands— cheap throwaway magazines chronicling the rapid-paced adventures of Tarzan of the Apes, the Shadow, the Spider, Buck Rogers, and numerous other prototypes of comic-book superheroes. From the pulps, comic books inherited a sensational storytelling style and, perhaps more important, a ready-made distribution network.

Publishers had been issuing reprint collections of newspaper cartoons as far back as 1897, but the sales potential of most of them was limited by a lack of color and original material. There was, however, a definite and underexploited market for strip reprints. After all, the comics supplement was the most popular section of many metropolitan newspapers. What publishers lacked was a cost-effective package they could sell to the masses. Finally, in 1933, Harry Wildenberg and Max C. Gaines, two employees with the Eastern Color Printing Company in Waterbury, Connecticut, devised a new format: a booklet measuring eight inches by eleven inches, roughly the size of a folded-over tabloid page. Their first effort was *Funnies on Parade*, a thirty-two-page magazine reprinting Sunday strips in color, which they sold to Procter & Gamble for use as a giveaway. When that proved successful, Gaines produced several more well-received magazines for corporate sponsors. Then he had an idea. People seemed to enjoy the comic-strip collections. Maybe they'd be willing to pay for them. A trial issue of a title called *Famous Fun-*

nies appeared in early 1934 with a 35,000-copy print run and a cover price of 10¢. The magazines sold out. In May, a sequel, *Famous Funnies* #1, hit newsstands, and the monthly comic book was born.

Offering an assortment of previously published newspaper strips such as "Joe Palooka" and "Mutt & Jeff," *Famous Funnies* didn't look much like the comic book of today. The funnybook concept needed refinement. That task fell to Major Malcolm Wheeler-Nicholson, a retired U.S. cavalry officer and former pulp writer. In 1935, Wheeler-Nicholson published *New Fun Comics*, the first title to feature original stories written and drawn expressly for the comic-book format. The magazine—an anthology of adventure, western, and humor tales starring knock-off characters such as Buckskin Jim and Don Drake of the Planet Saro—didn't break any sales records, but it set a precedent. Comic-book publishers no longer had to pay the exorbitant reprint fees demanded by newspaper-strip syndicates. In that Depression-ravaged time, there were plenty of young and unemployed artists who would leap at the opportunity to create brand-new stories for a meager page rate.

Many of those artists found work in the comic-art shop set up in 1936 by Harry "A" Chesler, a former ad man from Chicago. Chesler, who was heavyset and favored three-piece suits, figured out early that comic-book publishers would need a steady stream of cheap material. To fill that need, he rented a small office on lower Fifth Avenue and hired an assembly line of writers and artists. The Chesler Shop became a comic-book factory, with the artists seated at desks arranged in rows, and the writers in a room down the hall. In the beginning, they packaged entire magazines, covers included, for Wheeler-Nicholson and a competitor, and later for other publishers such as Centaur, Fawcett, and MLJ. Many of the pioneers from that golden age of comics passed through Chesler's doors, including *Sandman* artist Creig Flessel and 1940s trendsetter Charles Biro.

Outside the frantic action of the shop, two high-school buddies from Cleveland named Jerry Siegel and Joe Shuster were trying, unsuccessfully, to break into the newspaper-strip business. They found an eager customer in Wheeler-Nicholson. He published their *Dr. Occult*, a strip about a mystic detective, in *New Fun Comics* #6. With Siegel writing and Shuster drawing, they produced several more comic-book stories, but nothing with any staying power. Wheeler-Nicholson eventually took on two business partners, Harry Donenfeld and Jack Liebowitz, and together they formed Detective Comics, Inc., the company that came to be known as DC Comics. When the major's finances fell apart in 1937, his partners bought him out.

Soon after that, DC Comics editor Vincent Sullivan was casting about for a feature to showcase in a forthcoming title called *Action Comics*. Max Gaines, who was then working at the press that printed the company's comics, suggested a strip that Siegel and Shuster were shopping around about a hero who had superstrength, a near-invulnerable body, and the ability to leap tall buildings in a single bound. Sullivan saw that the character, though somewhat outlandish, had potential. He bought the feature, and *Action Comics* #1 arrived on stands in 1938 with a cover that sported a figure in a red-and-blue costume, hoisting a car high above his head. Superman had landed on Earth. And in his wake, the budding comic-book industry was changed forever.

With Superman leading the way, *Action*'s monthly circulation climbed to 500,000 copies. In 1939 another Superman title appeared; it was selling 1,250,000 copies per issue within a year. Dozens of entrepreneurs piled into the industry, many from the flagging pulp-magazine business. By 1941, there were 168 different comic-book titles. For their part in creating the character who sparked an industry stampede, Siegel and Shuster received $130. When publishers Donenfeld and Liebowitz paid out the standard $10 page rate for the first thirteen-page Superman story, they made the creators sign over their rights to the Man of Steel, establishing a pattern of abusive work-for-hire practices that persisted for decades. Although Siegel and Shuster enjoyed a few lucrative years of continuing work on Superman, they eventually left the company amid a lawsuit—which they settled unprofitably—over ownership of their work. While the owners of DC Comics raked in millions of dollars from their flagship superhero, Siegel and Shuster faded out of the limelight. Having turned on their former publisher, they found it increasingly hard to land assignments. Shuster spent much of his remaining life in near-poverty.

After Superman came Batman. He was different. Springing to life in *Detective Comics* #27, Batman lacked alien powers and had to rely on his shrewdness and Olympic-level physical training to trounce the criminal element. Then, a litany of superhero copycats: the Flame, Hawkman, Ultra Man, Cat Man, the Blue Beetle, Plastic Man, the Flash, the Sandman, and dozens more. In vibrant hues, they chased their arch-villains across the page and brought justice to a tilted four-color world.

To keep pace with the voracious demand for fresh material, comic-art shops swelled and multiplied. No two operations produced comics the same way. At Jack Binder's shop, a half dozen artists worked on a single story, with the tasks broken down into layout, main character pencils, secondary character pencils, main character inks, secondary character inks, and so on, with the result that Binder productions developed a common visual look. Lloyd Jacquet, by contrast, gave his artists their own characters and features, and they produced comics that were stylistically distinct.

The shops, staffed mainly with beginners and out-of-work illustrators, produced a lot of schlock but also some work of genuine quality, which is remarkable given the conditions that many artists labored under. In his memoir about that era in comic-book history, cartoonist Jules Feiffer paints a vivid picture of the shop atmosphere:

> Artists sat lumped in crowded rooms, knocking it out for the page rate. Penciling, inking, lettering in the balloons for $10 a page, sometimes less; working from yellow type scripts which on the left described the action, on the right gave the dialogue. . . . The "editor," who'd be in one office that week, another the next, working for companies that changed names as often as he changed jobs, sat at a desk or a drawing table—an always beefy man who, if he drew, did not do it well, making it that much more galling when he corrected your work and you knew he was right. His job was to check copy, check art, hand out assignments, pay the artists money when he had it, promise the artists money when he didn't. Everyone got paid if he didn't mind going back week after week. Everyone got paid if he didn't mind occasionally pleading.

Young cartoonists gathered to talk about their art, comparing swipes and conceiving new worlds, new heroes, new villains. Sometimes, they would team up and create shops of their own—drawing, always drawing, long into the night. "Eighteen hours a day of work," Feiffer writes. "Sandwiches for breakfast, lunch, and dinner. An occasional beer, but not too often. And nothing any stronger. One dare not slow up."

Around the time that Superman started taking off, Frank Torpey, a salesman for a comics-packaging studio, persuaded a pulp magazine publisher named Martin Goodman to try his hand at comic books. Goodman had already made a small fortune catering to the lurid interests of pulp readers. In 1932, when he was twenty-two years old, Goodman began his career producing cowboy-themed titles such as *Complete Western Book*, *Best Western*, and *Quick Trigger Western Novel*. Whenever new genres became popular, he released a spate of hastily assembled imitations, hoping to cash in before the market faded. His often-quoted credo was simple: "If you get a title that catches on, then add a few more, you're in for a nice profit." By the time Torpey approached him, Goodman was publishing twenty-seven pulp titles under several different imprints. (He divided his publishing interests into separate companies in order to spread out the financial risk and lower his overall tax bill.)

Goodman contracted Torpey's studio, Funnies, Inc., to create a new line of comic books. For their first title, the Funnies artists produced an anthology of features designed to capitalize on the current superhero vogue. Borrowing a titular theme from one of his old pulps, Goodman published the stories in 1939 as *Marvel Comics* #1, introducing two new characters who would go on to enjoy long funnybook careers. The Human Torch, created by Carl Burgos, was a fire-engulfed android who wreaked havoc with the searing heat produced by his unstable metallic body. Later, the Torch learned how to put his powers to noble use, dispatching evildoers with tightly packed fireballs and slender sheets of flame. The Sub-Mariner served almost as a counterpoint to the Torch; he wore swimming trunks for a costume and had powers derived from the sea. Invented by Bill Everett, the elfin-looking Sub-Mariner was originally a villain who waged a war of vengeance on humans for the destruction they had caused to his undersea kingdom. As time went on, however, he joined up with the Torch to battle far more pressing evils, such as Nazis and fifth column saboteurs.

The first issue of *Marvel Comics* sold well, and Goodman saw that he was on to something. After changing the book's name to *Marvel Mystery Comics*, he published more issues. He expanded his line to include *Daring Mystery Comics* and *Mystic Comics*, featuring such forgettable heroes as Dynaman, the Fin, the Human Top, and Flexo the Rubber Man. The Human Torch and the Sub-Mariner were also given their own magazines. Goodman gathered all of his comics titles under one banner: Timely Publications. The name stuck. Although he employed dozens of other company labels in subsequent years, Goodman's comics-publishing ventures during the 1940s are generally referred to as Timely comics.

Goodman lured Joe Simon, a twenty-four-year-old artist, away from Funnies, Inc., and paid him $12 per page to draw comics directly for Timely. The son of a tailor, Simon had worked as a newspaper illustrator and photo retoucher before hopping on the comics bandwagon in 1939. While freelancing for Goodman, Simon also became the editor in chief of Fox Publications, earning a handsome salary of $85 per week. Simon was doing as well as anyone then hacking it out in the comic-book industry, except perhaps the publishers.

In the Fox Bullpen, Simon met his future collaborator, Jacob Kurtzberg, a gifted young artist who signed his work with a variety of pen names, including "Ted Grey," "Jack Curtiss," and, most famously, "Jack Kirby." At the tender age of twenty-one, Kirby had amassed a modestly impressive resume as an animator at Fleischer Studios and a strip cartoonist for small newspaper syndicates. The son of Austrian-Jewish immigrants, Kirby had grown up poor on Suffolk Street in New York's Lower East Side. As a child, he ran with a gang and brawled with kids from nearby neighborhoods. He escaped into the dream worlds of fantasy and science-fiction books, leaving behind the cruelties of the ghetto. In comic strips, he found a career ambition to lead him out of poverty. "I thought comics were a common form of art and strictly American, in my estimation, because America was the home of the common man," Kirby once said. "It's a democratic art."

His artwork, with its raw kineticism and explosive vibrancy, reflected an upbringing steeped in urban and ethnic violence. Kirby was tremendously talented, and what's more, he was fast. In an industry that typically paid by the page, Simon could hardly have found a better partner. Kirby, for his part, got along well with editors and publishers, but he lacked a strong business sense. While at Fox, Kirby had been pulling down $15 a week, which he used to help support his parents. Within two years of teaming with Simon, he was making nearly twenty times that amount.

Simon soon found that his freelance career was more lucrative than his daytime job, and he quit Fox Publications. Kirby joined him some months later. The pair worked out of a small one-room office, producing features for a number of publishers, including Goodman's Timely. Initially, Simon and Kirby shared the creative responsibilities more or less evenly. Simon wrote the script on the illustration boards and sketched in rough layouts of the figures, and then Kirby drew the story in pencil. Simon would letter the balloons and ink Kirby's drawings with a brush. When deadlines were tight, they brought in other artists to lend a hand. In later years, Simon became the team's business manager, leaving most of the plotting and art chores to Kirby.

One of Simon's and Kirby's efforts for Timely, *Red Raven Comics*, tanked on the stands and was canceled after just one issue. Despite that failure, Goodman continued to sense a potential gold mine in comic books, and he employed Simon to edit the Timely line. For the thirteenth issue of *Marvel Mystery Comics*, Simon and Kirby turned out the Vision, a supernatural being who traveled in wisps of smoke. Then, in late 1940, Simon proposed a new costumed character who embodied many of the swirling patriotic themes of the day. The United States had not yet entered World War II, but there was widespread concern about Hitler's campaign in Europe and its potential to spill over to domestic shores. In the pages of some comic books, heroes were already taking on the Axis powers and other enemies of America. Simon's superchampion, whom he called Captain America, carried a liberty shield and was clad in red, white, and blue, neatly symbolizing the country's pre-war sentiment. The cover of *Captain America Comics* #1 depicted the star-spangled avenger exploding into a German stronghold, his body in mid-leap, as he lands a haymaker on the crumpled jaw of Adolf Hitler.

Captain America was an immediate hit, with sales rivaling industry heavyweights Superman and Batman. Goodman put the book on a monthly schedule, turning up the pressure on the already over-worked Simon and Kirby.

Before long, they asked for an assistant. Simon hired the cousin of Goodman's wife, Jean—a seventeen-year-old kid named Stanley Lieber.

STAN LEE, PLAYWRIGHT

When Stanley Lieber started working at Timely Publications in 1940, just a few months shy of his eighteenth birthday, he could hardly have imagined that he would be running the place only a year later. His initial duties certainly gave no indication of what was to come. As an assistant to comic-book editor Joe Simon, Stanley swept floors, refilled inkwells, and topped off the coffee can. When Jack Kirby finished a page, Stanley would erase the penciled drawings that lay under the inks, prepping the artwork before it was sent to the engraver. On his downtime, he blew on a recorder, banging out simple tunes such as "Yankee Doodle" and annoying his coworkers.

Timely had roughly a dozen employees at the time and, except for Simon, Kirby, and a few others, relied on freelance artists for material. The company was staffed mainly by relatives of owner Martin Goodman. His brother Abe ran bookkeeping, while Dave, another brother, shot photos for the magazine division. Artie Goodman, the youngest sibling, handled comic-book color guides. Martin's brother-in-law, Robbie Solomon, performed odd jobs and gained a reputation as an office busybody and a meddler. It was Robbie who originally told Stanley about the gig at Timely.

Working a job that was the 1940s equivalent of an internship, Stanley had little contact with Martin in those early days. But to others in the office, it was clear that the boss's cousin-in-law had ambition. Joe Simon recounted that Stanley, confident and extroverted, asked for a promotion within a week. "I know everything," Simon recalled him saying. At the time, most comic books included two-page text pieces in order to qualify for cheaper mailing rates. These stories were typically slapdash efforts that readers skipped over on their way to the next illustrated adventure. Text fillers were a chore, but when Simon assigned one to Stanley, it felt like a privilege and an opportunity to the junior staffer.

A few days later, Stanley turned in "Captain America Foils the Traitor's Revenge," twenty-six paragraphs of warmed-over pulp prose pitting the star-spangled avenger and his "gallant lad," Bucky, against three would-be assassins in a U.S. Army camp. It would be unfair to hold up the tentative scribblings of a teenager as emblematic of the work he would produce as a more mature writer. Nevertheless, some of Stan Lee's favorite motifs were evident in that ancient piece. At one point, Captain America, displaying comic-bookish panache, picks up Bucky by his arms and swings him at two thugs, knocking away their guns. Written straight, all words and no images, the passage is comically bad, falling short of camp even in retrospect. But it also presages the vigorous physical action that would characterize many of the early-1960s Marvel comics by Lee and his collaborators, Jack Kirby and Steve Ditko. Spider-Man, for example, didn't just lay into bad guys with his fists; he bounced over them, under them, flipped them head-over-heels like flapjacks, with the spirited verve of the heroes in the Errol Flynn movies that Lee once thrilled to as a child.

Stanley's debut story ended with Private Steve Rogers, Captain America's alter ego, receiving a tongue-lashing from the camp colonel for having slept through the previous night's excitement. "Captain America and Bucky mopped up three armed men by themselves and saved my life—and YOU were asleep!" yells the colonel. "Oh, why can't I have some soldiers like Captain America in this army—instead of YOU!" Steve Rogers smiles to himself. "*If the colonel only knew . . .*" Here, Stanley had identified the secret-identity conundrum, already a cliché in 1940: the superhero hogs the glory, while his alter ego can't catch a break. Clark Kent has no chance of scoring with Lois Lane until he ties on a cape. One of Lee's principal achievements at Marvel twenty years later would be to tweak that cliché, sending some characters to the poorhouse, others to the therapist, and forcing the spandex-costumed set to deal with "real life."

"Traitor's Revenge" ran in the third issue of *Captain America Comics*, cover-dated May 1941, with a byline that read "Stan Lee." Stanley Lieber had entered the comic-book field, but he checked his real name at the door. Simon related a conversation he had with his young assistant about the pseudonym.

"Who's Stan Lee?" Simon asked.

"I'm changing my name," Stanley replied. "For journalistic reasons."

"It would be better for a laundry."

"I hadn't considered that." Stanley paused. "I wonder what the comic book prospects are in China."

Back then, comic-book stories did not typically include credits, but when they did appear, aliases were common. Some artists, such as Jack Kirby (Jacob Kurtzberg) and Batman cocreator Bob Kane (Robert Kahn), chose to Americanize their names in order to disguise their ethnic roots. Others wanted a cover identity while they slummed in the field, so that their reputations would emerge untarnished when they moved on to better jobs in commercial illustration or advertising. Even artists who were unembarrassed to sign their given names used aliases to escape detection when they freelanced for competing publishers. So there was already an established tradition when Stanley Lieber split his first name, swapping the "y" for a second "e," to come up with the nom de plume that would eventually become his legacy.

"Lieber" is fairly distinguishable as a Jewish name, but Lee says that played no part in his decision to take on a pseudonym. He grew up with Jewish neighbors, hung out with Jewish kids in school, and therefore felt insulated from the anti-Semitism that was then in circulation. "I know it exists, but I've been lucky. I never ran into anti-Jewish prejudice," Lee says, adding that he was unhappy when he finally changed his name legally to "Stan Lee" in the 1970s because living with two identities had become too complicated. The original urge to cloak himself sprang from Lee's desire to eventually write in other venues, such as novels and screenplays. He wanted to reserve his real name for more prestigious writerly pursuits. Comic books were kiddie fodder, produced by folks who were held in the same esteem by the literary community as moonshiners would have been by the winegrowers of Bordeaux. For comics, "Stan Lee" would do.

Meanwhile at Timely, Simon and Kirby were blazing a trail within the pages of the million-selling *Captain America Comics*. Kirby's artwork had become more assured, displaying a solid command of human anatomy and an energetic sense of action. While most of his peers were still mired in the Dark Ages, limply depicting characters in awkward poses from standard, unimaginative angles, Kirby had style. Unleashed by his furious pencil work, Captain America danced from panel to panel, dispensing right hooks and sending the villains reeling in all directions—sometimes right out of the panel. Kirby's fight scenes unfolded smoothly, like a ballet, with such clarity that they required no explanatory captions. Simon and Kirby also experimented with page layouts, separating panels with jagged lines, framing dramatic moments with round backdrops, and effectively making the comics page a storytelling unit unto itself.

There were other great artists then working in comics—for example, Creig Flessel (*Sandman*) and Lou Fine (*Black Condor*). But none of them drew a book that could boast the sales figures of *Captain America Comics*. Kirby's work was the most visible of the early masters, and it set the standard for all comic-book stories to come. A slew of Captain America imitators soon followed: American Crusader, Commando Yank, Yank and Doodle, Yankee Boy, the Liberator, the Scarlet Sentry, Captain Freedom, Captain Valiant, and dozens more. Timely even tried to duplicate its own success with characters such as the Patriot, the Defender, and Major Liberty. They all failed to match the appeal of Simon and Kirby's original superpatriot.

Stan Lee's first comic-book script, "Headline Hunter, Foreign Correspondent," appeared in *Captain America Comics* #5, coverdated August 1941, and ran for eight issues. Concurrently, he wrote a series called "Father Time," about a costumed character who dispensed justice at the business end of a scythe. The first installment of "Headline Hunter" opened with a large splash panel that read "Story by Stan Lee," which was unusual for the time. Either by personal choice or editorial decree, comics writers rarely received credit for their work. Most writers turned out stories by the pound, at 50¢ or a dollar per page, with little concern for portfolio enhancement. Comics were just something to get them through lean times. To Stan Lee, though, the fake name notwithstanding, they were clearly something more. As more than one comics historian has noted, it seems as if Stan Lee pasted his name on all of his work: The signature "Stan Lee" appears in hundreds of stories from the 1940s and 1950s, many of which weren't even signed by the collaborating artists. Early on, Lee employed additional pseudonyms—"Neel Nats," "S. T. Anley" and "Stan Martin," among others—in order to make the company staff appear bigger than it was. Stanley Lieber may not have been proud of the path his life had taken, but Stan Lee was certainly enjoying himself.

Propelled by the ever-climbing sales of *Captain America Comics*, Timely's fortunes continued to rise. Martin Goodman was getting rich—or richer. Simon and Kirby, who had negotiated a profit-sharing arrangement with Goodman, were also making a decent sum, although, as it turned out, they should have been making more. As Simon recalled in his memoir, he found out from Goodman's accountant that the publisher was using slippery bookkeeping methods to shortchange Simon and Kirby on their cut of the profits. Disgruntled, the creative duo headed over to Jack Liebowitz at DC Comics and signed a year-long contract at $500 per week. Their plan was to create new projects for DC on the side, while keeping up their day jobs at Timely. In a small hotel room near the Timely offices, Simon and Kirby set up desks and drawing boards, converging there on evenings and weekends to hack out pages for the competition. "The work at Goodman's became a chore as we gathered every spare moment to retreat to our secret hideaway where we could work on the new features," Simon wrote.

The competition for talent was fierce during the gold-rush days of comic-book publishing, and companies commonly poached artists from one another. But that made it no less of a sin if you were discovered to be working for the enemy. Apparently, Simon and Kirby did a poor job of hiding their extramural activities. One day at lunch, when they were headed to their hotel room, Stan Lee tagged along, needling them about their intended destination. "You guys must be working on something of your own," Stan said.

Caught, or perhaps just exasperated, they told him their secret. Then, Simon wrote, they hired Lee to help out at their after-hours art shop. A few days later, Goodman confronted Simon and Kirby, demanding to know if they were moonlighting for other publishers. When they acknowledged that, yes, they were, Goodman fired them. Lee disputes Simon's account of his involvement in the events surrounding their departure, saying that he still has no idea why they left. For his part, Simon said he doubts that Lee was the person who tipped off Goodman, suggesting that it was probably a DC staffer hoping to score some points with the Timely owner.

If any element of that muddled affair is certain, it's this: the departure of Simon and Kirby gave Lee a terrific career boost. With Timely's editor and art director both gone, the bulk of the comic-book line's editorial duties fell into his eager lap. Goodman installed Lee as the editorial director on a temporary basis, with the intention of eventually finding someone else. At some point, Goodman must have stopped looking, because, except for a three-year hiatus during World War II, Lee stayed on as head editor for more than three decades.

Upon Kirby's exit, Al Avison, a young cartoonist from Connecticut, took over the penciling duties for *Captain America Comics*. Syd Shores, a Chesler-shop veteran who had been hired by Simon at $30 a week, provided the inks and also became the company's art director. The Timely line, with *Captain America Comics* leading in sales, boasted nearly a dozen titles, including *Young Allies, USA Comics, Mystic Comics, Marvel Mystery Comics*, and *All Winners Comics*, which presented Captain America, the Human Torch, and the Sub-Mariner all in one book. The sixth issue of *Mystic Comics* featured the debut of "The Destroyer," a series that Stan cocreated and wrote for several years across a range of Timely books.

Still operating out of the McGraw-Hill Building, Goodman hired a roster of staff artists to churn out an ever-growing amount of material. Crowded into a tiny room in the Timely offices, with a single window linking them to the outside world, the staffers sat hunched over their drawing tables, penciling figures into panels, inking each other's work, and filling letters into captions and speech balloons. George Klein, tall and quiet, had started his career as a painter, then segued into comics to make a living. He inked humor features starring characters with names such as Percy and Little Pan. Ed Winiarski came from the animation business. Dave Gantz, who was born in the Bronx the same month as Stan Lee, drew adventure stories before finding his voice in *Super Rabbit, Gandy Goose,* and other funny-animal titles. Dave Berg, who later gained fame at *Mad* magazine, also served a stint in the Timely bullpen. Carl Burgos and Bill Everett, the creators of the Human Torch and the Sub-Mariner, respectively, worked from home.

There were so many titles that needed to be filled with stories that staffers often took freelance work home. A typical page rate was $15—$8 for pencils and $7 for inks. With a quick hand, an artist could easily double his annual income through freelancing. Sometimes staffers competed to see who could finish the most work over the weekend. Mike Sekowsky, a skinny, tough-talking man and the most facile member of the bullpen, always won. He once showed up on a Monday morning with twenty-seven penciled pages. Gantz, who was no slouch, arrived with fifteen pages.

One highlight of that early Timely era was the striking comic-book covers by Alex Schomburg, whom Lee once described as "the Norman Rockwell of comics." Schomburg began his career drawing magazine covers for science-fiction publisher Hugo Gernsback. He later specialized in airbrushed erotic covers for horror pulps such as *Uncanny Tales* and *Mystery Tales* before moving into the comic-book field. Back then, when few artists had any following to speak of, and comics heroes lived and died at the whimsy of millions of dime-carrying kids, covers were the key marketing element of a comic-book package. The sales of a comic book soared or tanked on the quality of its cover. A snappy cover could even salvage the business prospects of a sixty-four-page tome of muddy-colored artwork and hackneyed writing—a fairly common scenario in those days.

Because they had such a direct impact on his bottom line, Martin Goodman supervised the assignment and design of covers very closely. Schomburg, a favorite of Goodman's, produced some of the best covers from the Golden Age of Comics. His artwork—lush, bright, and laden with fine detail—adorned *All Winners Comics, Captain America Comics, Daring Mystery Comics,* and countless others. He drew nearly 200 Timely covers between 1939 and 1945, many of which are highly sought collector's items today.

Stan Lee had his own office, spartan and unimpressive, from which he managed the comic-book assembly line and wrote scripts for *Captain America Comics* and features for various lesser-known superheroes such as Jack Frost, the Whizzer, and Black Marvel. Other stories were supplied by the artists and a cadre of freelance writers, including Mickey Spillane, the future detective novelist. Timely was by no means a one-man show. With production on an upward slope, more bodies were brought in to keep traffic flowing smoothly. Gantz and other artists pitched in on the editorial duties. "It was all very casual," Gantz told interviewer Jim Amash.

In the early days of Lee's tenure, Goodman kept a tight grip on the reins. "I had to show him everything," Lee recalls. Stan regarded Goodman, who sported fine, chiseled features and prematurely gray hair, with a kind of hero worship. In addition to Timely, Goodman's publishing empire encompassed magazines and pulps. Gradually, as Stan learned the comic-book business, he asserted more control over the Timely division and sought his employer's counsel less often. Still, Goodman held the purse strings, and that made him the man in charge. Goodman mostly stayed in his office, poring over sales figures, trying to identify trends, sometimes napping. But whatever else was on his plate, he always insisted on approving covers. According to Lee, Goodman also tended to avoid confrontation and difficult situations. When messy personnel matters arose in later years, such as a company-wide firing, he would send Stan in to mop up.

As a writer, Lee appeared to demonstrate more enthusiasm than his peers. Whereas another scribe might dash off a story and send it along by messenger, Lee would call an artist, say, Leon Winik or Chad Grothkopf, and dictate the script to him over the phone. "I thought [Stan] was the Orson Welles of the comic book business," artist Dave Gantz said in an interview. "He had energy and was young, tall, and good-looking. When Stan would try to explain an action scene, he'd say, 'Take it to its ultimate point. Don't give me the in-between stuff.'"

Lee also wrote quickly. Goodman paid him by the page for script work, in addition to his editorial wages, so the more stories he churned out, the more money he took home. Lee wrote two to three stories a week, sometimes more. It wasn't just the money that motivated him. As he soon discovered, he didn't have the patience for time-intensive writing endeavors. "Almost everything I've ever written, I could finish at one sitting," Lee says. "I'm a fast writer. Maybe not the best, but the fastest. Writing is a lonely thing, so I try to get finished with it as soon as possible."

Because the medium was so young, there was no formal training for comic-book scripters. Stan learned on the fly, picking up dialogue tips and storytelling cues from the work of more accomplished writers such as Charles Biro at Lev Gleason Publications and Bill Finger, who wrote for the Batman comics. "Nobody sat down and told anyone how to do it," Lee recalls. "Nobody had any respect for comics. It was the lowest rung on the creative totem pole." Few publishers asked for writing credentials. They were happy with "anybody who could put two words together and work cheap enough."

Unsurprisingly, the works produced in that creative milieu made little impression on the world of arts and letters. Who had time to develop themes or round out characters? The script was due at the publisher's office *yesterday*, and they didn't pay enough for that kind of literary attention. Lee, like most of the folks then pounding out ten- and fifteen-pagers, stuck to the basics. His writing was undistinguished but competent, at least good enough to give a twelve-year-old his dime's worth of diversion. "I'd have a plot in my mind, always the simplest plot in the world, and I'd start writing," Lee explains. "I'd try to think, what would the first panel be? Then I'd write a description of what the picture should be, then I'd think, what should the characters say? Or what caption do I want to write? Then I'd go on to panel two, and I'd keep doing it until I reached page ten, the end."

A small-town sheriff is revealed as gun-shy on page five. If he doesn't overcome his phobia by page nine, a gang of outlaws will kill his kidnapped son. Page ten brings the big shootout. Lee liked the improvisational nature of story creation, spinning out plot complications and character wrinkles as he typed. Working with an overly planned narrative would have ruined that process, he says. "The simpler the original idea, the more opportunity it gave me to come up with all kinds of interesting angles."

On his lunch hour or during lulls in the day, Stan went on long walks in the city to unwind. Occasionally he invited artists to join him. A freelancer might come back from such a walk with an earful of new story ideas and a dollar-a-page raise. Timely was raking in a lot of money, and Stan wasn't afraid to spend it. "Martin likes to brag about how much money we're spending to produce the books," Lee told one of his artists in the early 1940s. Because some titles were published sporadically and others were canceled or changed editorial direction on short notice, Lee amassed a lot of extra inventory, purportedly for fill-in or emergency use. If an artist called in sick or blew a deadline because he'd been out drinking the night before, Stan could pull one of those stories and drop it into an issue. At one point, he had tens of thousands of dollars worth of pages stashed in office cabinets, many of which were never published.

Lee got along well with most of his Timely colleagues. Few of the staffers seemed to resent taking orders from a recent high-school graduate, and those who did kept it to themselves. Whatever else Stan may have been—young, cocky—he was still the boss's relative. "I was writing stories, and they were as good as anyone else's stories," Lee says. "Besides, everyone was trying to make a living, and if I'm the guy who's buying the work, nobody is going to be rotten to me." Lee led an active social life, inviting the artists and writers over to his apartment for gatherings. "He was always the object of conversation, and the guys' wives would get jealous," Timely artist Vince Fago said in a magazine interview. "Stan was well liked by everybody."

By 1942, comic books had cemented their place in American pop culture, approaching mass-media numbers with 143 titles on stands and 50 million readers per month. Some public discussion had arisen about the increasing luridness of comics and their noxious effect on schoolchildren. "A poisonous mushroom growth" is how one wag described them. But the critics had minimal effect on business, and the dimes kept rolling in. It would be at least another decade before the anti-comics movement gained traction.

Superman and Batman were still pulling the ship at DC, while other companies found success with characters such as Captain Marvel and Plastic Man. Still other publishers ventured into uncharted waters, testing out genres ranging from teenage titles (*Pep Comics*) to literary adaptations (*Classic Comics*). Artists such as Jack Kirby, Will Eisner, Mac Raboy, Reed Crandall, and Lou Fine stretched the art form in new directions, incorporating bold cinematic techniques, exploding and reassembling the grammar and syntax of comics, and reinvigorating the field's sense of purpose. Through an informal system of swiping and homage, experimentation and refinement, the comic-book medium evolved.

Dozens of publishers littered the landscape. Many of them were small-time operators who printed their comics on credit, finagled their way onto newsstands, and then were swept away in a tidal wave of red ink. It was relatively easy to enter the comic-book business, but, as with most booming industries, very difficult to establish a going concern. Still, amid the clamor and chaos of those early days, some firms emerged as industry leaders. They included DC Comics, Quality Comics, Lev Gleason Publications, Fawcett Publications, Dell Publishing, and Martin Goodman's Timely Publications.

The secret to Goodman's success was the same as it had been when he was minting money with pulp magazines: Find a hot trend, milk it for all its profit, and move on. When superhero comics were selling, Goodman put out ten of them. The quality of the books barely mattered, so long as Timely collected its share at the newsstand. It was in this spirit that Goodman charted a new course for his company in early 1942. The year before, Dell had done well with licensed titles based on Walt Disney and Looney Tunes characters, as well as with a funny-animal book, *Animal Comics*. Sensing rich prospects in these genres, Goodman instructed Lee to create some titles in the same vein. Lee inaugurated Timely's humor campaign with *Joker Comics* #1, which featured Snoopy and Dr. Nutzy, Eustice Hayseed, and Stuporman, as well as the debut of Powerhouse Pepper, by legendary big-foot cartoonist Basil Wolverton. Lee also converted *Daring Mystery* into a title called *Comedy Comics*. The transition happened so quickly that the first two issues of *Comedy Comics* contained both superhero and humor stories. In its rush to capitalize on trends, Timely sometimes made it difficult for a kid to know what his hard-earned ten cents was buying. *Krazy Komics*, which focused on Disney-esque funny animals, came next, followed by *Terry-Toons*, a licensed title that eventually starred Mighty Mouse.

For Stan, the humor comics were an opportunity to try out fresh material and to draw on the radio and movie comedies he enjoyed as a child. While still keeping a hand in the superhero universe, Lee began scripting features such as "Little Lester" and "Ziggy Pig and Silly Seal," working with such artists as Vince Fago, a former animator, and Al Jaffee, the future *Mad* magazine cartoonist. Those efforts represented Lee's first tentative stabs at humorous writing, a style that he would refine in the coming decades, culminating in the irreverent, semi-ironic tone of the 1960s Marvel comic books. The comedy in Lee's scripts was broad, with sight gags and hare-brained schemes, but there were also hints of the playful innovations that would make Marvel so endearing to readers. In an installment of "The Ginch and Claude Pennygrabber," published in the August 1943 issue of *Terry-Toons*, the title characters get mixed up in high jinks at a military camp. At the story's end, they wind up, predictably enough, in the stockade. The Ginch, who resembles a junior version of Walt Disney's Goofy, sits obliviously in his cell, toying with a wooden gun. Pennygrabber, a good-natured but conniving fox brought low, stares out at the reader, imploring, "Please, please dear artist, don't put me in the same strip with the Ginch again!"

"I love humor. Comedy is one of the highest forms of entertainment," Lee says. But humor is more than just gags and one-liners, he adds. If a character delivers a zinger, it should be funny because of the context, what the reader already knows about the character. "Everything is characterization," Lee notes. "I'm not turned on by just jokes. It's got to mean something."

In due time, World War II caught up with the comics industry. Art shops and publishing houses emptied as writers and artists were drafted into service. At Timely and elsewhere, older artists, women, and others who were exempt from wartime duty came on board to pick up the slack. Comic books had long been leading the charge against the "evil Japs" and Hitler's Third Reich. Now, the business enjoyed a circulation boost from sales to the millions of young men on military bases who were tackling those menaces for real. When paper shortages hit, publishers such as Goodman and DC's Jack Liebowitz managed to secure generous allocations, and their companies thrived.

On November 9, 1942, Stan Lee enlisted and was assigned to the Signal Corps, the army's communication division. Stationed in

Astoria, Queens, and later at posts in North Carolina and Indiana, he wrote and illustrated training manuals, using many of the skills he had acquired as a comic-book writer. Lee created a cartoon character called Fiscal Freddy to help the army train its payroll officers. He drew a public-service poster that encouraged soldiers to visit syphilis-treatment stations after they had sexual contact with women overseas. And, inspired by his love of musical theater (and presaging some of his later cornball antics at Marvel in the 1960s), he wrote a marching song for the finance department, whose members sang it to the tune of the air force anthem while they marched. "I instilled a new morale and enthusiasm in that finance department," Lee quips. "I don't know why I didn't get a medal of honor."

When Lee left Timely to enter the service, he appointed artist Vince Fago to act as editorial director in his absence. Born in Yonkers, Fago was eight years Stan's senior and also an alumnus of DeWitt Clinton High School. After a stint in the animation industry with Fleischer Studios, where he worked on Popeye and Betty Boop cartoons, Fago joined Timely and drew funny-animal features such as "Frenchy Rabbit" and "Dinky and Rudy Rooster." Fago and Lee became friends, going for swims and on long walks together. As editorial director, Fago's salary jumped to $250 a week, a sum that he typically doubled with freelance work. Stan had handed him a prize gig, irking some of the employees who had been with the company longer. Granted, Fago's animation background made him a suitable candidate to replace Lee, particularly since Timely was stocking up on humor material at the time. But there were whispers about another motive. "I think Stan was protecting himself," Gantz remarked. "He didn't want anyone to upstage him. Vince had the type of nature that would never allow him to do a thing like that." Of course, Stan probably needn't have worried, given that he was technically a member of Goodman's family. Like a Mafia don, Martin Goodman always took care of family.

While Lee was gone, Goodman relocated his publishing outfit to more spacious offices on the fourteenth floor of the Empire State Building. Before the move, a group of prank-loving staffers decorated the walls of the McGraw-Hill headquarters with ink drawings, costing Goodman extra money to have them recovered. Not that he couldn't afford the expense. His firm was swimming in money. At one point, according to Fago, Timely included a subscription notice in *Miss America Comics* asking one dollar for twelve issues. Within weeks, 20,000 dollar bills had poured in, and Fago had to commandeer the art bins to store them all. Comic-book issues routinely shipped with 500,000-copy print runs, sometimes more, while distributor returns sank to near-insignificant levels. During Fago's tenure, Timely launched a raft of humor and funny-animal titles, including *Super Rabbit*, *Comic Capers*, *Krazy Krow*, and *Animated Movie Tunes*. By late 1944, Archie-style teen-humor books were hot, and Goodman entered the fray with *Tessie the Typist*, *Junior Miss*, and several other copycat titles.

Even though he was occupied keeping America's fighting forces free from VD, Stan still found time to write stories for Timely. In the late evening and on weekends, he churned out scripts at a dollar per page, communicating with Goodman and Fago by mail. A Lee-penned satire about army life, titled "Super Soldier," appeared in *Krazy Komics* #15, signed by "Pfc. Stan Lee." Other artists, such as Gantz, who was stationed at a replacement camp in Florida, kept working for Goodman too, drawing complete stories in rented hotel rooms, earning as much as $500 in a weekend. Finally, on September 29, 1945, after two years, ten months, and twenty-one days of service, Sgt. Stanley M. Lieber received an honorable discharge. His separation papers, which classified him as a playwright, listed no battles. He did, however, earn a good conduct medal during his military tour. Stan returned to New York City, installing himself in a two-room suite at the Hotel Alamac, and resumed his editorship at Timely. Fago couldn't envision being an assistant after having spent three years in charge, so he transitioned to a full-time freelance career.

In the postwar years, the comics industry continued to prosper. Demand was high for funny-animal and educational comics. Super-heroes sold well until the end of the 1940s, and then experienced a prolonged fadeout. A stream of new genres arrived—women's comics, romance comics, crime comics, western comics. The purveyors of four-color wonder threw everything they had at the newsstands, hoping a few ideas might find favor with their increasingly fickle audience. Stan and the Timely staff never initiated trends, but they were always quick to produce a slew of imitations. "They did takeoffs on everything," Gantz recalled. "When we were doing the teenage books, Archie became very popular. Stan noticed that Archie had crosshatching on the back of his head and told us to start doing that."

In the fall of 1947, shortly before his twenty-fifth birthday, Stan attended a cocktail party and met Joan Boocock, a redheaded, blue-eyed hat model from Newcastle-on-Tyne, England. He was instantly smitten. Joan was intrigued by the handsome young writer, who immediately declared his love for her and quoted poetry by Omar Khayyam over hamburgers at Prexy's. "He looked exactly like a young Leslie Howard," Joan told an interviewer. "He was totally a writer then. He wore his coat tossed casually over his shoulders and his hat worn at a jaunty, carefree angle. He had marvelous eyes and an incredible sense of humor." Their relationship faced only one obstacle: Joan was already married. She had arrived in New York City as a war bride. "I had only known my first husband twenty-four hours when we decided to get married," Joan said in a 1979 *People* magazine article. "It really was a great marriage in many respects. But after living with him a year, I was finding him sort of boring . . ." Within a few passionate weeks, Stan had persuaded Joan to file for divorce. She flew to Reno, Nevada, which granted divorces after six weeks' residence there. Stan followed, and on the day her divorce was finalized, they were married minutes later by the same judge.

Stan and Joan's first apartment was a spacious brownstone in Manhattan. Outfitted with a skylight and a terrace, their dwelling was a huge step up from the cramped, alley-facing apartment Stan lived in as a child.

Stan seemed to enjoy his role as a youthful editor in a still-blossoming industry. He even felt confident enough to write and self-publish a short book, titled *Secrets Behind the Comics*. *Secrets*, which Stan sold out of his apartment for a dollar a copy, was laid out in comic-book format, with illustrations by Ken Bald and other Timely mainstays. In a loose but entertaining fashion, it provided a behind-the-scenes look at the comic-book production process—a rare enterprise for those times. In later years, comics fans would dissect every detail of their chosen hobby, but back then, few people cared how the sausages were made. In his book, Lee revealed such insider details as how to recognize an artist's style and the proper formatting for a script. He also included several blank pages that comic-book wannabes could use to draw their own stories. Lee counseled aspiring writers to spend about an hour penning each page, although on days when ideas aren't flowing, he advised more time might be needed. In *Secrets*, Lee's writing, while a tad unpolished, nevertheless resonates with the jazzy, pitchman style that would permeate the covers of 1960s-era comics such as *The Fantastic Four* and *The Amazing Spider-Man*. For example: "Are you beginning to realize now why *The Secrets Behind the Comics* has been called the most complete book about comic magazines ever published . . . as well as the most exciting?" Even then, Lee had a flair for self-promotion.

Back at Timely, the offices were swelling with more artists, writers, production workers, and business staff. Lee oversaw a team of editors, including Al Sulman and Al Jaffee, who handled the different comic-book lines. He acted as a "supreme editor" of sorts, reporting only to Martin Goodman. For a brief period, Stan had three secretaries seated in plain view of the entire office, to whom he dictated stories simultaneously. "I was kind of cocky, and I think I enjoyed doing it," Lee recalls. "But then I said to myself, 'What the hell are you doing? You're a showoff. If I was someone else, I'd hate a guy like you.' So I stopped." During that time, Lee could hardly be said to have flourished creatively. Though an efficient editor, his imitative strategy was driven more by greed than any notions of artistic flattery. "I was just doing what my publisher asked me to do," Lee said in an early-1980s interview. "Being young, I enjoyed the feeling of importance of being editor and art director and head writer.

"It never occurred to me that what I was doing wasn't all that great."

PART II

"EXCELSIOR!"

BRING ON THE BAD GUY

Stan Lee entered the 1950s on a personal and professional roll. The Goodman comic-book line had found its publishing niche as an opportunistic follower of popular trends. Lee was taking home as much writing work as he desired, to the point that he could almost calculate household expenses and newlywed indulgences by the number of scripts he needed to complete. His marriage flourished. Joan Lee was happy as a homemaker, giving up her modeling and acting career at Stan's request to provide her husband a functioning household, a best friend in which to confide, and an oasis of interests and activities divorced from the ins and outs of the comic-book industry. Joan not only furnished the foundation for Lee's home life; she changed the focus of his career. Having a family to support increased Lee's general desire for greatness and sharpened his focus on very specific demands for the here and now. Stan Lee was now a provider.

The Lee family unit expanded twice during those early years. A daughter, Joan Celia (named in tribute to Stan's mother), arrived in April 1950. Stan's sixteen-year-old brother Larry moved in upon their mother's death in 1947, and stayed with them until he was old enough to live on his own. Needing more space, the Lees pulled up roots in the first of many restless moves between city and suburb. They moved into a remodeled carriage house in Long Island's Hewlett Harbor—a gated community incorporated from a private club in the 1920s and home to what local historians describe as the Island's most "socially prominent and very wealthy families." Joan Lee reminisced to interviewer Blake Bell about her neighbors: "They considered Stan as something of a lightweight inasmuch as he was writing these silly little magazines for little children." According to Mrs. Lee, Stan would dictate his notes into a wire recorder and type them up in the morning. Lee eventually found a way to reduce the pressures of the morning commute. With Martin Goodman's permission, Lee stayed home one, then two days a week. At home, he wrote comic-book scripts and received pages of art from illustrators living nearby. Lee wrote outdoors when the weather permitted, typing in a standing position facing the sun. He even hammered away at the keyboard as poolside parties went on around him. Martin Goodman's eldest son, Iden, who recalls the Lees' time on Long Island in idyllic fashion, was a constant visitor from the Goodman home two miles away. "I remember it as a very warm, happy place," he says, and the Lees were "very generous, very welcoming." Iden learned to drive a car in the Lees' driveway and once tangled up Stan's wire recorder, "the first I ever saw." It was a very different way of life than the one Stan Lee had experienced growing up in the Bronx.

Not everything went swimmingly for the new couple. Joan and Stan suffered a personal tragedy—which Stan later called the greatest of his life—when, in 1953, they lost a second daughter, Jan, at the age of three days. Still dreaming of a larger family, the bereaved couple was unable to negotiate the rigors of the adoption process. They had hoped for a son. The inability to add to their family was one of the few regrets the normally ebullient Lee would acknowledge in later years. But despite this source of sadness, their marriage remained strong. The proud parents doted on little Joan, and Stan's work was constant, profitable, and diverting.

Happier than he'd ever been, Stan Lee projected his fears of not being able to provide for his family onto an entire industry. If the comic-book industry were to shrink, if comic books were to fall out of favor, Stan mused on his long walks, then eventually Martin Goodman might dissolve his comic-book line. And what skills could a thirty-year-old editor and writer of America's least-respected form of creative expression hope to bring to more legitimate industries?

The specter of failure, of being let down by his field and, in turn, letting down those who depended on him, would continue to haunt Lee in palpable fashion until the early 1970s. Fragments of these concerns would pepper his conversations and interviews for decades after that.

Lee had reason to worry. Basking in the glow of its breakout success as a publishing phenomenon, the American comic-book industry experienced the fury of an anti-comics backlash several years in the making. This backlash was not specifically directed at Lee or the Goodman comic-book line, nor did Lee or his comics even act as major players in the direct confrontation between the comics industry and its self-appointed reformers. But the rigorous examination of comic-book content in the early 1950s was an industry-wide event. It changed the way comic-book professionals thought about their line of work, Stan Lee as much as anyone, and engendered economic consequences for the Goodman comics for years to come. Lee's personal story had found its bad guy.

Every popular American art form of the twentieth century suffered through a crucible in the name of the public good. Filmmaking experienced several rounds of public censorship battles, foreshadowing the controversy that would eventually engulf the comic book. The overwhelming popularity of movies in the 1910s and '20s made their excesses a bigger and more attractive target for critics. A pattern of legislative threats and promised self-censorship became locked into place as early as 1915, culminating in the establishment of the Hays Board in 1934. Comic books' direct antecedents, the newspaper comic strips, had been protested against for their crude and controversial nature in the mid-1890s. Newspaper boycotts by concerned educators and parents made headlines from 1906 to 1911. When the newspaper comics page moved from a preponderance of gag strips to embrace the adventure serial in the 1930s, a second generation of reformers noted its racier qualities. Citing the lurid violence of "Dick Tracy" and the femmes fatales of "Terry and the Pirates," concerned citizens voiced their displeasure to parents' groups and newspaper editors with increasing frequency.

The first major shot across the bow of the burgeoning comic-book industry came in May 1940, the same year Stan Lee entered the field. The popular newspaper writer, playwright, and eventual

Disney-adapted children's author Sterling North wrote an article excoriating comic books for the *Chicago Daily News*, which was syndicated to forty additional papers nationwide. North struck a nerve. Requests for reprints poured into the *Daily News* office for a full year after its initial publication. The article eventually saw widespread publication in pamphlet form as "A National Disgrace."

North's arguments focused on the early comic book's status as lurid, sensationalist junk. According to North, reading comics kept the average youth from developing healthier tastes in children's literature. Men like Martin Goodman, Major Malcolm Wheeler-Nicholson, and Max C. Gaines were responsible for creating a curriculum made up of cheap thrills, simply constructed sentences, and gaudy pictures that would ruin the vocabularies and stunt the imaginations of an entire generation. The only solution parents could safely embrace was to introduce Junior to the fruits of their local library. Any adult who eschewed this responsibility and allowed kids free run at the local newsstand, dimes in hand, was negligent.

North's article became the outline for a battle on educational grounds that dominated the next eight years of cultural dialogue about the comic-book industry. For North, as well as the concerned parents and conservative librarians who believed in him, the question was simple. How exactly did comic books impair the development of young readers, and what could be done about it? In library bulletins and local newsletters in New York, California, and Pennsylvania, educators debated various strategies for weaning children away from superhero comic books. Such articles considered everything from direct confrontation of the offending material in the classroom to bait-and-switch tactics in local libraries, whereby a child seeking out the latest adventure of Captain America might leave the stacks with a biography of George Washington.

One solution to the comic-book problem became a sizable footnote in the industry's publishing history. In a remarkable display of not beating but joining the comic-book menace, *Parents Magazine* released the debut issue of *True Comics* in 1941. *True Comics* featured wholesome, well-crafted stories about real-life heroes and events, and offered up an impressive "advisory board" of squeaky-clean child stars (including Shirley Temple) to vet them for their target audience. *True Comics* lasted for ten reasonably successful years, and it established a sizable market for "good-for-you" comics, stories drawn from literature or from real people worth modeling. The most popular title featuring adaptations, *Classics Illustrated*, appeared in October of 1941 and enjoyed a three-decade run for its publisher, Gilbertson, and multiple revivals by different publishers thereafter. Having never met a genre they didn't like and couldn't exploit, Stan Lee and Goodman produced a few comics roughly analogous to Gilbertson's bestsellers. *Idea—A Classical Comic*, which lasted four issues from mid-1948 into 1949, adapted historical novels of a classical type, if not pedigree. Although many Goodman adventure comics, such as *Men's Adventures* and *Man Comics*, proclaimed that their stories were taken from true life, both the claim and the stories themselves were less than truthful. By the early 1950s, such magazines were producing straightforward, but fictional, war stories.

The parents' groups and cultural critics were successful in propagating a view of comic books as a debased form of literature, harmful junk food that was a waste of a child's time. Even the more wholesome comics seemed to offer up material that was derivative of more substantial written work. Comic-book publishers countered with a claim they still use to promote their product today: A child reading a comic book was at least reading something, and, given time, a curious child would move on to more challenging material. This argument became so ingrained in the consciousness of industry professionals that in 1978 Stan Lee proclaimed to Nelda Clemmons of the *Tampa Times*, "I learned to read by reading comic books." Considering all evidence to the contrary, including Lee's advanced age when he claims to have first encountered comic books, his boast is best understood by taking into account the pressure of decades spent justifying his livelihood.

Like all media, comic books enjoyed a respite from the grinding of critics and commentators beginning in December 1941. A country focused on the immense task of winning a war had little time to debate the merits of popular forms of entertainment. Comic-book companies received an additional boost from the kind of unabashed patriotism that detectives and superheroes and kid gangs displayed by punching out Axis spies and slaughtering the occasional battalion or two of demonized, subhuman soldiers fighting for the other side. Timely flagship character Captain America was credited with a million dead Japanese in one memorable war-era story, a body count that fans of Jimmy Stewart could only dream about.

The calls for censorship returned in the late 1940s, intensified. Postwar America squirmed with threats of nuclear Armageddon and whispers of an erosion of Western society from the inside out. One of the most alarming threats, driven in part by a news media trying to hold onto its audience in an increasingly crowded market, was juvenile delinquency. The popular conception of a transitional, teenage period between childhood innocence and adult responsibility was beginning to gain acceptance. Now there were wide-ranging reports of this new breed gone bad. The type of crimes being committed by teenagers and the regularity with which they were reported seemed aberrant to police authorities in major East Coast cities. Desperate for an explanation, social reformers turned to the study of environmental causes for behavior, a line of inquiry popular among working psychiatrists of the day. One environmental factor that distinguished the immediate postwar generation was a childhood spent reading comic books.

The postwar comic books were different, too, as new genres jostled with the superhero for market ascendancy. In 1942, Lev Gleason Publications changed the name of its *Silver Streak* title to *Crime Does Not Pay*. Under the direction of editor, writer, and artist Charles Biro, *Crime Does Not Pay* offered up grim and lurid morality tales. Never before had a comic-book title suggested the tone of the work inside so well. Biro's books were a sensation, and in the late 1940s he enjoyed a small measure of celebrity as the man whose magazines sold as many copies as *Life*. One admirer was Stan Lee, who, according to Biro, often called asking for the secret by which he might imbue his copycat efforts (like 1948's *Lawbreakers Always Lose*) with Gleason's winning box-office formula. "The secret," Biro reportedly told Lee, "is Charlie Biro."

Other comics companies enjoyed similar success with the attention to detail and real-world pulp thrills favored by Biro. By the early 1950s, EC (Entertaining Comics) was the industry's most admired publisher. EC had the most glittering array of talent yet assembled at one company—artist-writer-editors Harvey Kurtzman, Johnny Craig, and Al Feldstein; much-admired illustrators Wally Wood, Graham Ingels, and Jack Davis; even the occasional writing contributor like Ray Bradbury or publisher William Gaines himself. EC specialized in crime, war, science fiction, and horror stories told in a voice that, while still relatively unsophisticated, refused to speak down to the reader as blatantly as many youth-targeted comics did. Many EC comics contained elements of social commentary or satire, science-fiction stories that commented on racism, or war stories that were critical of heroic outcomes. EC comics were the most effective, confrontational, and beautifully rendered comics on the stands. They were the kind of comics that turned thousands of kids into single-company snobs—"EC Fan-Addicts"—and sent writers like Stan Lee scrambling after their own versions of EC's best-selling titles, even if only the gaudier surface qualities could be copied. The end result was a comic-book newsstand awash in blood, gore, and muck.

Stepping into the breach against these new comics was a loose confederacy of parents' groups and teachers' committees. The National Office of Decent Literature of the Catholic Church even maintained a list of comics it found harmful. In 1948, *Parents Magazine* spotlighted the Committee on the Evaluation of Comic Books, a Cincinnati-based group whose sole purpose was to read and rate comic books to aid parents in making decisions about the reading material their children were bringing home. *Parents Magazine* also began publishing the yearly CECB list in its pages. Other responses were less measured. In December 1948, *Time* reported on a comic-book burning in Binghamton, New York, a form of protest that would in the next few years spread to cities including Indianapolis, Oklahoma City, Phoenix, and Sacramento. Local laws were also passed against the publication and sale of comic books in New York and California.

In response, a few comic-book publishers put together advisory boards to ensure the safety of the readership and to act as a publicity shield. Some industry professionals were able to point to a small but potent body of literature from psychiatrists and educators that treated the comic book with moderation or even kindness. Martin Goodman's company was more aggressive than most in resisting the creeping tide of negative public opinion. Goodman hired noted psychiatrist Jean Thompson of the New York City Board of Education's Child Guidance Bureau to advise on book content from June 1948 to November 1949. She was trumpeted in the pages of the comics as an editorial consultant. "Dr. Thompson's professional examination of our magazines, as advisor to our staff, is *your* guarantee that the Marvel Comics Group magazines are striving to bring you the very best in reading matter," proclaimed a strident editorial that ran in May 1949. Thompson developed an in-house code and reviewed every periodical released. The Marvel editorials went so far as to criticize Dr. Fredric Wertham, the leading authority on comic-book dangers, and stressed the public's right "to read what they wanted to read." Lee even wrote a punchy short story, "The Raving Maniac," a direct parody of Wertham, for the April 1953 issue of *Suspense*.

Wertham was the comic-book industry's Savanarola. The New York–based psychiatrist was popular and well regarded in his field, particularly among reformers. His expertise relied on the study of the impact of social factors upon the individual psyche. Wertham provided testimony on the egregious effects of segregation that was used by lawyers in the landmark Brown v. Topeka Board of Education case. He worked with the destitute, abused, and neglected in Baltimore and Harlem. Wertham was also a writer, stumping in magazines and books for social reforms based on his fieldwork. The doctor's writing style careened wildly from table-thumping didactics to descriptions both dramatic and intense—Lee remembers Wertham's second book, the 1941 case study *Dark Legend*, not for its social critique but as a macabre thriller about a boy who murdered his mother.

Wertham first wrote about comic books in the article "The Comics . . . Very Funny!" which appeared in the *Saturday Evening Post* in 1948. For the next seven years, he enjoyed a profitable sideline writing and speaking about the dangers of the comic book, culminating in 1954 with the publication of his book *Seduction of the Innocent*. That volume was excerpted in both *Ladies Home Journal* and *Reader's Digest*, where his views received their widest audience yet. Wertham first identified the comic-book threat, citing statistics (which some contemporary scholars believe to be generous by a factor of two) that the publication of ninety million comics a month led to a child reading a comic book a staggering one billion times a year. He then went on to describe why the vast majority of these comics were unsuitable for children. They denigrated positive feelings in favor of a considered cynicism. They taught children to hate authority figures and were primers on how to commit deviant and criminal acts. They were sexually charged and luridly violent, and they promoted homosexual relationships and racial intolerance. Based on his readings of the four-color texts—he even had bad things to say about comic books based on Disney characters—and his own experiences seeing juvenile offenders express their love of comic books, Wertham could only conclude that these were an evil that needed to be controlled through legislation.

In April 1954, a United States Senate subcommittee convened to consider that notion and to investigate the comic-book matter for itself. It was steered by Estes Kefauver, who had come to national prominence four years earlier investigating organized crime. Kefauver was interested in the potential electoral springboard another high-profile series of hearings might bring. The entire comic-book industry watched—veteran artists and writers, including Lee, would decades later recall, with the clarity most reserve for the remembrance of a presidential assassination, how they heard about a day's events. Wertham testified, as did EC publisher William Gaines, with a series of answers that became famous for their cheeky absurdity. (Hopped up on medication, Gaines denied that one lurid cover was tasteless by describing a cover that was ten times worse.) Newspaper cartoonists Walt Kelly and Milton Caniff were brought in as expert witnesses. In the end, it was clear that the hearing had been conceived as a publicity ploy to frighten comic-book publishers into controlling their own excesses. In its report released on March 5 the following year, the subcommittee urged the comic-book industry to take steps to better regulate itself, even though no causal relationship between comic books and juvenile delinquency had been established.

The industry was a few steps ahead of Senator Kefauver. The summer of 1954 was rich with debate among comic-book professionals as to what concessions the industry might make to forestall the negative publicity that could come with a harsh subcommittee finding. An earlier attempt, in 1948, at self-regulation had failed miserably for lack of participation. It was unclear whether a new effort would be better received. Martin Goodman was encouraged to resist any attempts to appease Wertham and the reformers, not only by Lee and the freelancers but by his company's longtime lawyer, Jerry Perles. "My own feeling was that comics didn't need the *Good Housekeeping*–type seal of approval. There was more patriotism in a comic book than in a roomful of 'do-gooders,'" Perles recalled in 1987. Goodman reacted with decisive and effective public denials to charges against his company, including rebuking an assertion that he obscured his ownership of the comics line so that he could avoid responsibility for their content.

By September, at the urging of EC publisher Gaines, the Comics Magazine Association of America had formed. Gaines hoped the new body would combat public outcries through research and legal advice, and would act as an effective counter to Wertham's views. Instead, the larger publishers who dominated the CMAA, caring little for EC's right to publish and eyeing its market share, established a Comics Code Authority to regulate comic-book content. According to its charter, the CCA would screen books at every step of their formation and offer a stamp by which distributors and retailers would know these "approved" comic books to be the kind that didn't lead to bad-for-business protests. Wertham turned down the CCA's chairmanship, believing such a self-patrolling effort would in the long run prove toothless. Retired New York judge Charles Murphy took his place, and named five women to the board in order to maximize its "inherent sensitivity."

The Comics Code adopted by the CMAA in 1954 changed the field for decades to come. The code constricted content. It demanded that, in all instances, good defeat evil. It forbade comics from ever showing a criminal act in sympathetic fashion. Authority was to be respected at all times. Violence of all sorts, but especially that involving guns, was limited. Touchstone words including "crime" and "terror" could no longer be used on covers. Artists were required to draw women in a respectable manner, without lingering over physical features. Many of the more ghoulish monsters could not be drawn at all. Any subject matter that could have been construed as unsuitable for children by the broadest standards of 1950s America was banned, and with it went many of the creative devices by which the industry could be made more interesting for older readers.

There was business fallout as well. The cumulative effect of several years of intense scrutiny had taken its toll on the industry. The number of comic-book titles declined by almost two-thirds, and several major companies that had been around since the industry's inception went under. William Gaines attempted to transform the EC line into code-friendly books, but eventually gave up and canceled all of its titles except *Mad* magazine. Even the successful companies remained somewhat scarred—no one ever looked at Batman and Robin the same way after Wertham was done interpreting their relationship. With television entering more homes and providing intense competition for a child's leisure hours, it was a historically inopportune time for a faltering entertainment medium to be further weakened by public controversy.

The Goodman line suffered more than most. Despite the advice of his lawyer and his own basic feelings regarding the First Amendment, Martin Goodman couldn't opt out of the Comics Code. He lacked the market clout of Dell, with its Disney-licensed titles, or the sheen of semi-legitimacy that Gilbertson enjoyed with *Classics Illustrated*. Adapting the Goodman line to the code made for disruptions for many on the freelance rotation. "I lost *The Ghost Rider* on account of the title," says artist Dick Ayers. Plot points also needed to be negotiated differently. Horror, already declining in popularity, was out entirely. Guns were used more sparingly, a touchy proposition when it came to westerns. Production became a more extended process, as Lee was forced to have the books approved and to make any corrections demanded by the CCA. Many of the changes seemed bizarre and arbitrary—Lee would speak for years about having to change a single gun or item in a way that decreased the violence very little, only heightening its absurdity instead. But any potential increase in the editorial workload that came with the code was mitigated by the relatively inoffensive state of the Goodman line. "We were tame before Wertham," Lee says. The biggest change for Goodman's line was yet to come. In the early 1950s, Martin Goodman engineered a split from newsstand distributor Kable and started his own distribution company, Atlas News Company. The timing of the controversy over comic-book content weakened many distributors and, with the rise of television, was one of several factors contributing to a general sales decline in the comic-book field. Seizing control of distribution had simply exposed Goodman to another level of business risk. By 1957, this problem would come to a head with disastrous results.

In addition to the real business fallout of this time period, the crusade against comic books had an effect on Stan Lee's attitudes toward his job and his industry. The writings of Dr. Wertham made Lee's accidental career more disreputable than ever in the eyes of the public. Other comic-book industry figures—none of them as bright or quick on their feet as Lee—were the ones asked to testify on the field's behalf. Even newspaper strip cartoonists Kelly and Caniff, despite reading a statement of support into the record from the National Cartoonists Society, gave off the air of respectable family members appearing at a morally lost cousin's bail hearing.

In his autobiography, Stan Lee wrote about a series of public debates between Fredric Wertham and himself. It is a highly emotive but vaguely phrased discourse, and it appears in the text without the slightest bit of factual confirmation. No record exists of a series of Wertham/Lee debates. Wertham displayed little interest in hearing from comics professionals, even refusing to allow those from the comic-book industry in attendance to speak at a 1948 symposium. He likened comics professionals to liquor distributors at a conference on alcoholism. And Lee was only one professional among many. Lee now admits that he never debated Wertham, although he claims to have participated in a few public discussions on the issue of comic-book censorship with "followers" of Wertham. "One of them was in a school gymnasium," he says. Given the helplessness felt by comic-book professionals in the mid-1950s, it's not surprising Lee would write himself a better, more active role in his industry's defense. "I hated the idea of what was happening with Wertham," Lee says. "I hated the fact that he was tarring every comic book with the same brush, but there was nothing we could do about it. We had to live through it."

THE BIGGEST COMIC-BOOK COMPANY IN NORTH AMERICA

Mad magazine stalwart Al Jaffee had the young Stan Lee pegged. Lee's same-age peer in the comics industry and a close professional acquaintance, Jaffee would eventually write one of the more insightful tributes to Stan Lee's varied career. In 1995, speaking of the period decades earlier when he worked with Lee as a comic-book editor at the Timely offices, Jaffee penned: "The one thing that impressed me greatly about Stan was his 'can do' attitude. No matter how many new titles were thrown at him at the last minute, he somehow never failed to meet the deadlines. I remember the first time I was called in for a cover conference. I was an associate editor at the time, responsible for about twenty teenage titles. I figured this would take the better part of the day. No way! Stan said, 'Read the titles off one by one.' I started, and instantly he rattled off a cover idea quicker than I could rough-sketch it. This went on for no more than thirty minutes, until all twenty or so covers were done. . . . It was a bravura performance."

Jaffee's story captures a forgotten and under-appreciated chapter in Stan Lee's life. Before he was Stan the Man, Stan Lee was in many ways the hardworking embodiment of the postwar era in the American comics industry. In the decade and a half after 1946, comic-book companies were rarely measured by their books' quality, their success at scoring film deals and licensing options, or their asserted cultural significance. Comic-book publishers in the postwar era were most significantly defined by how many units they moved from printing press to spinner rack. As much as Marvel Comics, with its dynamic and quirky superheroes, came to represent American comics from the 1960s to the present, the Goodman comic-book line in all of its earlier incarnations, featuring a relentlessly shoddy and shameless exploitation of popular trends, was equally emblematic of the comic book's disreputable teenage years. The field was a long time in growing up, and Stan Lee seemed in no extra hurry to guide it into adulthood.

This middle phase of Stan Lee's career, between falling backward into a comic-book job in the 1940s and swooping in out of nowhere to help revitalize the field in the 1960s, has been for the most part ignored. The main reason for this is that the majority of his work from that period was largely forgettable. Lee spent the 1940s and '50s writing hard, fast, rote genre stories. His primary goal was to meet deadlines and bolster his paycheck. He encouraged similar stories as an editor, whether from in-house staff, freelancers, or the occasional writer slumming from his regular job at Magazine Management, the parent company of all Goodman's publishing concerns. If Stan hadn't insisted on working against comic-book tradition and signing his work wherever it might appear, it would be hard to discern from content alone exactly which scripts he contributed. He was one of several dozen undistinguished writers working the field. Without the revival that his career experienced in the 1960s, there would be little to no interest in the content of Lee's pre-Marvel stories at all. Indeed, Lee himself has buried his comic-book career between 1946 and 1961, making it the wilderness of vocational disappointment from which he and Marvel Comics emerged. Lee has spent the last three decades poking fun at features such as "Fin Fang Foom" and "Ziggy Pig and Silly Seal," citing them as examples of the kind of brainless pap he was churning out before he was struck by the inspiration for Marvel.

Managing the comic-book line of a company that was hell-bent on maximizing its sales offered a special set of challenges. Upon returning to Timely from active duty in the war, the first item on Stan Lee's editorial plate was continuing Vince Fago's work in capitalizing on the latest trends. Timely had already succumbed to the pressure for girl-friendly characters by adding Otto Binder's Miss America superheroine to the cover of *Marvel Mystery Comics* in 1943. Miss America soon moved into her own title and immediately incorporated features designed to appeal to young girls—dating, makeup tips, and recipes. Lee returned to a full-time position in 1945. *Patsy Walker*, launched that same year, became the company's longest-running and most successful female-character-based title. Patsy was soon joined by *Tessie the Typist*, *Millie the Model*, and *Nellie the Nurse*, giving Timely a full complement of boys-and-dating adventures with which to soak the market. These comics brought in an impressive female readership, and they also led to women being hired by the male-dominated company. Miss America's first artist was Pauline Loth, hired by Vince Fago out of the animation industry. Ruth Atkinson was the debut artist for both *Patsy Walker* and *Millie the Model*. Stan Lee has ever since enjoyed a significant reputation as a female-friendly editor.

Whether he was devoted to female audiences or just audiences in general, Lee didn't stop with a few titles explicitly devoted to girls. The young editor grabbed every last bit of market share he could with as many conceptual gymnastics as the "girls' comics" concept would allow. Female superheroes were a natural development in Timely's remaining superhero titles, taking over even as their male counterparts' popularity was fading in the postwar, peacetime era. The Blonde Phantom began a three-year run in 1946, solving crimes in a red evening gown and black mask that writer Les Daniels called "an outfit even less suited to adventuring than leotards." In April 1948, Captain America's young but unfortunately male partner, Bucky, was rewarded for his years of service to the Timely line by being shot by thugs and hospitalized; he was replaced by the female adventurer Golden Girl. August of that year saw the launch of three more female superhero titles: *Namora*, featuring the female cousin of the Sub-Mariner; *Sun Girl*, the fiery counterpart of the Human Torch; and *Venus*, the adventures of the Goddess of Love as she slummed among mankind as a reporter. That year was the height of Timely's efforts to appeal to female readers. Female-comics historian Trina Robbins estimates that thirty of forty-eight titles offered by Timely in 1948 were directed to a female readership. But, like most trends, this one soon died down and was transformed. Namora and Sun Girl both lost their titles by year's end, while Venus, despite an impressive number of changes, never found her way past issue #19. Most of the other books were converted into romance comics.

Some of Lee's maneuvers on behalf of a potentially saleable genre worked much less effectively. Superheroes were a nearly hopeless cause by 1947, as audiences for comic books made their preference known for the sturdier realism found in other genres. In 1946, Lee tried unsuccessfully to replicate the "superteam" success enjoyed by DC Comics and other companies by joining Captain America, the Sub-Mariner, the Human Torch, and newer characters the Whizzer and Miss America in the All Winners Squad. That attempt lasted only two issues. And, while Bucky's debilitation might have been a good career move for Golden Girl, it didn't do much for Captain America—the last regular issue of the title bearing his name appeared in 1950. The Human Torch and the Sub-Mariner left comics in 1949, the same year that the former superhero flagship *Marvel Mystery Comics* came out with its ninety-second—and last—issue. By the decade's end, the superheroes were dead and no amount of editorial gimmickry was going to resurrect them.

The loss of a once-popular genre hardly caused Stan Lee a moment's worth of grief. He busied himself with managing and contributing scripts that exploited new trends. Timely began publishing crime comics in 1947 with *Official True Crime Cases* and *Justice Comics*, a title converted from *Wacky Duck*. The company soon added several similar titles. These comics owed their style and approach both to the early EC crime comics created by Johnny Craig and to the leading work in the field done by Charles Biro for Lev Gleason Publications. At least three Goodman comics—*Lawbreakers Always Lose*, *Crime Can't Win*, and *Crime Must Lose!*—even aped the title of Gleason flagship *Crime Does Not Pay*. Other titles included *All True Crime* and *True Complete Mystery*. Many of the company's most undervalued artists, such as Jack Keller, did some of their best work on those titles. Lee wrote only a tiny handful of crime stories, exclusively for the title *True Complete Mystery*. He was better suited to the western trend, which had been brought about by the increasing popularity of the genre in movies and was sustained by the spread of such films as programming on early television stations. His first western comic book was March 1948's *Two-Gun Kid*, which, with *Annie Oakley* and *Wild West*, launched Timely's western efforts. *Two-Gun Kid* foreshadowed numerous titles built around various "Kids" and names with hard "t" sounds (*Kid Colt*, *Tex Morgan*, and *Tex Taylor*).

Lee also contributed to the shape and character of the comic-book line through his occasional scripting efforts. The artists particularly enjoyed his western fillers. Artist Al Williamson recalled: "They were four-page, five-page stories. They were simple little stories, but they had a nice moral to them. The guy would come in, clean up the town, you know. And there would always be a nice moral behind it. But it was always so much fun to draw." None of Lee's writers, nor Lee himself, could make much from the blending of westerns and love comics found in the sagebrush romances of the late 1940s and early 1950s. Titles such as *Rangeland Love* and *Cowboy Romance* were extreme examples of the editorial mission to capitalize on popular trends, a comic-book contribution to American kitsch that Lee and the Marvel artists of the 1960s helped the medium to largely outgrow.

By 1950, comic books had firmly established themselves as disposable, mainstream entertainment, and the Goodman line was perhaps the most disposable and eager-to-please group of titles on the stands. Coming out of the war and into this fertile period, Goodman's comics were produced under a bullpen system. In a suite of offices on the fourteenth floor of the Empire State Building, the bulk of the company's artists worked on salary, rather than at home as freelance contractors. They assembled on workdays in one large room that was reminiscent of the "shop" setups that had been prevalent at the dawn of the comic-book age but had since gone out of favor. The Goodman setup was a large room with enough space for approximately thirty artists, from veterans including Carl Burgos and Syd Shores to baby-faced newcomers such as Dan DeCarlo and Gene Colan. The bullpen was a genial setting where artists argued over which New York–area baseball team to listen to on the radio. "When we worked, we worked," said artist John Buscema, "but if something interesting came up, we might stop for a discussion, especially during the baseball season." There were also workplace advantages. Younger illustrators like Buscema and Colan could watch veterans like Burgos at work, picking up various artistic hints and tips that, because of the industry's lack of respectability, were not taught in most art schools. "Syd Shores was there to straighten us out if we had any questions about the work," Colan says.

For his part, Lee loved the energy of the bullpen and the easy access to artists. After a decade as a writer and editor, Lee was becoming more set in his ways, and one of his habits was seeking corrections the moment they occurred to him. Although Syd Shores supervised the bullpen, Lee enjoyed being able to bounce in to have corrections done or to call an artist directly into his office to explain why a certain page wasn't up to production quality. Having a staff of artists on call suited Stan's frenetic way of getting work done immediately. Years after the company no longer enjoyed a formal bullpen, Lee would still drag freelancers in from the waiting area and into his office to make a correction or two.

Lee also felt at home as the slightly juvenile leader of a band of zanies. He loves to tell the story of going up the elevator at the Empire State Building with various bullpen members in their disheveled clothing, as if they were playing hooky from the kind of buttoned-up jobs the rest of the grim-faced businessmen were trudging to and from. Lee would often play an ocarina, stand on his desk, or sit on a filing cabinet to make proclamations. Colan remembers his first encounter with Lee before being hired in 1948. When Colan arrived at the Goodman offices looking for work, he found Stan sitting in his office, playing cards with another editor. Lee was wearing a beanie cap with a propeller, which spun every time a gust of wind came blowing in through the open window. "Stan asked me to sit down and he said to me, clowning around, 'You want to get into this business, right?'" Colan recalls. "I said, 'Well, that's why I'm here.' He hired me right on the spot and told me I'd be working in the bullpen with other artists."

Lee learned a hard lesson in 1950, when the bullpen was closed due to structural changes at Magazine Management. Goodman would tinker with the inner workings of his company for the next several years. It was during this period that he began his move into distribution. Goodman had always been fascinated by the distribution process, and his defining characteristic as a publisher of comic books was his devotion to scouring behind-the-scenes reports and rumors about which titles were selling and which ones were not. By starting Atlas News Company, which was anchored in part by the eighty-two monthly titles that Stan Lee and the boys were producing in the comic-book division, Goodman could increase profits by eliminating the middleman. He could also respond much more rapidly to evolving trends and sales figures.

Goodman was confident that Lee could maintain the comic-book line's healthy production by working with freelancers instead of in-house staff. Many companies employed a system whereby artists and writers worked at home or in studios as independent contractors. Stan himself preferred to write at home. Goodman had discovered one of the ways that Lee had been able to keep on top of the demanding schedule. The company was loaded with inventory, a backlog of completed scripts and finished comic-book pages, already paid for. All companies kept an inventory, but Lee was hoarding enough pages to fill a closet—and according to industry scuttlebutt, he had literally done so. Because of the surplus, the in-house art staff was fired. "When I came back to work on Monday, all the artists were out of a job," says Colan. Others remember a more gradual elimination process, but one just as definite.

Lee would later refer to this time as the beginning of the "Black Days," a period of business reversals when the standard way of operating was either changed or foiled outright because of the needs of the larger corporation. Professional lives for which Lee felt at least partly responsible were changed, if not outright disrupted, by such machinations, and even if no one blamed him directly, the bad news was his to bring to the artists and writers. Most of the staffers were let go in a series of fits and starts beginning around Christmas of 1949. Luckily, Goodman's plans did not involve curtailing production. Although he was asked to use some of the collected inventory, Lee was able to offer a sizable amount of freelance work to former members of the bullpen by the end of 1950 and into 1951. Stan remained relentlessly positive about the work atmosphere, but some undefined quality of carefree creative ferment had been lost. A decade later, when casting about for an image with which to present the professionals working on the Marvel superheroes to their growing audience, Lee offered up a fictional bullpen that sounded a lot like the old setup in the Empire State Building. But back in 1950, the offices emptied, and the company that had made its name as Timely Publications would now forge a new reputation as Atlas Comics. Lee soldiered on.

Another business-driven possibility helped bring about a brief revival of the Timely superheroes. A Superman television show that hit the airwaves in February 1953 was a solid ratings success. George Reeves's portrayal of the Man of Steel drove additional licensing sales of DC Comics' most recognizable superhero character and helped maintain interest in the comic book. Superman's TV success led to interest in a possible series for the superpowered fish out of water, Bill Everett's Sub-Mariner. As a businessman, Goodman was also intrigued by Atlas getting back into the business of publishing superheroes, a genre with a once-lustrous sales pedigree.

A closer look at his then most recent foray into superhero comic books, a two-issue series released in 1950 featuring a character called Marvel Boy, might have dissuaded Goodman. Unlike his predecessors, Marvel Boy was not tethered to World War II. In the early 1940s, superheroes acted as colorful avatars of action for readers denied the chance to pound on the world's very real bad guys. Marvel Boy's plots were a reflection of the early 1950s, and closely resembled a fever dream of red-scare paranoia and acceptance of nuclear proliferation. Flying saucers did not merely reflect fears of a Soviet invasion, as they did in many sources of pop culture from the 1950s and '60s; in *Marvel Boy*, strange ships in the sky were most likely arriving from a communist planet.

A similarly enthusiastic and unsubtle updating of superhero tropes doomed the Timely superhero revival almost before it began in December 1953. Bill Everett—one of the artists on *Marvel Boy*—provided what may have been the tightest and loveliest art of his career for the new Sub-Mariner stories. But the television show never panned out. Russ Heath and Dick Ayers, two solid craftsmen, provided art for the new Human Torch stories that appeared in *Young Men* and then in the character's own brief title. Captain America was drawn by a young John Romita, an artist who was not only trained as a commercial illustrator, but also a cartoonist who took the comic-book industry's history seriously. When Romita drew Captain America, it was in obvious homage to the Kirby-

Simon version, all exaggerated action and panel-breaking fight scenes. Yet the scripts doomed the character's solo title revival to almost immediate extinction. This new Captain America proudly proclaimed himself a "commie smasher" on the covers of his adventures, and inside he could be seen boldly slugging his way through Cold War hotspots and thwarting poisonous influences at home with the moral certainty that he had brought to the Nazi conflict ten years earlier. Upon the near-immediate cancellation of the revived *Captain America Comics*, Lee told a distressed Romita, who feared his art had proved commercially unviable, that readers had simply reacted poorly to the stridently conservative tenor of the scripting. Everett's Sub-Mariner lasted slightly longer, perhaps due to the broader range of stories the artist was turning out, but more likely because of continuing television show negotiations. By October 1955 it was canceled as well. It would take more than a simple transposition of old ways of storytelling into new settings for the Goodman line to successfully revive the superhero.

As much as they were temporarily enamored of the past, Stan Lee and Martin Goodman had a different model in mind for Atlas during much of the early 1950s. By the decade's start, EC Comics had begun to hit its stride as a publisher in multiple genres. Its comics featured the finest group of illustrators ever assembled in one place in the industry's short history, and a team of skilled writer-editors who could also act as illustrators, frequently communicating their narratives to the artists via thumbnail sketches. For some cultural historians, EC Comics' exquisitely crafted, challenging stories represented the first, brief flowering of a truly adult sensibility in the American comic book. While there were certainly more commercially powerful companies in the early 1950s, no comic-book publisher enjoyed the artistic influence of EC. Its books were widely read in bullpens and among freelancers, including those who worked for Goodman. Lee admits that he studied the books as editor at Atlas, and that for a brief period it seemed that every comic book Goodman suggested Atlas might explore was a takeoff on something that was working for EC.

EC also held some fascination for Lee as an editorial enterprise. He was captivated by the way publisher William Gaines was able to create an identity for the entire line despite the fact that EC, like

Atlas, always worked in multiple genres. EC rewarded fans for their passionate interest, creating a fan club for "EC fan-addicts," spotlighting their talent, and running letters pages that reflected more of a clubhouse atmosphere than a respectful exchange between reader and editor. EC seemed to get more and better work out of some of the same talents who worked for Lee. Harvey Kurtzman was one of EC's primary editors, writing a number of morally complex war stories and the social satire-minded *Mad* magazine for Gaines. Kurtzman went to EC after having been employed by Goodman doing single-page gag strips that were noteworthy for their play within the confines of the comic-book form. Where Lee had attempted to keep Kurtzman busy, Gaines had given the same talent free rein to create a series of successful books and one breakout hit magazine. Lee would respond to EC's example at Atlas by creating similar works in similar genres, even copying the art direction and general look in his attempts to duplicate the success of *Mad* magazine. Lee had some minor successes in that regard, but he wouldn't learn the more general lessons from Gaines and his bunch—the importance of catering to fans, loosening up the letters pages, and giving greater creative leeway to the top talent—until the 1960s.

Like every comic-book company, Atlas was hurt by the acceleration of comics' general sales decline that came with the overwhelming criticism of comic-book content dominating the 1950s. But as a self-distributing company with a flexible editor and freelance staff, the Goodman line might have been in a position to suffer less than most. In 1955 and 1956, Atlas added a number of titles in multiple genres, even as EC was making the moves that would eventually boil the company's output down to a single publication, *Mad*. Lee also took advantage of the industry disruptions to bolster Atlas's freelance talent pool. It wasn't always a good match. Some artists weren't accustomed to working in the mighty Atlas manner. Bernard Krigstein, a painter who worked in comics in part because of a belief in their artistic potential, had created several semiotic masterpieces for William Gaines at EC. In "Master Race," a late-period EC story about a Jewish concentration camp victim encountering his camp commandant in a city subway, Krigstein innovated new ways to communicate the passage of time on newsprint that thrill academics even today.

Unfortunately for Krigstein, formal innovation was not in demand at Atlas, nor was it a practical course for an artist, considering what Atlas was offering as pay by the latter half of the decade—an anemic $27 per page. His work for Atlas from 1950 to 1954 and again from 1955 to 1957 was of a high quality. But the experience of working with Lee and Atlas left a bad taste in Krigstein's mouth, which increased as the decade progressed. He didn't think much of the scripts he was given to work with. "I thought the plots that Stan Lee was using at the time weren't that bad, but their treatment was very banal. As far as possible I tried to transcend that written treatment to bring out the idea behind the story, and to give them a lighter touch," Krigstein later recalled. He also ran up against the company's then-standard practice of providing as many features per issue as possible, at the expense of extended stories that facilitated complex narrative solutions. Krigstein went so far as to refuse Lee permission to add dialogue to a clever pantomime section of a story called "Phantom of the Farm." He eventually left the company, frustrated by the limits placed on artists by Lee's approach to comic books.

The artists who worked well with Stan tended to be those who had worked with him for a longer period of time and who had a particular talent for being prolific in addition to their illustrative skill. Joe Maneely, lightning-fast and versatile, was the signature artist of the Atlas era. Highly gifted in multiple genres, he could accurately embody the classic Timely look on a superhero cover as easily as he could draw in the loose, energetic style required for humor comics. Lee claimed that Maneely could do seven pages of complete comic art—pencils *and* inks—in a single workday. Maneely's was the example that the Atlas editor hoped younger artists would follow. Lee sent a very green John Romita to Maneely's studio for a day's tutelage in the specifics of comic-book production, and Maneely held court while working on multiple pages of highly detailed period comic art. "I may have learned more that day than any other," Romita recalls. Maneely's adventure art was showcased in a rare Atlas period adventure serial, *The Black Knight*, the first issue of which was written by Lee, while his covers and interiors were an anchor for the modest but steady-selling western genre that was the backbone of the company.

Lee not only valued Maneely as a vital cog at the workplace; he genuinely liked him. "Joe was not only the best artist, but the greatest guy to work with," Lee says. "He had not an ounce of temperament." Lee describes their relationship as close—in a life that, outside of a few couples with whom he and wife Joan socialized, was not exactly distinguished by its number of close industry friendships. Lee was friendly and amiable with Maneely in a way that he was with few comic-book artists. Although Lee didn't move in the social circles Maneely did—like Bill Everett, Maneely liked to drink, and the pair would often lose entire days to carousing—theirs was a fruitful workplace relationship that spilled over into the outside world. Together Lee and Maneely worked on side projects that had the potential to move them into the much more respectable world of newspaper comic strips, selling the strip "Mrs. Lyon's Cubs" to a syndicate in 1957. Then tragedy struck: Maneely died at the age of thirty-two in 1958, falling in front of a moving commuter train. Stan was deeply saddened, and he still speaks fondly of the artist. "Bright, fast, he could draw faster than Jack Kirby. Versatile. He could draw anything," Lee says. Romita remembers his one-time tutor as someone who would have been as important an artist to Stan's 1960 superhero comic books as Jack Kirby and Steve Ditko. And with Maneely's speed, "it might have been hard for the rest of us to get work," Romita comments. Lee suggests that if Maneely had survived, there might not have been any Marvel superheroes: "I think if he hadn't died, I would have eventually maybe quit Marvel and gone off with Joe and done other stuff."

Lee's personal tragedy in losing Maneely came on the heels of his most severe professional setback to date. A sales malaise began to catch up with Atlas, not because of the efficient office manned by Lee, but due to the distribution arm. Lee reduced page rates to help offset the decline, but that merely drove many of the artists with young families to more stable companies or out of the field altogether. The biggest change came in a disastrous set of circumstances surrounding distribution. Frightened by the decline in comic-book titles and the potential effects of the Senate hearings and the Comics

Code, Goodman closed Atlas News in November 1956 to sign a deal with the largest comic-book distributor of the mid-1950s, American News. But the larger distributors had been the ones hurt the most by the scare surrounding comics. They had lost multiple magazine clients to other distributors, publishers trying to distance their companies from the unsavory comics business. Goodman's decision to close his own distribution arm—encouraged by a business manager named Monroe Froelich—was the worst business move of his career as a comic-book publisher. American News left the market in early 1957, forcing Goodman to scramble for another distributor. Desperate not to cease publication, he signed a hugely repressive deal with DC, which made its offer only when Goodman agreed to limit his line to eight published titles per month. Suddenly, Stan Lee was saddled with a shadow of the company he had helped build.

The collapse at Atlas was immediate, and it can be traced almost directly to a work stoppage in late April 1957. Titles were pruned from the schedule in direct and brutal fashion—nearly thirty that were cover-dated August alone. The Goodman line dropped the Atlas designation and published sixteen bimonthly titles built around its core strengths of yeoman westerns and light romance. And until another batch of inventory was exhausted, Lee stopped hiring for those few comic books. Lee was devastated, particularly as it was up to him to communicate the change in the line to the various freelancers who counted on him for part of their living. One industry account said Lee went to the restroom after each face-to-face meeting and vomited. John Romita recalls that he was asked to send in the story he was working on at the time—for which he wasn't paid—and then was told he was out of a freelance gig not by Lee himself, but by one of his secretaries.

For the next few years, Lee toiled in a small, two-office space at Magazine Management's offices on Madison Avenue. It was a great distance from the fourteenth floor of the Empire State Building, both physically and emotionally. The comic-book business was a small part of the Goodman publishing empire, which included major book and magazine divisions. David Markson worked alongside Lee at Magazine Management for almost two years, but says, "I don't think I ever knew where the comic-book offices were." Lee was generally well liked in the offices. "I thought he was very brave, always chipper," says Bruce Jay Friedman, who worked for Martin Goodman from 1954 to 1965. Friedman remembers Lee's tiny workspace and single secretary, in contrast to the sea of employees he had enjoyed previously. Remembering Goodman as a publisher he considered both a supportive employer and a stern businessman who had the respect of every editor at Magazine Management, Friedman suggests that it might not have been the company's survival that Goodman had in mind by keeping Lee in-house. "The comics had tailed off, and I have the feeling that Martin Goodman was trying to squeeze him out, not quite fire him, but humiliate him into leaving." After running through some inventory, Lee hired back the core Atlas artists on a freelance basis with the now nameless Goodman comic-book line, including two important late-period hires, the young artist Steve Ditko and the veteran Jack Kirby. Both men were formidable artists who would influence Lee's career for years to come. Together with Don Heck and Paul Reinman, they anchored Lee's late 1950s and early 1960s efforts with the Goodman line.

For a brief period—one that is often inflated because of its proximity to the superhero comics that would transform the company in the 1960s—Lee's most notable titles were in the genre of light-hearted science fiction. Beginning in December 1958 with *Strange Worlds*, which would soon be followed by titles such as *Tales of Suspense*, *Tales to Astonish*, *Worlds of Fantasy*, *Strange Tales*, and *Journey into Mystery*, Lee and his brother, Larry Lieber, wrote science-fiction stories of aliens and monsters that were rendered with a high level of charm and energy by the remaining freelancers. By their second year, the highlight of most issues was a monster story drawn by Jack Kirby, featuring a giant, rampaging, Godzilla-like monster and the efforts by humans to protect themselves from its fury. Kirby was enamored of monster stories as a kind of universal campfire fodder for the ages, a way for humankind to show its mastery of the world around it by defeating a rampaging enemy, often of its own creation. Lee had fun making up strange names for the creatures—Taboo, Vandoom, Zzutak, Grottu, Fin Fang Foom—and helping devise ways to explain their downfall.

Although Lee dismisses the monster comic books as weak in contrast to their superhero successors, the content of the stories remains interesting despite their pedestrian narratives. The monsters and aliens by Heck, Kirby, and Ditko were more visually sophisticated characters than those in the vast majority of comic books that Goodman had published in healthier times. Lee allowed the artists to drive the works, and the result was more intriguing than stories about a monster stepping on people and knocking over buildings had any right to be. With his silly names and panicky dialogue over the impressive, sometimes moody art, Lee and the artists achieved an early version of the blend of silly and serious that made his 1960s superhero comic books so appealing. By working fast and loose, Lee had secretly uncovered seeds of the revolution to come: he began to trust his artists, and react to their visual narratives in a way that flattered both parties.

Stan Lee was one of the most efficient and productive managers during the American comic book's period of greatest mainstream availability. At the beginning of the 1950s and again at the decade's midpoint, under two radically different styles of management, Lee was the editorial director of what was, by most accounts, the industry's most prolific company. But the next stage in both the comic book's development and Lee's career would be about something entirely different, something Lee had largely neglected before—the content between the covers.

JOLLY JACK AND STURDY STEVE

Stan Lee never created anything alone. As a writer working in a visual form, he depended on artists to bring his ideas and words to life. For Lee, the most significant event of the fertile monster-comic-book period of 1959–1961 was the establishment of two creative relationships that would later propel him to his greatest achievements. An industry giant, Jack Kirby was far and away the top artist on the Goodman monster books. A relative newcomer to the field, Steve Ditko employed a consistency and visual élan that soon established him as a can't-miss talent and a solid third option behind Kirby and Don Heck. Lee's partnerships with Kirby and Ditko, solidified in the late 1950s over dozens of short stories featuring rampaging behemoths with silly names, would eventually flower into the best work of each man's career. With Jack, Stan would participate in the creation of the bulk of the Marvel superhero line, including its flagship title, *The Fantastic Four*. With Steve, Stan would breathe life into the most popular comic-book character of the last forty years, Spider-Man. Unlike many of the other important collaborators in Stan's life, both Kirby and Ditko brought a wealth of artistic skill and creative ego to the table. Their professional lives stood in stark contrast to Lee's own.

When Jack Kirby returned to the Goodman line for good in 1958 and took up the mantle as that company's premier artist, he was midway through a career that, like those of Will Eisner, Harvey Kurtzman, and Carl Barks, defined the American comic book. Like Kurtzman, Kirby made his impact in multiple genres. When Kirby wasn't innovating methods of comic-book storytelling or instigating successful, widely copied genres, he was giving those genres some of their best representative works. Jack Kirby made comics of solid craftsmanship and raw power. If for Stan Lee the Marvel superheroes of the 1960s represented an unheralded period of creativity after years of self-described hackwork, for Kirby the Marvel superhero line was one significant period of inspiration among many. For Lee, Marvel would prove to be everything; for Kirby, Marvel was the joyful afternoon of a long day in comics. Jack Kirby's career during the years 1941–1961 was everything Stan Lee's was not.

Following their controversial departure from Timely for DC in late 1941, the team of Joe Simon and Jack Kirby settled into a comfortable groove exploiting the adventure-comic phenomenon with Kirby's signature panel-to-panel action. Having created Captain America, the most popular patriotic superhero, Simon and Kirby next started the successful subgenre of boys-gang comics. Based loosely on movies like the Dead End Kids series, with their broadly played, incorrigible boy characters and a homespun sensibility derived from neighborhood values close to Kirby's Lower East Side heart, titles such as *Boy Commandos* and *Newsboy Legion* were among the most popular comic books of the World War II period, and they remain definitive representatives of that era's mass entertainment. Simon and Kirby also continued to create athletic superheroes such as Manhunter and the original Sandman character, properties that DC Comics continues to utilize today.

Like Stan Lee and most working writers and artists in the comics industry, Jack Kirby was drafted for service in World War II, entering the army in 1943. Whereas Lee served stateside in a creative position about which he would later brag, and continued to do as much comic-book work as he could squeeze in, Kirby fought in Europe with the infantry, rarely spoke of the experience, and whatever artwork he could muster went into foxhole sketchbooks or letters to home. Lee and Kirby held very different views of the war, emotionally opposite reactions to a shared experience. Comics critics would later claim the war years told the difference between their respective creative contributions to the comic-book field. In war and in comics, Stan Lee was the ebullient careerist, always looking for a way to continue his breadwinning, while Kirby was the silent achiever surviving in the trenches.

After being discharged, Kirby renewed his partnership with Joe Simon. They quickly reestablished their reputation as creative thoroughbreds, cranking out comics for publishers DC Comics, Hillman, and Harvey Comics in the explosion of genres and styles that marked the postwar funny-book market. In their next significant contribution to the form, Simon and Kirby created the first romance comic with 1947's *Young Romance*. Romance comics, with their overwrought soap-opera plotlines and mostly conservative values, would be a staple for comic-book publishers through the early 1970s. Simon and Kirby gave their readers agonized heroines for whom the tortuous quest for true love was played out in a series of self-reflective word balloons and teary-eyed body language. Stan Lee would copy the Kirby/Simon formula diligently in dozens of romance comics for the Goodman line. Even today, the original Simon and Kirby stories are effective totems of kitsch. The tearful heroine biting back tears as she debates telling her paramour some dark secret is an easily recognizable contribution to American visual iconography and pop-culture shorthand.

Jack Kirby also contributed to the flexibility of the mostly staid, conservative comics business. Instead of working as a freelance production team, Simon and Kirby had taken their romance comic concept to a publisher, Crestwood/Prize, in return for a fifty–fifty return on profits. Soon they were running nearly an entire comics line for Crestwood, including the titles *Headline*, *Justice Traps the Guilty*, *Western Love*, *Young Love*, and *Young Romance*. In order to produce the hundreds of short stories necessary to sustain those books, Simon and Kirby employed several artists, including skilled veterans such as Mort Meskin and Bruno Premiani. Everyone there drew in a style reminiscent of Kirby's, creating a house look similar to the visual debt Marvel's superhero artists in the 1960s and '70s would owe him.

At the end of his first full decade in comics, Kirby had become a seminal comics artist, one whose work anchored every publisher he worked with and was copied by dozens of working artists.

A second wave of titles for Crestwood, including *Black Magic*, *Young Brides*, and *The Strange World of Your Dreams*, was eventually published, but the seminal Simon and Kirby comic book of that era was produced for humor specialist Harvey Comics. *Boys' Ranch* was a western comic that recalled the jaunty group dynamics of titles like *Boy Commandos*. But Kirby was hardly the same artist he'd been before the war. Now Kirby was able to supplement the energy of fight scenes with panels of profound stillness and atmosphere, where the shapes on the page took on weight and dramatic intensity by their spacing within the panel rather than simply by their movement. Like many artists with a signature style who seek to broaden their style's effect, Kirby was overshadowed in this period by the stars of William Gaines's EC stable, which included Wally Wood, Bernard Krigstein and Alex Toth, and the increasingly slick line work from the regular artists at DC Comics.

The last great achievement of the Simon/Kirby partnership was the broadly satirical *Fighting American*, produced for Crestwood in 1954. *Fighting American* was the first significant superhero title to enjoy a purposeful subtext, as Simon and Kirby used the powerful but simplistic icons of the previous decade's patriotic superheroes to satirize and explore the murkier political waters of the Cold War. Less significant but still worthy of note, the effectiveness of *Fighting American* was enhanced by a fan's knowledge of comics tropes and previous stories, making it perhaps the first comic to specifically reward longtime comics readers in a field that traditionally viewed complete reader turnover every few years as an unavoidable reality. That same year, Simon and Kirby made an attempt to become comic-book publishers themselves. Their Mainline Comics produced titles such as *Police Trap*, *Fox Hole*, and *In Love*. Like most companies, including Stan Lee's Atlas, the Simon/Kirby strategy was to cover every popular genre of the period with a representative title. Of course, the last thing the publishing world needed at that moment was another comic-book company. The industry turmoil caused by the juvenile delinquency scare and the growing popularity and affordability of television was driving even the established companies to near bankruptcy. Many of the Mainline Comics titles lasted fewer than five issues.

With the failure of Mainline, Simon and Kirby began to drift apart. They worked together very sporadically thereafter, and each man found his primary focus as a solo act. Simon continued with the romance comic work, moved back into drawing, and eventually created the long-running *Mad* competitor *Sick*. Kirby moved back to the large publishers and explored newspaper syndication. Two of his efforts in particular presage the Marvel superheroes.

In DC Comics' *Challengers of the Unknown*, Kirby gave comics fans a precursor of the modern superhero team. *Challengers* featured four rugged adventurers of varying hair color and macho vocations banding together for adventure after sharing a near-death experience. The Challengers shared a centrally located headquarters and wore professional jumpsuits rather than gaudy, decorative costumes, and their adventures consisted of matching their various skills and personalities against outsized obstacles. In basic conception and in the progression of the individual adventures, *Challengers of the Unknown* would not have been out of place as a Marvel comic a decade later, although Marvel was never to publish a title with characters quite so bland.

Starting in September 1958, Kirby also drew the syndicated daily space-adventure newspaper strip "Sky Masters," the kind of mainstream showcase after which many in comic books, including Stan Lee, consistently pined. It was never more than a minor success in terms of client newspapers, and save for an eight-month run when it was inked by Wally Wood, "Sky Masters" rarely stood out artistically. But the fact that Kirby was drawing a syndicated strip in addition to carrying a hefty monster-comic workload may help explain the unparalleled explosion of output that came into play during the early Marvel superheroes period, beginning in 1961. It was a creative geyser that erupted only a half-year after Kirby departed the newspaper strip.

Kirby had landed on Stan Lee's doorstep for good in 1958. A contract dispute over "Sky Masters" had driven a wedge between the artist and DC Comics, and his raw, dynamic approach to action-adventure comics was falling further out of vogue with the editors who purchased stories. Although he wasn't exactly an artist "at the bottom of the barrel," as described later by one Marvel editor in chief, Kirby was no longer a rising star in a growing industry. Kirby himself felt that comic books were dying, but with a chance at a more successful strip unlikely and a move into the world of slick advertising art nearly out of the question, he had no choice but to throw himself into the comics work offered, like most industry veterans with a mortgage to maintain and children to feed. Kirby's art for the Marvel monster line reflected that workmanlike approach; it was stripped down to bare essentials to allow for the highest number of pages per month. Even so, Kirby's monsters had power and incredible visual appeal. The horror in his comics came from an unstoppable force wreaking destruction on an otherwise peaceful countryside and populace, and that force was portrayed in spectacular fashion. Such stories recalled the invasiveness of war, and the monsters were particularly evocative stand-ins for the atomic violence that nations then stood on the brink of delivering to one another with the press of a button.

By working with Jack Kirby, Stan Lee wasn't simply engaging the talents of a capable veteran artist. Lee had on his freelance staff perhaps the most important creator in comic-book history, a dynamic artist slightly out-of-favor who remained at the top of his game. Jack Kirby was a formidable industry presence. He possessed a peerless visual imagination, and he was sublimely fast. All of these factors would come into play in the heady years of 1961 to 1965, when a universe of pop culture was brought to life on Jack Kirby's drawing table—the Marvel Universe.

Like Jack Kirby, Steve Ditko possessed a personality that stood in stark contrast to Stan Lee's, and his career diverged wildly from those of both men. Ditko was one of the few important artists who entered the comic-book field after the flush period of the postwar era. Unlike the previous generation of artists, most of whom viewed comic books as a temporary stop on their way to more satisfactory work in commercial illustration or fine art, Ditko had admired the early comic book entirely on its own merits. He came to New York City from his childhood home in Pennsylvania for the sole purpose of seeking a career in the field. Ditko brought a different style to Martin Goodman's monster line than Jack Kirby or Don Heck, and he approached it with a completely new sensibility, a passion that was more in touch with the comics of today than anything else published at that time. Ditko was the new kid on the block, the comics artist of the future, the one for whom comic books deeply mattered.

Steve Ditko is the most mysterious major figure in comic-book history. He has refused to be photographed or interviewed since the early 1960s, and personal information remains sketchy and unfulfilling. Ditko was born in 1927 in Johnstown, Pennsylvania, to immigrant parents of Eastern European descent. A precocious teenage artist, Ditko was a fan of DC Comics' *Batman* and master storyteller Will Eisner's Sunday newspaper supplement feature "The Spirit." He spent weekends with his brother tracking down these publications and copying their art. Both Batman and the Spirit were square-jawed heroes with upstanding, rigorously applied moral codes. Their adventures featured some of the best and most stylish art of comics' early heyday, acting as aesthetic confirmation of each character's inner goodness.

Upon graduating from high school, Ditko enrolled in New York's Cartoonists and Illustrators School, where he was greatly influenced by Jerry Robinson, a solid, veteran comic-book artist best known for his moody work on the early *Batman* stories. Ditko began to work in comic books in 1953. The beginning of his career was spotty and unremarkable. He returned home to Pennsylvania for a full year (it has since been rumored that he was recovering from tuberculosis) in the mid-'50s, sabotaging any early momentum he might have enjoyed as a freelancer. Ditko eventually moved back to New York, this time for good, and by 1960 he was a regular at the Charlton publishing house—and Stan Lee's favorite freelancer with the Goodman line.

Ditko's art was as visually imaginative as that of any artist Stan Lee utilized, including Kirby's, and more atmospheric. The abnormalities present in a Ditko thriller would often seep past the depiction of the monster itself and into the backgrounds, yielding greater psychological effect. Ditko drew stylish figures whose tortured body language suggested simmering emotional turmoil. While other stories in the line featured relentless physical assaults, crushed buildings, and broken limbs, Ditko's best work focused on invasions of body and mind, dangers that snuck in sideways or under the skin. In a Ditko story, the horrors of the physical world were conveyed in the expressions on a victim's face. Titles such as the reconfigured *Amazing Adult Fantasy* were tentatively aimed at older readers, due in great part to the strengths Lee saw in Ditko's evocative approach.

Despite his polite, withdrawn personality, which was nearly the polar opposite of Lee's chatty effervescence, Ditko managed to cultivate a "go-to" reputation with his writer-editor, one that would serve him well in years to come. "He helped me out so many times when we had an emergency and I needed an artist to do something quickly," Lee says. "He was a joy and a pleasure to work with." But still waters ran deep with the implacable artist, who, at that point in his life, was developing a rigid moral code that would later find full bloom under the objectivist teachings of Ayn Rand. When Ditko moved out of monsters and onto *Spider-Man*, Lee was engaging the services of a comic-book true believer, someone who as an artist trusted the form, and as a man was devoted to the morality upon which its stories were traditionally built.

During his two decades in the industry, Stan Lee had never worked with artists as significant to comic-book history as Jack Kirby or Steve Ditko. These creative relationships would prove to be very different from the friendly camaraderie Stan had felt with Joe Maneely, Dave Berg, or Vince Fago. Kirby and Ditko were every bit as formidable as Lee himself, no matter how many hats Stan wore at the company or to whom he was related. Stan Lee, Jack Kirby, and Steve Ditko would spark a comic-book revolution derived as much from their differences as from their shared values and creative synergy.

None of the men would survive the experience unscarred.

THE ESCAPIST

Stan Lee felt trapped.

The comic-book industry was neither as exciting nor as fun in 1961 as it had been when comic books ruled the newsstands and Lee was their boy prince. With a well-crafted, monster-heavy take on science fiction, revenue of Martin Goodman's comics line had grown slightly but solidly since its distribution crisis in 1957. But in many ways, the creative wind had gone out of Lee's sails when the company contracted, and there was little sign that it would ever return. As much as he tried to inject a sense of playfulness into the work, Lee's comics writing remained unsophisticated and hacked out, both by market dictates and publisher decree. He began to chafe at the restrictions. And Lee no longer enjoyed the slight status that came from working at the country's most prolific publisher. The status itself had never been that important to him in the first place, but he was now filled with a sense of letting down fellow professionals for whom he could no longer provide freelance opportunities. "They were working out of a closet," says artist Gene Colan. "They didn't have any work. I'd call Stan for work and he'd say, 'I'm sorry, I just don't have it.'" Approaching forty, Lee could sense nothing in his accidental profession that would continue to sustain his interest, let alone provide avenues to the wealth and respect he still dreamed of attaining.

Lee wanted out, and he was willing to take on as many new ventures as he needed to find his creative escape hatch. He spent a growing percentage of his time exploring his options as a writer, folding outside work into his already furious schedule. He knew he could write, and he figured that was the talent that would sustain him and his family no matter what else happened. Lee had always kept a number of freelance irons going at any one time. He worked for Goodman's magazine division on what publishing insiders called the "sweat mags"—pulpy concoctions of girlie photos, true crime stories, and sports profiles. A 1950 issue of *Focus*, credited to "Stan Lee, Editor," featured articles with such promising titles as "Traveling Salesmen Beware" and "The World's Loveliest Legs." Lee also claims to have done a small amount of writing for New York–area television, and by 1961 he was in his fifth year of scripting duties for Sol Brodsky on a series of giveaway comic books for the Big Boy restaurant chain. Still, Stan wanted more. His comics future very much in doubt, Lee turned to slightly more upscale writing projects, both with Magazine Management and with his own imprint, Madison Publications.

In 1961 Madison published two humor books, *Blushing Blurbs* and *Golfers Anonymous*. Subtitled "A Ribald Reader for the Bon Vivant," the anonymously penned *Blushing Blurbs* consisted of cheesecake photos onto which Stan placed humorous quotes, either playing on a detail or humorously commenting on the picture as a whole. The sultry photo on the book's cover featured as its model none other than Stan's wife, Joan, leaning against a lamppost in come-hither fashion. It was accompanied by the caption, "But honey, you TOLD me to take up a hobby!" *Golfers Anonymous* mined a similar vein of what Stan calls non-sequitur humor, such as a caption under a photo of two golfers and a dog approaching a green: "It wasn't bad enough giving him a full membership! NOW he's got the lowest handicap in the club!" Perhaps unconsciously, Lee was drawing on one of his skills as a comic-book writer, directing the audience to a desired reaction by putting words into the mouth of an existing image. He was working to one of his personal strengths: prodigious flippancy summoned in rapid-fire fashion. The work was fast, easy, and satisfying. Lee claims to have sold 10,000 copies of each book, although he never went back to press on any of them.

Lee would utilize the photo/caption concept for two noteworthy projects at Magazine Management that began in this period and ran well into the mid-1960s. *Monsters to Laugh With*, a magazine of B-movie monster stills accompanied by Lee witticisms, began in 1964 and, with a mid-run title change, lasted a total of seven issues. Some of Stan's gags found a second life in the 1970s in *Monster Madness*. "I loved doing them," Lee says in his autobiography. "I think they helped me get over the blues at a time when I felt my day job was becoming more and more of a dead end." A series of perfect-bound paperbacks called *You Don't Say!* appeared on newsstands previous to the monster books. For this project, Lee placed captions on top of photos of national and political leaders culled from the UPI wire service, tapping into the insouciant satire made safe for mass consumption by angry coffeehouse trailblazers such as Mort Sahl and Lenny Bruce. Lee's third volume, *More You Don't Say!*, was set for a late-1963 release and featured President Kennedy on its cover and on twenty-four of its ninety-six pages. When Kennedy was assassinated in November of that year, the volume suffered a quick and ignominious fade from the marketplace. Although Lee would later make extravagant claims for the series' quality, comparing its audience to that of William Shawn's *The New Yorker*, it's clear that he regretted the loss of a potentially successful mainstream franchise.

Lee reminisces that his vocational crisis lasted for a short time in 1960 and 1961. But many of the projects in which Lee claims to have briefly found solace, such as the photo books, lasted well into the middle of the decade. Even at that late date, Lee failed to realize he had already begun his life's work, the writing that would one day bring him the celebrity and wealth he desired. As *You Don't Say!* faded from the newsstand, Lee's other early '60s publishing project began to cohere into a cultural juggernaut and industry-revitalizing force. By 1963 Stan Lee was focused on writing and editing superheroes, and it was superheroes that would finally save Stan Lee from his career malaise.

Superheroes were as unlikely a rescuer as Lee could have imagined. Not only did they represent a genre in which Lee had experienced little previous success, but the comic-book industry in 1961 was hardly enamored of men and women in capes and tights. As a publishing phenomenon, superheroes were widely considered a relic of the last World War, or at best another trend to be exploited at some future date, when public tastes moved in that direction. In 1959, the president of Harvey Comics had bluntly told creator Joe Simon, "Superheroes are dead." Most comic-book companies had settled into a genre or two that did particularly well and were hanging on through an extended period of torpid sales. Archie had its humorous teenage residents of Riverdale High. Harvey Comics concentrated on its children's line of friendly ghosts and poor little rich kids. Dell had the Disney licenses. Charlton offered low-rent versions of them all. And under Stan Lee, the Goodman line had come to mean clever westerns and punchy monster tales.

Superhero comics had only one champion, but it was an important one. DC was the comic-book industry's gold standard in 1961. Its bustling offices, dedicated solely to the making of comic books, were a far cry from the tiny, two-office space Lee had managed to carve out of a forgotten corner at Magazine Management. DC's highly trained staff was the envy of the industry: career comic-book people working diligently in their areas of specialization. At DC, editors were editors, art directors were art directors, and the publishing machine ran smoothly due to the well-compensated excellence of its employees. Stan Lee, in comparison, wrote most if not all of the Goodman company's comics in any given month, edited the line in its entirety, and served as de facto art director on the covers. DC controlled the distribution of its own product, and after 1958, it controlled Martin Goodman's, too. Ownership of distribution provided a sure venue for DC's comics and comprehensive information on what sold and what didn't.

DC stood on a foundation that included superheroes. Unlike other companies born during the medium's initial boom, DC had never stopped publishing its big-name characters. Superman, Batman, and Wonder Woman appeared in DC comic books uninterrupted by genre trends, industry shake-ups, or the whims of public taste. DC's superheroes were easy to understand conceptually and visually, and they won their place as comic-book icons based on the clarity of their concepts and the ubiquity that came with two decades of monthly presence on the newsstand. When Stan Lee began to write a new kind of superhero comic book in 1961, he did so in DC's shadow, in response to genre conventions that DC had established and maintained, and as a continuation of the revitalization of the capes-and-tights crowd that DC had begun five years earlier.

Starting in the mid-1950s, DC launched several series that would lead directly to Lee's superhero renaissance. In 1956, DC published *Showcase* #4, which introduced a brand-new version of the speedy superhero the Flash. Industry veteran Gardner Fox and artist Carmine Infantino gave their comic-book stories the veneer of square-jawed soap opera and a recurring humorous motif: much to his eventual wife's consternation, the "Fastest Man Alive" was late for everything. These were storytelling baby steps compared to the dramatic paradigm shifts that Lee's comics would later unleash on readers, but for the first time since World War II, a new voice had come to superheroes in a way that was commercially and creatively viable.

The Flash revival established a trend of taking old characters and thoroughly rewriting them for current audiences. This satisfied readers on two levels. The emerging baby boom generation got superheroes they could claim as their own, while a small cadre of dedicated older comics readers could delight in connecting these new stories to the comics of ten and fifteen years earlier. By 1959 the Flash was spun off from *Showcase* into his own title. This led to a similar revival for the character Green Lantern, his magic ring from years past now a tool of space-age alien technology. By 1960, DC had enough characters, between the various newcomers and their "Big Three"—Superman, Wonder Woman, and Batman—to launch a team book. The marketing impulse behind team books was simple and had remained the same since the early days: if one character was good, then several must be great, and if one character's fan base was good, then the combined readership of seven superheroes should make for a bestseller. Slipping into its own title in October 1960 after a quick tryout in *The Brave and the Bold*, DC's Justice League of America quickly grew in popularity.

Industry figures took notice, including Martin Goodman. Various accounts exist about how Goodman might have received information regarding the sales of DC's emerging flagship title. A story later claimed by Goodman himself to be largely apocryphal, but repeated by Marvel in its official histories and by Lee at his most expansive, had Goodman on a golf course taking in a game with DC's Jack Liebowitz and learning of the Justice League's success in the form of a good-natured ribbing. A more cynical account, which was popular among that era's freelancers, had Goodman employing various spies housed with his distributor, who regularly reported to the publisher not only on Goodman's sales, but also on those from DC's line. The fanciful back story matters little in comparison to the events set in motion by Goodman's directive. In a sober, straightforward version relayed in an interview in 1983, Lee recalled being summoned into Goodman's office one day in early 1961 and receiving one of the publisher's typical "get-this-done" suggestions for the most anemic part of his magazine empire: "Maybe we ought to do some superheroes." Without either man knowing it, Goodman had set Stan Lee free.

PART III

"THE MARVEL AGE OF COMICS HAS TRULY BEGUN"

THE WORLD'S GREATEST
COMIC MAGAZINE

It's been a bad week for strange sightings in Central City. Today thousands choke through a gigantic, smoke-filled flare that advertises some product or group no one has heard of: "the Fantastic Four." Crowds begin to panic. Rumors abound of an alien invasion.

The smoke invokes a ripple effect of weirdness for dozens of blocks in all directions. A young society matron reports the sudden, inexplicable disappearance of a guest during tea. A man declares he hears a ghost; perhaps the same one a taxi dispatcher reports took a cab ride, leaving a one-dollar tip. A prominent haberdasher claims a monster destroyed his storefront—with two veteran police officers as witnesses, one of whom discharged his weapon. A man files insurance claims for striking the same monster, while a homeowner calls for assistance to remove from his garage a car that had been melted by its owner. Finally, the United States Air Force fires a nuclear missile at a teenager-sized comet, a missile that fails to explode over a heavily populated area only because it is snatched from the sky by gigantic human hands and tossed to sea. "I don't know how to explain it," says the chief of police, "but there's something weird happening in Central City!"

Meanwhile, four people gather in a nondescript apartment. The tall, skinny one is named Reed. His fiancée, Susan, is blonde and storybook beautiful. Her brother Johnny, a different shade of blond, stands with youthful confidence. In the back of the room lurks Ben—he is short, stocky, silently brooding. They are bound by crime and failure. "You all heeded my summons!!" Reed declares. "Good!! There is a task that awaits us . . . a fearful task!"

Flash back to an earlier meeting, in another plainly furnished room. A portentous argument, filled with undercurrents of jealousy and arrogant recklessness. *We must beat the commies into space!* Donning purple jumpsuits, the unlikely and largely inexperienced flight staff sneaks aboard a rocket ship of Reed's design and launches it into space. Almost immediately upon leaving Earth's atmosphere, mysterious green "cosmic" rays bombard the impromptu crew. The foursome experiences sickening episodes of extreme physical trauma and the rocket crashes back onto land. Everyone survives.

A heated, accusatory argument erupts among the four, driven by the disappointment of the failed mission and the fear of disfigurement from the strange rays. "What'd you expect?" Ben mutters. Much to everyone's shock, Susan briefly disappears and reappears, her body slipping into nothingness as if she's being erased from the page. When she returns to sight and collapses into the arms of her fiancé, Reed, a confrontation between Reed and Ben turns ugly. "I'm sick and tired of your insults . . . and your complaining! I didn't purposely cause our flight to fail!" Reed shouts.

Ben replies, "And I'm sick of you . . . period! In fact, I'm gonna paste you right in that smug face of yours!"

The spat careens into violence as Ben transforms into an angry, orange, and poorly complexioned apelike creature. He snaps a tree off at its base to use as an impromptu weapon. Reed becomes rubbery and jointless to a miraculous degree, enabling him to fight off the enraged Ben. Suddenly Johnny, the teenage brother of Susan, bursts into flame and, in ejaculatory fashion, fires himself off the ground and into flight. After miracle upon miracle, the four become reflective and dazed, all of their disagreements melting into one shared thought. "We've changed! All of us! We're more than just human!"

Placing their hands across one another's in the way of four children making a campfire pledge, Reed, Ben, Susan, and Johnny dedicate their newfound abilities to an ongoing altruistic effort to help their fellow man. "You don't have to make a speech, big shot!" Ben snaps at Reed. "We understand! We've gotta use that power to help mankind, right?" They take on special names. Susan Storm becomes the Invisible Girl. Johnny Storm, the Human Torch. Ben Grimm takes the others' reaction into account and becomes the Thing. Reed Richards names himself Mr. Fantastic. Together, they are the Fantastic Four.

The apartment meeting, called by a signal flare weeks later, is the first opportunity the Four have to make good on their crash-night pledge. Reed shares photographs with his former late-night rocket crew that show large holes forming at atomic installations around the world, the result of massive ground shifts beneath each base. A radar machine owned by Reed shows that another cave-in is about to occur. It happens, in a portion of the Dark Continent called "North Africa," where three French sentries barely survive the total destruction of their installation by a gigantic green monster, who pulls the structure into a hole with him. The monster, impervious to heavy artillery, is controlled by a small, mysterious figure, who shrieks orders when its mission of destruction is complete: "Enough! Return to Earth's core! Our mission here is finished! Go!!"

After analyzing data from this latest incident, Reed informs the other three that the cave-ins are likely coming from Monster Isle. Making their way to the remote location via a private jet, the four are soon confronted by a three-headed creature that immediately tries to kill them. It attempts to eat Susan, but she turns invisible and the creature misses her completely. Reed lassos the beast with one rubbery arm and sends it out to sea, telling his traveling companions that the creature may have been a surprise to everyone but himself. "I had heard there was a giant three-headed creature guarding this isle . . . but he shall guard it no longer!!"

Before any of his teammates can ask him what else Reed might know about any forthcoming monsters, Reed and Johnny fall down a secret passageway, find a trapdoor, and are immediately blinded by a roomful of giant diamonds, to the point of losing consciousness. After being dressed in more appropriate glare-reflective jumpsuits while passed out, the pair revive to have their host introduce himself.

He is the same figure who controlled the monster at the atomic installation in North Africa. He wears a green jumpsuit and carries a staff. Broad blue eyeglasses that would look comfortable across the nose of a pop singer settle on his gigantic proboscis, with only the tiniest slits for eyeholes. Short and squat, the man has Edward G. Robinson's bearing, Howard Cosell's hairline, and large, pointy ears. He introduces himself succinctly. "And as for me—I am the Moleman!!"

While Ben and Susan defend themselves from other monsters on the surface of the well-named island, Reed and Johnny are forced to listen to the Moleman's biography: small, hunched over, and possessing obvious physical deformities, the Moleman had, in his former life, found himself frequently abused by office cutups with cheap mustaches, haughty women, and bespectacled, mean-spirited bosses. He decided to become an adventurer instead of an office drone. It proved to be an isolating job, but one that suited him: "Even this loneliness is better than the cruelty of my fellow men!"

On an expedition to find a place to live beneath the earth, a land where he felt he could be king, the Moleman fell down a rock shaft, similar to the one that delivered Reed and Johnny into his grasp. United with the object of his quest in a way he did not foresee, the Moleman carved an underground kingdom for himself in this subterranean world, acquiring along the way the total control of scary, installation-destroying monsters and advanced skills in stick fighting, which he demonstrates on Johnny. His sinister plan, now on display for their benefit, seems to be more of the same atomic-plant treatment seen earlier, carried out to such an extent that it will eventually lead to a saturation point of despair among citizens, bringing him world domination.

Ben and Susan stumble in unexpectedly, and the lengthy demonstration of the underground king's prowess dissipates into a quick fight. Lumbering forward with meaty paw outstretched, Ben flushes out the Moleman, forcing the diminutive would-be global dictator to call forth one of his biggest monsters. The monster is chased off by Johnny's flame, and Reed nabs the escaping Moleman with one rubbery limb. The Moleman makes a last-ditch effort, releasing all of his monsters at once. With a fiery swath, Johnny weakens the cave walls and traps all of the beasts underground forever. Flying away in the private jet, Reed declares that the Moleman has joined his monsters. Reed has left him behind. "It's best that way! There was no place for him in our world. . . . Perhaps he'll find peace down there. . . . I hope so!"

Susan has the last word. "I just hope we have seen the last of him."

Thus ends the first issue of *The Fantastic Four*, cover-dated November 1961.

Stan Lee is thirty-eight years old.

SECRET ORIGINS

"Any idea is merely an ephemeral entity existing in a vacuum until it can be fleshed out—until the reader is made to care *about it."*
— STAN LEE, IMPACT MAGAZINE, 1977.

The Fantastic Four ushered in the so-called Marvel Age of Comics, but they weren't Stan Lee's first 1960s-era attempt at superheroes. That honor belongs to Dr. Droom, a little-known sorcerer who appeared in *Amazing Adventures* #1, cover-dated June 1961, and who served as a model for Lee and Steve Ditko's later hero, Dr. Strange. The Dr. Droom series appeared as a backup to other oddly named features such as "Sserpo!" and "The Escape of Monsteroso!" before being laid to rest around the time that *The Fantastic Four* #1 hit stands. Dr. Droom was a failed attempt by Lee to pursue the reemerging market for superhero comics, but it proved a useful template for determining how a slightly different approach to costumed heroes might find a place in the Goodman adventure line.

The Fantastic Four was another experiment. Judging by the publishing record, it came at a time in mid-1961 when Lee and Goodman had still not fully embraced superheroes. The title was on a bimonthly schedule until its sixth issue. Its earliest issues came out less frequently than did *Amazing Adult Fantasy*, and contemporaneously with several non-hero books, such as the workplace romance *Linda Carter, Student Nurse*. Stan Lee didn't wake up one day with an insatiable urge to write superheroes and then jump headlong into the genre. At Goodman's behest, he dabbled in them. And in that dabbling, through a combination of luck and clever improvisation, he and his artistic partner Jack Kirby hit upon a winning formula. The Fantastic Four weren't as invincible as Superman or as crafty as Batman. They didn't even wear costumes until their third outing. Sure, they had superpowers, but they were defined as much by their weaknesses as their strengths. The FF teammates felt resentment, got depressed, and bickered among themselves like family. In short, they were human. Or they were at least closer to possessing human qualities than any of their spandex-clad predecessors.

A superhero comic book was a new challenge for Lee at that point in his career. Superheroes were a resurgent genre for DC, but no one else had capitalized on their sales success. This forced Lee and Goodman out of their accustomed role as followers of a well-established industry trend and put them in the riskier position of trying to create the breakout success that defines such trends. In addition, DC had always published superheroes. It was a traditional strong point for the company. A new DC superhero comic could be expected to carry a modest amount of weight in the marketplace. Goodman had his Big Three, but the 1950s effort to bring back the Sub-Mariner, Captain America, and the Human Torch had been a resounding dud. No one knew how many superhero titles the potential market could bear. To top things off, Lee had never enjoyed a great deal of success with superheroes.

Complicating matters even further, Lee no longer did business the way he used to. Five years earlier, a decree from Martin Goodman to delve into a specific market would have served as a direct order to put several new titles into production, the kind of prodigious allocation of resources and tight management of inventory with which Lee was greatly experienced. But the American comic-book industry had changed drastically since 1957, and no company that was still publishing felt that change more strongly than Goodman's. Magazine Management's distribution contract with DC-owned Independent News allowed for only eight books to be published in any single month, no matter how many pages Lee and his artists could produce. Those titles had to encompass every saleable genre in which the company wished to be represented. Asked to add a genre to Goodman's mix of westerns, romances, and monster books, Lee faced a complicated chess game of production management. Each new superhero title demanded that a distribution slot be freed up. Lee could move a monthly title to bimonthly status, cancel a title outright and replace it with a new one, change features within an already existing title, or rename a title. He could also petition Independent News for a special exemption to produce an extra title until the line could be adjusted, or produce one anyway and hope no one noticed.

It was through the last kind of maneuver that *The Fantastic Four* became the legendary seventeenth title in Goodman's sixteen-title lineup. "There was nothing else that was canceled to make way for *Fantastic Four* #1," says comic-book historian Dr. Michael J. Vassallo. "Stan Lee and Martin Goodman obviously 'snuck' it in." To introduce the remaining titles that together would one day constitute the Marvel superhero "universe," Lee utilized all of the scheduling tactics at his disposal, many of them at the same time. He retitled books, launched new ones immediately upon canceling others, and slipped superheroes into anthologies where other genres had previously held sway. The Goodman line was a bonsai tree amid the great oaks of the other companies, one that Stan slowly pruned from a monster shape into that resembling a superhero. As a comic-book production manager, the Stan Lee of the early 1960s was without peer. What has often been described as the startling genesis of a new way of doing comic books was really a lively but considered transformation of an existing comic-book line. It would take almost four years for the first group of Marvel superheroes— a family of characters and titles midwifed by Lee, and given illustrated life by multiple artist collaborators—to be worked into the marketplace.

By 1962, however, it was clear that the superhero experiment had paid off. Fan letters poured in to Lee's tiny workspace at 655 Madison Avenue. The reaction to *The Fantastic Four* was overwhelmingly positive, and far stronger than for any other title then in Stan's lineup. He immediately got to work making room for more heroes. Lee and Kirby replaced *Teen-Age Romance* with *The Incredible Hulk*, which featured a radioactive monster who rampaged his way into superhero-style adventures. Next, Lee converted *Journey into Mystery* into a superhero title starring the Mighty Thor. Another Lee/Kirby creation, Thor was a Norse god who wielded a mystic hammer as he battled his adopted brother Loki and an assortment of other mythological villains. *Tales to Astonish* and *Tales of Suspense* underwent similar conversions to introduce Ant-Man— a character whose life among the ants had previously been portrayed in a monster story—and Iron Man, respectively. Lee and Ditko's Dr. Strange, a master magician who was the most elegantly bizarre character of that era, debuted in *Strange Tales*. The final issue of *Amazing Fantasy*, a summer 1962 release, contained an eleven-page origin story for an arachnid-like, red-and-blue figure named Spider-Man.

Despite the restrictions on what he could produce, Lee enjoyed several advantages as a one-man writer-editor about which the conservative bureaucracy at DC could only dream. In a field run by careerist managers, Stan was, relatively speaking, an editorial auteur. On any given project, he could choose an artist without fear of upsetting other editors. He had the leeway to decide what kind of title would be published within Goodman's parameters or market demands. And, as an editor and writer, he could greatly influence content at two stages of production. The fact that Lee had not taken full advantage of this freedom in previous decades underscored his lack of creative ambition at the time regarding comic books and the blinding speed with which Goodman's line was traditionally produced. The 1957 distribution deal had taken care of the latter problem—Lee now had time to mull over every creative decision.

He also had motive. Lee assembled *The Fantastic Four* #1 in the midst of an overall effort to improve his professional position, both within and outside of the comics industry. He was pursuing extracurricular freelance work at Magazine Management, was publishing his own books, and had even nudged one of his comic-book titles, *Amazing Adventures*, toward a slightly older audience. Lee was approaching middle age, and he desperately wanted out of comics. He was well paid, but frustrated. "It was like doing a radio show, and you have no idea if anyone's listening," Lee says. As Lee tells it, his wife, Joan, encouraged him to persevere. She told him to take one last shot at respectability, to be as serious about the content of his new hero titles as he was about his other efforts. And so he did.

Lee was not a skilled superhero writer, but he was an engaging scripter of character-driven romances and an effective plotter of outrageous monster books. He was also accomplished at presenting humor through dialogue. So instead of rehashing earlier superhero efforts, Lee applied what skills he had to a blank page. The resulting blend of genres under the superhero umbrella changed the industry's perception of what could be done with such stories, and provided much of what was interesting and remarkable about those first Marvel superhero comic books.

Lee's other great advantage over his industry peers was his proximity to artists like Jack Kirby and Steve Ditko, and his way of working with them that maximized their talents, not just as imaginative artists but as storytellers. Kirby in particular grounded Lee's stories with a visual authority few in the comic-book field could match. Lee and Goodman were blessed to have Kirby available for *The Fantastic Four*. He was one of the few active creators whose past work in superheroes was considered innovative and financially lucrative. Almost from the moment of his arrival in Goodman's offices, Kirby had been pushing for another stab at superheroes—either a relaunch of the Timely characters or a variation on his own idea for "science heroes," plainclothes adventurers roughly equivalent to the very mortal, jumpsuit-toting Challengers of the Unknown he had created for DC. The closest Kirby had come to realizing this dream for Martin Goodman was three issues of *Yellow Claw* on which he freelanced before his full-time return. Kirby's take on the feature mixed real-world intrigue with science-fiction elements including UFOs, aliens, and sleeping cities. But the feature was short-lived. One thing was clear to any casual reader: Kirby could draw almost anything, and he invested all of his art with an energy that drove even the most uninspired plot. Lee knew that Kirby gave him his best shot for a successful new title, and that, at this tireless point in the artist's spectacularly prolific career, he could do so without diverting crucial energy away from the rest of the line.

Kirby was given incredibly wide latitude in his working relationship with Lee. On becoming the primary writer for the Goodman line in the late 1950s, Lee popularized a little-used system of creating comic books that later came to be known as the "Marvel Method." In the traditional way of making comic books, writers created full scripts that were then illustrated by artists. Scripts included detailed breakdowns of panels per page, what the reader would see in each panel, and any dialogue to be spoken. Artists rendered each page as closely as they could to the scripts' directions. It was a way of working that guaranteed tight editorial control and maximized the economic benefits that came with specialization, but it practically guaranteed a sameness and lack of inspiration in the final product.

In Goodman's downsized late-1950s comics operation, Stan Lee was a busy writer, by his own testimony too busy to craft full scripts. Lee turned to a way of working that emphasized synopses, an infrequently used method that had been employed most notably by Harry Shorten on MLJ's superhero comics in the 1940s. Lee fashioned his variation out of necessity. To his most visually accomplished artists, Lee gave a typed synopsis rather than a complete script, later adding dialogue to the penciled art. Steve Ditko described their working method on *Amazing Adult Fantasy* in a 1990 essay. "Stan provided the plot ideas. There would be a discussion to clear up anything, consider options and so forth. I would then do the panel/page breakdowns, pencil the visual story continuity, and, on a separate paper, provide a very rough panel dialogue, merely as a guide for Stan. We would go over the penciled story/art pages and I would explain any deviations, changes, and additions, noting anything to be corrected before or during the inking. Stan would provide the finished dialogue for the characters, ideas, consistency, and continuity. Once lettered, I would ink the pages." This method of production allowed Lee to maintain a heavy writing workload.

While much of the early superhero background material has been lost to the ages, two pages of the first *Fantastic Four* script survived and were eventually reprinted in the fan magazine *Alter Ego*, published and vouched for by longtime Marvel employee Roy Thomas. Stan's script describes the first thirteen pages of *The Fantastic Four* #1 in a conversational synopsis, almost a casual letter from Lee to Kirby. "I hope this won't seem to [*sic*] sexy in art work," Stan writes in one aside. "Better talk to me about it, Jack—maybe we'll change this gimmick somewhat." Lee breaks down the characters—Reed Richards, Susan Storm, Johnny Storm, and Ben Grimm—and the basic story of an illicit rocket-ship ride and exposure to cosmic rays. The characters as they exist on the typed page are well realized in comparison to those in traditional superhero comic books, and the basic thrust of the plot appears to have been conceived by Lee.

But what also becomes clear on comparing Lee's contribution and the final product are the significant differences between the two—fundamental changes that could not have simply reflected editorial input from Stan late in production. In the Kirby-drawn story, the spaceship with our heroes does not head to Mars, as Lee had suggested in his synopsis. The depiction of the powers in the stories is streamlined: Lee wanted the Invisible Girl to remain invisible and Mr. Fantastic to suffer immediate pain upon stretching; Kirby, in his typical freewheeling style, disregarded both instructions. An entire opening sequence crafted by Kirby from an offhand suggestion of Lee's ("Story might open with a meeting of the Fantastic Four") sets the issue apart from the sunnier stories of the good citizens in DC's Justice League. Kirby's realization of the synopsis also includes a direct conflict at the spaceship crash site adding a level of physical danger between the protagonists that is barely hinted at in Lee's typewritten missive. Stan Lee may have created a Fantastic Four on paper, but the book as it sprung to life on the comic-book page was clearly the result of Lee and Kirby together.

Thus began the most fruitful stage of Stan Lee's career, working with Kirby and the other Goodman line artists to bring life to a world of superheroes around the Fantastic Four. Future characters were less ambitious, drawn from more traditional sources of pulp creativity—already existing characters, high-concept ideas, or an artist's particular area of enthusiasm. *The Incredible Hulk*, an update on the Jekyll-and-Hyde story, was given pop currency by making the title character the result of radiation poisoning. The Hulk's uncontrollable rage, simmering beneath the surface, was similar to the creative energy that Kirby was letting loose in the pages of this comic book and across the line. Spider-Man, who graduated to his own title in early 1963, was a twist on kid sidekicks and the teen-comics genre. Thor brought in fantasy elements and touched on Kirby's fascination with mythology. The Ant-Man stories drew on the popular science-fiction-movie conceit of people thrust into adventures in a familiar world suddenly made too big for them. The "Iron Man" serial blended elements of war comics, spy novels, and science fiction. *Sgt. Fury and His Howling Commandos* was a straight-ahead World War II comic that featured the kind of dressed-down heroism popular in movies and on television at the time. (The comic book was rumored to be the remnants of a Kirby newspaper-strip offering that never found a home.) Dr. Strange dressed up Steve Ditko's effectiveness as an artist of the supernatural in superhero's clothing. In September 1963, Martin Goodman finally launched a title to compete directly with *Justice League of America*, creating a similarly conceived team of Marvel characters for the comic book *The Avengers*. At the same time, Jack Kirby's idea of a single event creating both heroes and villains was given its first voice in the last distinctive concept of Marvel's early years, *The X-Men*. *Daredevil*, which appeared in early 1964 and would be the transition character between the early 1960s and the Marvel that was to come, was a throwback to old-time acrobatic superheroes, freshened by soap operas and the lead character's blindness. After the first few years, Lee's glib writing became sharper, the overwhelming presence of monsters and science-fiction elements was toned down, and individual artistic touches made their way into the characters.

The various back-and-forths between artist and writer, designer and plotter, staffer and freelancer distinguished the new Goodman company superhero comics from everything that had come before—to the line's lasting benefit. No character exemplifies this point better than Spider-Man. In Lee's later account of Spidey's creation, he said the character burst wholly formed from his imagination after—depending on which version of the story he tells us—the writer either recalled a favorite pulp character or viewed a spider making its way down a window pane. But the Spider-Man who appeared in *Amazing Fantasy* #15 was more precisely the product of different creative impulses competing with each other for final voice. In early 1962, Stan Lee expressed the desire to do a teenage superhero using the spider motif. Jack Kirby had long wanted to do an insect-related superhero. (With Joe Simon, he had previously created the Fly for Archie Publications.) With Lee's input, Kirby began to craft an introductory tale, rejecting some of the more fantastic Lee story elements, grounding the character in a domestic situation featuring a kindly aunt and uncle, and giving the superhero a secret origin revolving around a neighbor who happened to be a scientist. At Lee's request, the character was turned over to Steve Ditko who, working from a synopsis and Kirby's pages, produced an inspired visual take on the character that drove its story for decades—bottle-thick glasses, slumped shoulders, and a homemade costume. Ditko was nearly as sharp as Kirby when it came to shaping characters in ways that would make them effective on the page. The Spider-Man millions of readers came to know and love got his youth and voice from Stan Lee and his human frailty from Steve Ditko, and he was presented to the world for the very first time through a dynamic cover pose drawn by his Uncle Jack.

Stan Lee's most significant contribution as an editor of American comic books was to use his relative autonomy to facilitate greater contributions from the artists. This editorial strategy would cause deep and enduring controversy. When in subsequent years the new Marvel comics became successful, who created which character, to what extent, and when became important questions, both legally and ethically. But in the early years, as the new formula books spilled out of Marvel's offices with as much speed as the restrictive distribution deal could manage, simply producing the books took precedence over everything. The way to ensure the best possible new superhero line, created on the run, was for everyone involved to contribute whatever ideas they had when they had them. For every synopsis from Stan Lee's desk that survives today, there exists an undocumented act of primary creation from a Marvel artist. Jack Kirby, whose career in comics was distinguished by his ability to create whole universes from start to finish, can be felt near the heart of almost every Marvel comic book and character on which he worked. In a more innocent time, Stan Lee could even refer to Dr. Strange as Steve Ditko's idea.

Stan presided over an editorial environment in which everyone, not just the top artists, could take part in establishing a new kind of comic book. As the number of creative people who were involved with Marvel superheroes expanded between 1962 and 1965, it was clear that Lee had fostered a new approach to a staid genre—a way of working that could be utilized by a variety of artists and writers. Lee's brother, Larry Lieber, could take a break from his work in westerns to help write Thor's adventures, artists Bill Everett and Wally Wood could add their pulpy visual flair to *Daredevil*, Don Heck could utilize matinee-idol figure rendering on Iron Man's suave Tony Stark in *Tales of Suspense*. All of their efforts could be claimed by Marvel. All of it was a reflection of Stan Lee.

WHAT MARVEL DID

"[It was] like watching The Odyssey *being written."*
—GEOFFREY O'BRIEN ON 1960S MARVEL
COMICS, FROM *DREAM TIME*.

Looking at them now, forty years after they came rolling off the presses, it's hard to imagine Stan Lee's Marvel comic books as objects of artistic or cultural significance. They are crude even by comic-book standards, suffused with the pent-up power of outsized figures frozen in motion and filled with lurid, flat colors barely soaked up by the cheap newsprint. The cover copy bellows with a carnival barker's glee, promising mysteries solved, worlds endangered, spectacles on display—all yours to take home for a cover price of 10¢, and, later, 12¢. Inside, every sentence of dialogue ends with a question mark or an exclamation point. No one in a Marvel comic book speaks in declarative sentences. No one does *anything* quietly or deliberately. Jack Kirby's art, which was everywhere on those early titles, seethes with a fury angry enough to set the entire world on fire. Kirby drew a world haunted by memories and echoes of war, a world of men and supermen who shuffle from gray building to gray building in heavy overcoats. Gone were the good cops and solid citizens of DC Comics' Main Street America, replaced by grotesque angels and sympathetic devils hammering one another with blows and blasts of chaotic energy that crackle beneath the reader's fingertips. Martin Goodman's comic-book line became Marvel Comics in May 1963; its rapidly expanding superhero effort was a visceral punch in the nose for millions of comic-book readers, a lightning-strike break from the medium's increasingly irrelevant past, and the template for forty years of hip, aware, and deeply heartfelt pop culture. And all of it was presided over by Stan Lee.

Marvel's first title, *The Fantastic Four*, became the flagship of the new Goodman superhero line. In its pages, Lee and Kirby developed the basic approach that would eventually characterize all of Marvel's comics by ignoring the rigid way earlier superhero stories had been told in favor of blending elements from multiple genres. The clash of styles they utilized was telegraphed in Jack Kirby's cover of *The Fantastic Four* #1. A group of strangely powered people with code names (a classic superhero story element) makes declarations about what is going on around them (in the manner of romance comic characters) while fighting a gigantic creature who has burst through a city street (just as in a monster comic). Lee and Kirby set their strange brew against largely pedestrian backdrops, playing up the resulting clashes in style and energy for all they were worth. The Invisible Girl might use her powers in a hair salon, while the Human Torch might slip away from his teammates to work on a car in a garage, or even spend the night slumming in a flophouse. This not only made for the strangest superhero stories ever read by comic-book audiences, but also allowed readers an easier transition between Lee and Kirby's more established efforts, like the monster stories in *Tales to Astonish*, and this new take on superheroes.

The early Marvel superheroes seem tethered to works that were already established in the Goodman line. The first dozen or so issues of *The Fantastic Four*, for example, feature alien invasions and rampaging monsters that would not have been out of place in a Kirby or Ditko eight-pager for *Journey into Mystery*. Lee and Kirby also derived a great deal of their narrative momentum from romance comic-book plot twists. The Thing gains a blind girlfriend, Alicia. In the title's memorable ninth issue, the superheroes have trouble paying their rent and are evicted from their headquarters. In the hands of Stan Lee and Jack Kirby, the superhero story proved a much wider umbrella for different kinds of tales than anyone had guessed.

Lee and Kirby were formally innovative as well. In 1940, Kirby had revolutionized the superhero comic book with his kinetic Captain America stories, straight-ahead action potboilers best known for their panel-bursting explosions of limbs and torsos. With *The Fantastic Four* and his other early Marvel superhero work, Kirby mixed the unstoppable energy of his action set pieces with skills he had picked up as an artist on the wide array of work he had performed in the intervening decades. Kirby could slow down the action with a panel or two of bodies at rest, or trip up the reader with an establishing shot in which meticulously rendered machines or an impressive view of the New York skyline overwhelmed any superhero action that might take place in a panel's foreground. Kirby brought a new sense of pacing to the early Marvels, a sense of calm and stillness and shifting perspectives that made the frequent storms of action that much more immediate and impressive.

Stan Lee did Jack Kirby one better, at least compared to where American comic books had gone previously. With Kirby handling the basic construction of the stories according to their collaborative method of working together, Lee had more time to focus on the dialogue. Indeed, Lee *had* to focus on dialogue. It was his main tool for shaping the story in the direction he wanted it to go, a way to infuse some of his own personality back into the intense artwork submitted by Kirby. Lee drew on his skill with romance and humor books to provide livelier and more fulsome dialogue than had ever been seen in a superhero title. Lee's dialogue indicated not just character type—good guy, mad scientist, street thug—but helped differentiate the characters among themselves in their closest groupings. At his best, Lee gave each major character a verbal stamp of identification equal to the visual imprint made by the artists. Lee's Thing seemed less educated and generally angrier than Mr. Fantastic, who came across as stuffier and more deeply arrogant than the teenage Human Torch, and so on. Each major early villain also received his own vocal fingerprint. A comic-book reader in the early 1960s might have argued that the elegant competence of DC's superhero artists was somehow preferable to Kirby's rocket-charged virtuosity, but no one could make a compelling case for writing in broad strokes, with all of the characters sounding alike. Few comics had offered writing that could be enjoyed on its own, and none of them had been superhero titles. Twenty years of benign neglect and creative contempt for the superhero now worked in Kirby and Lee's favor. Even their smallest changes seemed radical and daring.

By audaciously combining genres and ignoring the limitations that had settled in on the superhero, Lee and Kirby were free to foist on their readership a fantasy setting better realized than anything that had come before in the American comic book. Lee and Kirby were presiding over the kind of world-building that would become commonplace in movies and television. *The Fantastic Four* quickly became a friendly place to reintroduce a few of the more interesting elements of the Goodman line's superhero past. Lee and Kirby both admired Bill Everett's Prince Namor, the Sub-Mariner, Lee particularly, and so the character made his first appearance in the Marvel universe in the fourth issue of *The Fantastic Four*. In decades past, Everett had depicted an undersea antihero wary of men but redeemed by a shared contempt for the worst mankind had to offer. Under Lee and Kirby, the Sub-Mariner remained Everett's antihero but was transformed by the new book's context into a dangerous free agent in healthy conflict with the title's characters. The Sub-Mariner was a perfect foil for a genre-mixing book: he could fight the Fantastic Four in terms of monsters (he gave a particularly big one the task of destroying New York), romance (he had an eye for the Invisible Girl, who vaguely reciprocated), and superheroics (several pages of vintage Kirby slugfests). He was a handsome character that Kirby could draw in action or at rest, and his history as a crown prince of an undersea kingdom gave Lee his vocal hook. When fights between the Fantastic Four and the Sub-Mariner ended in a standstill, with a retreat to their respective neutral corners of superhero headquarters and undersea kingdom, it became clear to readers that the Sub-Mariner might have been wrongheaded, but perhaps not completely wrong, to mistrust the heroes and the "surface world" they inhabited. In simply reviving an old character, Lee and Kirby had injected a hint of moral ambiguity into their stories that was completely unknown to superhero comics before 1961, and they had done so in a way that sidestepped the objections of the Comics Code. They had also provided a connection to the faded comic-book glories of the company's Timely and Atlas past, creating a context for their new titles that included a vivid wartime superhero history. Both moves excited readers. Stan and Jack simply raced to the next deadline, barely cognizant of the creative possibilities they were leaving in their wake.

Marvel's next few books expanded and improved on the formula of fantasy clashing with the mundane. *The Incredible Hulk* was, on a conceptual level, a retelling of Dr. Jekyll and Mr. Hyde. The backdrop, however, was the U.S. military, and the transformation into "Mr. Hyde" was brought on by an explosive dose of radiation poisoning, giving the story pop relevance. In terms of the monster comics Lee had helped plot, the Hulk was another rampaging behemoth causing trouble in an environment dedicated to bringing him down. But now that the context was superheroes, the Hulk became an antihero. Unlike the superheroes of the past, and DC's then-current crop of do-gooders, who either relished the opportunity to put on a costume and slug a bad guy or shouldered their responsibilities in a manly, positive way, scientist Bruce Banner didn't want anything to do with his alter ego, the Hulk. Taking on a superhero's role messed up his life in the way of a massive drinking problem, with many of the same symptoms—blackouts, trashed apartments, ripped clothing, and a hazy memory. By mixing genres and wallowing in the incongruities that resulted, Lee and Kirby created a resonant character that would outlast his atomic age origins.

The Mighty Thor serial, which began in a 1963 issue of *Journey into Mystery*, went the opposite direction from *The Incredible Hulk* into sunny, absurd fantasy. As a mythological figure, Thor encountered a vast number of monsters as bad guys from the feature's beginning, and he kept running into them for a longer period of time than any other character had done. Everything about the standard Marvel mix of genres took on oversized implications in Thor. The character's signature weakness was his secret identity as a lame but noble doctor, into whom he would transform between adventures. His romantic dilemma was that the doctor misunderstood the signs of affection wafting his way from beautiful nurse Jane Foster. The fantasy elements in the Thor stories gave Jack Kirby free license to be as imaginative in his settings and as bombastic in his fight scenes as he could muster. A mythology buff who had clamored for such a character in the Goodman line, Kirby produced his most beautifully detailed artwork, putting a visual stamp on Norse mythology that sometimes dwarfed the rich source material. As dialogue writer, Stan Lee took advantage of the humorous opportunity to give his lead character a kind of television comedian's Shakespearean dialect, all "thees" and "thous" and "shalts." The contrast between the superhero and the pedestrian world in which he found himself was even more pronounced in Thor than in the other books. It was therefore a much better opportunity for humor from both Kirby and Lee. Seeing Thor forced to endure "mortal" indignations was not just a funny sight gag, it also gave Lee a chance to have the character moan about it to himself like a spoiled, befuddled Prince Valiant.

If Thor showed the strength of the Marvel formula when Lee and Kirby played it loose, Spider-Man was the character that spoke most clearly to the dramatic effectiveness that could be mined from the new approach. This time, the art chores—and thus the lion's share of the design and a portion of the active plotting—fell to the emerging star of the pre-hero Goodman books and Lee's personal favorite, Steve Ditko. The artist's take on the character was radically different than the conception supplied by Lee and the few pages of art that remained of Kirby's aborted attempt at an origin story. With Ditko as the copilot on Spider-Man's earliest adventures, the comic strayed from the teen-hero model that Stan had originally envisioned. It became instead an emotionally brutal and funny examination of the frustrations of being a teenager that was as far from Archie Andrews and the gang at Riverdale High as Dustin Hoffman's star turn in *The Graduate* was from Mickey Rooney's Andy Hardy.

Lee would later praise Ditko for his ability to draw characters that seemed less than heroic, not quite larger than life. This was an accurate assessment in terms of contrasting Ditko's ability to Kirby's, however much it might underplay the versatility of each artist. When, in Spider-Man's origin story in *Amazing Fantasy* #15, the hero takes off his mask to confront the burglar who murdered his uncle, Ditko's Peter Parker looks frail, shaken, and out of his depth more than he does a brave hero suffering a moment of anguish. Ditko's strength was the emotional authenticity he invested in the character, the tortured quality he gave to Spider-Man's high school existence. The romance-story twist that Lee emphasized in early issues of *The Amazing Spider-Man*—that Spider-Man was popular among the kids at high school, whereas Peter Parker was not—was realized by Ditko as the kind of schoolyard injustice experienced by every teenager. Peter Parker didn't see any of the humor in his situation—he was not the bigger man—and Ditko drew a character who was racked with pain and anger and insult. Ditko was also a strict moralist. Working with Lee's teenage protagonist allowed him to explore the nature of growing up, the need to become more reliable, and the spectacular ways in which a young person might be expected to fail. Together, Lee and Ditko were exploring what it meant to be a heroic, responsible adult, making Spider-Man a character with true emotional resonance for teens, and his title the first to genuinely explore the deeper meanings of its genre.

Lee met Ditko's emotional realism with a steady hand and a light touch in the dialoguing that helped cool down the artist's intensity. Ditko was skilled at drawing an urban landscape of rooftops and skewed perspectives. Lee helped fill it with a series of terrifically bad adult role models for the teenage hero. Spider-Man was the first Marvel character that lacked an easy-to-peg connection to the Goodman monster comics, or even a sense of his own status within the larger world. Spidey didn't usually save the universe, was not called in by the president, and enjoyed no status as the world's most important representative of anything. He largely lived in his own world, an unpleasant place full of rotten people with personal grudges and ungrateful peers who couldn't see past Peter Parker's glasses. When Ditko became fond of showing the hero in moments of reflection following particularly troubling encounters with the world at large, Lee turned them into character-driven soliloquies, giddy and agonized ruminations on the character's troubles and woes. Spider-Man could solve one set of problems physically, but other troubles, particularly those shared by Peter Parker, had to be worked out emotionally. The fact that any superhero had so much on his mind that he felt compelled to spill his guts like a troubled Elizabethan hero made perfect sense to Spider-Man's readers. It also held a certain degree of fascination for those outside the traditional comic-book reading profile who happened to stumble across the issues. By 1965 Spider-Man offered an irresistible hook for outside observers—a Holden Caulfield who punches bad guys—and a well-developed sense of emotional authenticity for those who were absorbed in his stories.

It was that kind of high-concept formulation that drove the fleshing-out of the Marvel line in its first few years. As an editor, Lee now turned the attention he had used previously to explore other creators' comics to pinpoint what was working about his own. With a greater understanding of a concept that Lee would later boil down to "heroes with feet of clay," new characters were designed to take direct advantage of the line's strengths. Thus began a march of slightly less inspired characters, all with different takes on the Marvel formula. Iron Man was a playboy superhero in the mold of Howard Hughes. His personal handicap was a bad heart, his romantic troubles consisted of an abortive love triangle between himself and two loyal friends, and his antagonists were a series of villains who threatened Tony Stark's wealth and Iron Man's metal shell. Dr. Strange was a magician superhero. His personal handicap was an arrogant, mortal past that subjected his magical powers to very human limits. His focus was on magical matters, and his villains were those who challenged his mystical abilities and threatened his physical well-being. Daredevil was an acrobatic superhero whose disability and superpowers were the same—a lack of vision that resulted in superheightened senses. His romantic troubles came in the form of a workplace love triangle. His villains were often the people he met in the course of his work as a lawyer, or those who managed to take advantage of his blindness.

The X-Men was conceptually different from the early Marvel titles. Cyclops, Marvel Girl, the Beast, Iceman, and the Angel were born as superheroes, "mutants" affected by radiation at birth. The villains they encountered shared the same origin in that they were also born with their powers, reinforcing the idea in other Marvel comic books that one's heroic nature is a moral choice rather than an accident of fate that bestowed superpowers or a scarred visage. But the title was extremely suffocating, and it recycled the same villains and heroes with regularity. Jack Kirby drew the early issues like he did the early issues of most Marvel titles. He was fascinated by the mythological resonance of heroes and villains sharing the same starting point. But while *The X-Men* was filled with colorful action, it lacked the emotional intensity Steve Ditko invested in Marvel's other teenager-focused title, *The Amazing Spider-Man*. Later artists and writers would capitalize on the metaphorical depth present in *The X-Men*, making the comic a sometimes strained commentary on racism and prejudice. But as an early Marvel title, it was notable for its depiction of outsiders wanting to become a larger part of society, a message that was not entirely lost on the legions of alienated teens who made up a significant portion of Marvel's growing readership.

Stan Lee was doing what any smart editor would do. He was striving to find methods to replicate the success of his new titles across a majority of his line. He gave his best talent all the work they could handle, found a way of working that maximized their artistic gifts, and helped others on the freelance staff to produce material that was similar to that which was moving titles. He also built awareness of the line through constant crossovers and aggressive appearances by characters in each other's titles—misunderstandings and fistfights and eventual team-ups that made the work of a few talented individuals look like a considered house style, and a collection of scattered titles seem like one long, continuous, heroic story. It worked. By 1964, sales had increased to the point that Marvel was able to move out of Magazine Management's offices and into a space of its own on Madison Avenue.

The early Marvels were remarkable not only for their breadth of new characters but also for the way they enabled the company's stable of artists to develop their craft. Unlike the monsters, westerns, or romances that used to dominate the Goodman line, the superhero stories were more than twenty pages long per issue, the stories continued between issues, and artists were encouraged to settle on at least one title for an extended run. Kirby and Ditko used the wider canvas to create the most popular and accessible work of their careers. During his run on *The Amazing Spider-Man*, Ditko became more adept as a page designer, working in shapes and shadows that began to make his work as pleasing to look at as it was compelling to read. As the regular artist for the Dr. Strange stories in *Strange Tales*, Ditko provided a progression of scary, dreamlike visuals that would match any comic-book artist's imagination. Jack Kirby worked an intensely rigorous schedule, and created from whole cloth hundreds of future lead and supporting characters and odd-looking villains as if he were being paid by the idea. Kirby's impressive stream of visual creations in the first few years of the Marvel line would constitute the bulk of the company's mainstay characters for the next forty years.

Stan Lee also progressed as a creator, albeit in a different direction from his top artists. His dialogue and caption writing became looser and more confident. He mastered the internal hero turmoil—given expression in Iron Man's thought balloons or Spider-Man's rooftop speeches—and by the middle of the decade his writing was as much fun as the visuals his best artists could conceive. Lee's work on Ditko's Dr. Strange stories allowed him the opportunity to riff on gibberish totems, secret idols, and heathen gods called on in spells that amused readers with their tongue-twisting quality without going so far as to spoil the moody atmosphere provided by Ditko's art. Dr. Strange fought villains that went by names like Dormammu, and called upon the "all-seeing eye of Agamotto" and "the eternal Vishanti" in his time of need.

By 1965, Stan was the most entertaining dialogue man in comics by a wide margin. Then he began to do something even savvier. Lee's writing started to become more solicitous of the readers, pointing out various fourth-wall absurdities or even speaking to them directly. The tone always flattered the readers, praising them for their intimate knowledge of past adventures and the high standards they brought to the work in front of them. It was the same tone of voice that he brought to the letters and commentary pages he had instituted in the new titles, that of the kindly "with-it" uncle.

It added another layer of enjoyment to Marvel's superhero titles, and it spoke to an older, hipper readership who delighted in the comic books' genre-bending qualities without taking their content seriously. Lee's showy writing also helped him transcend the traditional writer and editor roles to become Marvel's host, the man responsible for bringing the readers the entertainment, a kind of comic-book Ed Sullivan who was never too far away from the side curtains. Stan Lee was offering front-row seats to the Greatest Show in Pulp, and readers were lining up in droves.

PART IV

"A MARVEL POP-ART PRODUCTION"

LIVE AND ON CAMPUS

Stan Lee may have cocreated the Marvel Universe, but he deserves full credit for his own enthusiastic, comics-soaked public persona. Artists like Jack Kirby, Don Heck, and Steve Ditko were necessary to give Lee's story ideas visual life. Use of the Marvel Method meant that several of the ideas that made it into the final product came directly from the artists themselves. But Lee had fuller control over how he was perceived as an editorial presence in the books. Just as the financial imperative of having one writer script an entire line of books resulted in the shared creative burden of the best Marvel comics, economic factors motivated Lee to make himself known to the readers. Simply put, talking directly to the readers was a cost-effective way to advertise. More than any figure in comic-book history, Stan Lee maximized every opportunity to forge a deeper connection between reader and comic book, with himself as intermediary.

There were only a few significant predecessors of Lee's extended publicity push. In its brief heyday, EC Comics had forged an identity across its line through a consistently high level of craft, a recognizable story style, and overtures that sought to emphasize that the EC experience was aimed directly at its fans. Notes from the publisher weren't uncommon in the pages of comics, including those from Atlas, and a successful line of comic books had led to some media coverage for crime comics czar Charles Biro. Certainly the grand editors at DC Comics were somewhat of a known entity among the more dedicated fans. Newspaper-strip cartoonists enjoyed a degree of mainstream popularity. Some became minor celebrities, and many kept in contact with their audience through correspondence, gifts of original art, or even public lectures. Lee himself had run letters pages—although the letters tended to be less-than-inspiring cursory statements, perhaps stating a preference for one kind of book over another—and enjoyed a reputation as someone who signed absolutely everything he wrote. Creator credits were an early nod toward fashioning a relationship between Marvel's creators and its readers.

Lee wanted to promote Marvel's new books to all facets of his potential audience. Comic books had attracted a new group of fans by the early 1960s—enthusiastic, frequently older readers who treated comics as something more than disposable reading. As collectors who held onto their comics, and as interested observers who noted trends and which genres sold, many of these readers were energized by the superhero comeback that DC had initiated in the late 1950s. "The impetus for much of the formation of comic fandom in the early 1960s was the reemergence of superheroes," says cultural historian Bill Schelly. This interest extended to any tentative steps other publishers made in the genre, such as Archie Publications' Jaguar, or Dell's Brain Boy. Marvel's effort was greeted with the same kind of hunger. Many fans noted the subpar printing of the early issues of *The Fantastic Four*. But the stories crackled, even stretching over dozens of pages a month. Jack Kirby proved an exciting addition to those artists who had returned to working with capes and costumes, and *The Fantastic Four* reintroduced golden-age icons the Human Torch and the Sub-Mariner.

Just as Marvel's stories injected a spirit of irreverent fun into the staid superhero comics that directly preceded them, Lee's editorial presentation was a welcome relief to a growing fan community that up until then had been immersed in the seriousness of DC's editorial staff. Lee began slipping editorial commentary into the Marvel comic books from day one, speaking directly to the readers as early as in *The Fantastic Four* #1. Sometimes this was an attempt to explain a plot point that the line's dedication to more naturalistic dialogue kept Lee from articulating in spoken exposition; other times it was simply a narrative tool to break up the seriousness of the action. "I think Stan's iconoclastic tendencies were extremely appealing to his teenage fans," Schelly says. "His comics had an almost 'anything goes' feeling. For example, sometimes he'd comment on the proceedings in a caption, like 'Don't worry, frantic ones! This will all make sense eventually—we hope!' Readers felt like Stan was kind of whispering in their ear, as he would to an insider. He was also self-deprecating in print, admitting mistakes freely. We liked that sort of thing."

Lee paid attention to the organized fan communities by making a concerted effort to respond personally to letters and questionnaires sent by fan-magazine writers. Within two years, Marvel began to crack DC's domination of the fan-based Alley Awards, with Lee winning multiple awards between 1963 and 1967. When Marvel entered into its richest creative period in the mid-1960s, the fan community followed in rapt fascination, writing articles in tribute to the breadth and scope of the superhero stories Marvel was publishing. "Marvel always had the best-written fanzines," says Gary Groth, who eventually moved from writing his own fan publications into editing a trade magazine for the comic-book industry. "Some of them were pretty intimidating."

In his intense press to make a successful publishing effort out of the unlikely superhero line, Stan Lee did everything he could to replicate his successes in organized fandom with comic-book readers who did not belong to clubs, collect older comics, or trade correspondence with other fans—the more casual fans who made up the bulk of the comic-book readership. Fan letters to Marvel about the early superhero efforts were important to Lee because he was working in a genre in which he had little experience, and with only eight titles a month there was little room to carry a book that wasn't working. Lee needed the feedback. Marvel experienced a surge in correspondence after the first issue of *The Fantastic Four*, and by 1963 Lee publicly put the estimate of letters received at a hundred per day. He seems to have put some stock in them—it was response from fans that prompted Lee to have Kirby put formal superhero costumes on the Fantastic Four. But mostly he was encouraged by the enthusiasm and the volume of the response. By devoting space in each publication for a sampling of the letters and extending his routine as genial, self-mocking host to his responses, Lee created a secondary level of involvement for readers and promoted the sense that Marvel cared about its fans. Rather than arguing with fans about story mistakes made in various issues of the comics, Lee instituted the Marvel "No-Prize," an empty envelope festooned with Marvel's return address and a message: "This envelope contains a genuine Marvel Comics No-Prize which you have just won!" The No-Prize was a way of rewarding reader involvement while at the same time deflecting the emphasis from nitpicking at the details.

Stan also devoted space to the company's promotional news. In a special announcement section, readers could peruse a mix of press-release-type information and personal gossip, and scan a list of on-sale issues from Marvel. These bulletins eventually included a personal note from the editor, in offsetting yellow, that came to be known as "Stan's Soapbox," where Lee would hold forth on various issues in longer form. This was Lee in full-on promotional mode, selling all things Marvel with a combination of sneak peeks and a jargon derived in part from his days in the military: "Face Front, True Believers," "'Nuff said," and "Excelsior!" (the New York state motto meaning "ever upward" that became Lee's signature) all got heavily worked into these columns. Some cynical readers suggested that Stan may not have written all of the columns, particularly in the later years. But the "Bullpen Bulletins" and Lee's soapbox column were a basic component of Marvel's comic-book presentation from the mid-1960s until long after Lee had stopped actively editing the line. For years, they were as direct a link into Stan's expressive side as any selection of his comic-book dialogue—the carnival barker and center-ring attraction rolled into one.

Also in 1965, Marvel created its own fan community with the Merry Marvel Marching Society. The club crystallized Lee's happy-go-lucky public persona. Announced in the January books, those who joined for the price of $1 received a package consisting of a membership card, stickers, a membership button, and a letter of introduction signed by "The Bullpen Gang." In part because Lee had dropped casual mentions of a mysterious M.M.M.S. into the comics for months preceding the formal announcement, the initial response was overwhelming, and the office was flooded with dollar bills. The club's most fondly remembered premium was a disc containing a recording of various writers and editorial people—Steve Ditko notably declined to participate—cracking jokes about comic books and each other. The society even had its own theme song. Much like the hint of irreverence that Lee brought to the comic books, the fact that he treated the M.M.M.S. as a goof allowed many readers to participate without feeling as if they were joining a kiddie club. The Marching Society was successful as part of Lee's continuing efforts to increase fan involvement by spotlighting the personalities involved in making the comics—including secretary Flo Steinberg, whose otherwise unglamorous work involved running personal errands, answering letters, bundling art together for the printer, and blocking any visiting young people who tried to make a break for Stan's office. The club soon became unwieldy, however, and Martin Goodman eventually killed it. Marvel's next sizable attempt at a fan organization, the F.O.O.M. ("Friends of Ol' Marvel") effort of the mid-1970s, would be outsourced.

Several chapters of the M.M.M.S sprung up at universities, and it was to college-age kids that Lee would direct one of his more considerable publicity efforts. Lee's career as a college lecturer began inauspiciously. One early letter dated March 24, 1964, from Isabelle Kamishlian and J. Geoffrey Magnus at the Special Committee Programming Bard College Science Club Lectures, suggested an honorarium of fifty dollars. Once the details had been worked out, Lee received another letter from the same pair dated May 7 with suggestions for bus and train travel, and presenting the difficulty of how to get Lee dinner. "Aldo, who runs the only decent restaurant in this part of the valley, has a slight idiosyncrasy in that he refuses to serve a fast meal. That means either you can get here quite a bit, like one and one-half hours, before the lecture and eat there, or else we could slip you a quick sandwich before the lecture and humor Aldo after the lecture." This was followed by an advertisement by the "Bard College Committee for the Promotion of Anti-Intellectual Activities" promoting a June 5th lecture by Dr. Stan Lee. Lee was apparently a hit at Bard, and he received letters following the lectures from fans who'd been happy to have the opportunity to meet him, as well as from attendees who had enjoyed the lecture so much they picked up a few Marvel comic books for the first time. Lee even received one letter from a student a year and half later, in which he proclaimed the lecture "legendary" and "spoken of wherever the older students gather in a hushed tone of awe and reverence."

A biographical sheet about Lee later released by Marvel called the general subject of Stan's college lectures "Comic Books and the World About Us." But on most occasions Lee's talks consisted of a few jokes and an extemporaneous speech about Marvel's approach to comics, followed by as many questions from a usually fan-packed audience as would fit into the allotted time frame. "Regarding my own lecturing style," Lee wrote a student at Brown University in 1969, "I hate to make speeches as much as I hate listening to them." The benefits were enormous and wide-ranging. The lectures themselves were good publicity. Stan was quick on his feet and funny, and his subject matter stood in direct contrast and welcome relief to the majority of lectures one was likely to hear on a college campus in the 1960s. Lee could also count on some accompanying publicity—at the very least, an article written by a fan of the comics for a student newspaper. The mere fact that a comic-book editor was appearing on college campuses was a journalistic hook for many local media sources. Lee's 1966 appearance at Princeton University—where the Merry Marvel Marching Society chapter, headed by Timothy and Thomas Tulenko, sported its own formal letterhead—led to a flurry of media interest and invaluable word-of-mouth among college-speaker committees. Lee hired the first in a series of agents to handle his lecture business, and his speaking fee slowly began to climb. Soon the trips became a respectable secondary source of income. By 1975 Lee could produce a list of colleges he'd spoken at that read like a bright child's wish list of prominent universities. He was invited to speak everywhere: the University of Washington, Yale, Harvard, Notre Dame, Duke, Vassar, the University of Manitoba, and even the student-run Lancaster Arts Festival in England. He also briefly entertained a spin-off career as a corporate speaker, lecturing on the subject "Communicating with the Teenage World."

The college lectures put Lee at the forefront of the Marvel superhero renaissance, making him the public face for what he and the artists were accomplishing. They also suggested that, one day soon, Lee might have a role in the comic-book industry that did not involve the day-to-day work of editing, co-plotting, and scripting a comic-book line. By 1967 Lee had firmly established himself as the central figure in any and all press coverage the company received. After a few years of operating beneath the wider culture's radar, in 1965 Marvel began to attract the attention of mainstream journalists. Articles covered the line's growing financial success—as in a profile in *The Wall Street Journal*—and most writers were also quick to grasp the artistic significance of what Lee and the artists were doing with the books. Sally Kempton's April 1, 1965, article in the *Village Voice*, "The Super Anti-Hero in Forest Hills," noted that Marvel's books allowed for adult escapism, in part because the characters received and utilized their power in ambivalent, often ironic, ways. Lee was accessible to the reporters, was eminently quotable, and, when he started to read what they were gleaning from his comic books, was able to grasp the essence of what they were saying and repeat it back to other journalists from other magazines. Press people understood Stan Lee as a fellow writer, and while many articles used art from the various comic books, and some extended their description of Marvel's inner working to include the artists, it was always Stan who played the starring role. In many cases, he was the only nonfiction person profiled. When reporters wrote articles about Marvel as a cultural phenomenon, Lee was noted as the writer and animating consciousness behind the books. When they wrote about the inner workings of the comic-book company, as Nat Freedland did in his January 1966 piece for *New York*, Stan granted them as much access as they needed, and in the resulting articles he came across as a lively, creative presence. Whether on college campuses, in written correspondence with fans, or in his office with a feature writer, Lee discovered he was naturally adept at dealing with the public. Stan Lee was making a name for himself, and the thrilling content of Marvel's comic books would continue to make that name shine.

STAN LEE, EDITOR

In an offhanded personnel move that would prove to have long-term significance, Stan Lee hired Roy Thomas away from DC Comics in 1965. Lee was looking for a measure of relief as the primary writer of Marvel's new superhero titles. While veterans such as Larry Lieber could fill in on individual issues or for brief runs on the secondary titles, what Stan really needed was someone who could replicate his style without requiring a close, guiding hand. Thomas was a rarity in comics in 1965—new blood. He had sidestepped a fellowship at George Washington University to take an assistant's job under DC's Mort Weisinger. New in town, he reached out socially to Lee. "I wanted to meet Stan Lee, because despite my admiration for [DC writers] Gardner Fox and John Broome and others, I knew Stan was writing the most vital comics around," Thomas recalled in 1981. "So I just sat down one night at the hotel and—I wrote him a letter! Not applying for a job or anything so mundane as that—I just said that I admired his work, and would like to buy him a drink sometime." Lee remembered Thomas from his fan magazine *Alter Ego*, and while he declined the drink, he asked Thomas if he'd be interested in a writer's test. Thomas took the test on a Friday, passed, and an hour later received a writing assignment due the next Monday.

Thomas was a competent writer who could manage his own version of the Marvel style, but he understood comic books in a much different way than Lee. A well-connected and respected member of the small but vital comic-book fan community, he had presented Lee with the fan-voted Alley Award as best writer and editor before his hiring. Thomas could look at the early Marvel comic books and divine where Kirby and Lee had each contributed to the final effort. He knew what the Marvel creators were accomplishing in the contexts of their individual careers. Thomas could even discern, in the manner of a literary critic, aesthetic predecessors. "There was the influence, whether conscious or not, of Bill Everett's Sub-Mariner, his 'people are no damn good' attitude," Thomas said of the first few issues of *The Fantastic Four*. Thomas understood and felt affection for comic-book history and the larger sense of a connected story that the individual books implied. He also regarded the larger spectrum of pulp to which comic books belonged as a dignified tradition. Through a detail here, a borrowed archetype there, Thomas helped Marvel arrive at a grander conception of itself. And the symbolic meaning of Thomas's move from DC to Marvel confirmed to many Lee's elevated standing in the fan community, which contained the opinion leaders of the comic-book marketplace.

Kirby and Lee still burned at the heart of the Marvel comics empire, and nothing matched their output of the late 1960s. They presided over a true comic-book universe: vast, interconnected, and cosmically sound. In building a series of titles, Lee and his artists had frequently used other Marvel heroes as guest stars. Such crossovers were a tried-and-true method of calling the fans' attention to other books they might be interested in buying. DC had long made special events out of their team-ups, regularly scheduling affairs featuring square-jawed good citizens, like lodge meetings in tights. In contrast, the Marvel superheroes frequently spent their crossovers beating the tar out of each other. Spider-Man tussled with the Fantastic Four, the Avengers battled the X-Men, and the Hulk fought everybody. This circle of violence drove home yet another creative difference between Marvel and the competition, and, one imagines, it gave Lee and his artists a rest from creating a new villain every issue. The constant run-ins also made sense to fans, as the arrival of an alien with bad intentions in a crowded city street was likely to attract the attention of any hero within shouting distance, whether or not his name appeared on the front cover.

Marvel was creating brand loyalty by paying attention to a wider Marvel tale, offering crucial details of a continuing and interconnected story to those fans who cared enough to look closely. The sense of a fantasy world so deeply realized it could stand up to as much obsessive attention as any kid could muster did as much for brand loyalty as the visually dynamic, verbally playful Marvel style.

As Lee's responsibilities continued to expand, he grew to depend on his best artists more and more. In 1965 the top artists were Jack Kirby and Steve Ditko. Kirby had gone from the workhorse of the entire line—doing covers and early issues and fill-ins for nearly every major character Marvel introduced—to settling in as the full-time illustrator on a select suite of titles. Kirby began to produce stories that ran from one issue to the next without stop—less individual installments in a series than chapters in a sprawling saga that was limitless in scope. In *Journey into Mystery*, Kirby added a series of straight fantasy backup stories called "Tales of Asgard," featuring Thor and the other Norse gods. In the main features, he began to blend that fantasy world into the exploits of Thor on Earth. The result was a captivating mélange of the divine and mundane, using the interference of godlike characters into the affairs of men as the kind of abstract playing-out of the moral ideals for which gods had stood for years. In their Captain America stories for *Tales of Suspense*, Kirby and Lee fashioned a pulpy reminder of the power that Nazi Germany still had on the imagination of 1960s America. The threat was still with Cap, in stories of deadly robots called Sleepers. Both the comic book and the character were reluctant to see the 1960s as a better time.

Kirby's finest work remained *The Fantastic Four*. During one period from late 1965 to 1967, Kirby produced enough resonant characters to start yet another superhero line. The misunderstood and freakish family of outsiders known as the Inhumans, the first major black superhero, the Black Panther, and the noble but suffering Silver Surfer all sprang to visual life from Kirby's pencil in slightly over a half-year's worth of comic-book issues. It was an eye-popping show. The highlight of that run—and perhaps of Marvel's publishing history—was *The Fantastic Four* #s 48–50, in which the first family of modern superheroes faced down Armageddon in the form of a god named Galactus who sought to consume the planet's energies. It sounded like an old monster-comic plot, and certainly other company's superheroes had saved the world from imminent doom many times. But Kirby had become so effective at drawing the use of world-bending power, and the readers had become so invested in the characters, that the stakes felt extremely high. Kirby unrestrained was an awesome thing, and it was all Stan Lee could do just to hold on. Lee's own work on Thor seemed fully invested in Kirby's moralizing, with witty, philosophical points being made between hammer blows. In *The Fantastic Four*, Lee kept the heroes straight and the audiences interested by attending to various nuances in their characterizations and keeping the dialogue from descending into mawkishness. Like the fans, Lee, too, was falling in love with the cosmic scope and authority of Kirby's stellar output, and particularly with his visually compelling characters, such as the nearly translucent Silver Surfer.

The Amazing Spider-Man continued to build on its early success, marking out distinctive aesthetic territory in New York neighborhoods much less fancy than those inhabited by heroes like Captain America and Iron Man. For those in the comic-book industry, it was Spider-Man's success that proved the most baffling. Steve Ditko's art was even cruder than Kirby's overworked output on the early issues, and the hero was self-absorbed and unappealing. Yet the book was by far Marvel's most distinctive, and the character would become emblematic of the company's new superhero line. When DC Comics tweaked Marvel in the 1960s, they almost always did so through Spider-Man: Jerry Lewis became "the Fearless Tarantula" in an issue of *The Adventures of Jerry Lewis*, while a teenage DC hero in the "Legion of Superheroes" serials compared himself, quite favorably, to the webbed wallcrawler.

The initial competitors' backlash gave way to a growing respect for what Lee and Ditko had accomplished. A few artists could make out the distinctive point of view informing Ditko's visual style—the eerily accurate rooftops, the hunched-over figures. Even Ditko's critics conceded the artist's development from the comic book's earliest issues. But behind the scenes, Lee and Ditko began to disagree on the title's direction. By issue #25, and perhaps several issues earlier, Ditko was plotting the book himself and turning over the penciled pages to Lee, who filled in the dialogue. "I didn't know what he'd be bringing me. It was almost like doing a crossword puzzle," Lee says. By the time Roy Thomas joined the company as assistant editor in 1965, Ditko and Lee were no longer speaking to each other, using intermediaries to communicate. "There wasn't a lot of anger, it was just that they got to arguing so much over the plot lines," Thomas later recalled.

Then, one day in early 1966, Ditko walked into Marvel's offices on Madison Avenue, delivered a stack of pages, and quit. The lore repeated in comic-book circles is that the final straw was a dispute over the unmasking of the villainous Green Goblin in the Spider-Man book. In keeping with his view of the universe, Ditko wanted the Goblin to turn out to be someone who hadn't been seen before. Lee argued that he should be an established character so that readers wouldn't feel cheated. Lee remembers the disagreement over the Green Goblin, but doesn't think that's what prompted Ditko's resignation. "I really don't know why he left to this day, and he's never told me," Lee says. Regardless, Ditko's dissatisfaction was a well-known fact. The day Ditko quit, Sol Brodsky had been alerted to offer the artist a page-rate raise. But the depth of the artist's dissatisfaction took everyone by surprise.

Even now, the only person who knows for sure why Ditko left Marvel is Ditko. For many years, he remained silent about his collaboration with Lee, both publicly and privately, holding fast to his belief that the past is best left in the past. Decades later, Ditko broke his silence in a series of essays in *The Comics*, a small-circulation newsletter about the history of comic books. The decision to break his silence, Ditko wrote, was due to a few public incidents, including a 1998 article in *Time* that credited Lee as the "creator" of Spider-Man. Yet as eloquently as Ditko wrote on matters of general creative credit, and as strangled as his lengthy theorizing on the underlying causes of such conflicts could be, Ditko had almost nothing to say about his once-sudden departure. He wrote simply, "I know why I left Marvel but no one else in this universe knew or knows why. It may be of mild interest to realize that Stan Lee chose not to know, to hear why, I left."

Lee turned to John Romita as a replacement. Romita was one of the young stalwarts of the Atlas era who had been pruned from the roster when the distribution deal with DC severely limited production. Instead of leaving comics entirely when things went bad for many freelancers in the late 1950s, Romita had found refuge in the relative hinterlands of DC's romance department. Romita chose a return to Marvel over both a potential editorial position with the romance books and a berth at an advertising agency. He worked out an arrangement whereby he would do his freelance work at Marvel's offices. He became a fixture there, with Lee turning to him with great regularity as a kind of artist-in-residence; he eventually took on a full-time position as an art director.

Romita firmly believed that the job of a second artist on a feature was to continue the success of the original illustrator, something he had put into practice with several issues of *Daredevil*, when the creative partnership of Wally Wood and Bill Everett snapped. Romita tried to do what he thought was "a passable Ditko" for his first couple of issues—"I thought he might come back," he says—but soon more and more of his own style began to seep through. Romita's *Spider-Man* featured handsome men, beautiful women, clean storytelling with a minimum of distracting visual elements, and an elegant sense of superhero costume design. Romita was soon offered as much of a creative voice as any of the artists save Kirby. Lee would often give Romita a single word describing the next issue's villain—the Kingpin, the Shocker—and Romita would puzzle through and try to deliver something that made story sense but that was also fundamentally well drawn, the kind of picture that could be identified from a silhouette at greatly reduced size. Lee and Romita seemed to have more in common creatively than Lee and Ditko ever had, and Stan's scripting became a matter of emphasizing Romita's strong points rather than the compelling clash of divergent points of view. Stan Lee and John Romita's Spider-Man dropped the anguished teenager routine, straightened his spine, and embraced the romantic headiness of those first few years as a free-to-choose adult. With that subtle shift in emphasis, Spider-Man surged to the forefront of Marvel's sales and eventually challenged the DC characters as the industry's most popular.

Romita was one in a series of major artists Marvel hired that allowed for company expansion in the late 1960s, and the look and feel of the early issues was passed down to younger illustrators. By the mid-1960s, several DC artists had begun to do occasional work for Marvel, avoiding the wrath of DC editors in time-honored comic-book fashion by using false names. Lee also managed to get as much work as he could out of many veteran artists, including several loyal contributors to past Goodman efforts—illustrators perhaps not naturally suited to the kind of dynamic visual style that Marvel was attempting. EC veterans Johnny Craig and Wally Wood did work of varying quality for Lee—the incorrigible, sometimes insecure, and immensely talented Wood yet another artist whose personality stood in complete contrast to Lee's own. Lee may have lost for Marvel a chance for artistic diversity by making many of these artists adhere to a kind of Kirby dynamism, but as an editor Lee could always see what was working. Except for Ditko, who existed in a corner of the marketplace all by himself, what worked for Marvel was Jack Kirby.

Lee managed the twin feat of encouraging beautifully idiosyncratic work from his best artists and driving his less distinctive artists to provide work in roughly the same visual neighborhood. Getting a Marvel comic out of Jack Kirby was one thing; Stan Lee got material that was recognizably Marvel from *whomever* he had available. When Romita began working in-house, it was his job to communicate to artists the kind of art Lee wanted—advice that included such practical tips as making sure a speaking character had his or her mouth open. No editor in comic-book history did a better job at communicating a house style without losing the creative elements that made the line stand out in the first place.

Lee was fond of artists who had range to match their skill. When he found one who could work within the Marvel concept established by Kirby, he was willing to do whatever it took to make best use of that artist's time. DC veteran Gil Kane, an iconoclast who championed the idea of comics as a form of personal expression when very few others did, eventually became interested in what Marvel was doing. Kane was particularly good at illustrating covers and drawing dynamic figures, so Marvel made use of him on cover after cover and in the pages of various adventure titles.

After Romita, the most important hire of the 1960s was John Buscema, a Goodman bullpen artist in the late 1940s who had moved into advertising when the industry contracted. Lee sought Buscema out in 1965 and personally recruited him back into the fold. Buscema was a more facile artist than anyone at Lee's disposal, including Kirby. Stan Goldberg, who drew Marvel's teen romance books, later declared, "John Buscema was not *one* of the best artists to work in comics—he was *the* best artist who ever drew comics." Buscema understood not just how to draw dynamically, but how to get the maximum effect from the minimum effort, a vital skill for a workhorse freelancer. He was so quick that he was asked to run workshops on how to draw effectively and quickly, talks that were later distilled by Lee and Buscema into the book *How to Draw Comics the Marvel Way*. But back in the 1960s, Buscema was simply an artist with the talent to do anything asked of him, like a five-tool baseball player called up from the minor leagues whom Stan Lee could work into the lineup wherever he wished.

In 1968 Lee and Buscema created a solo title starring the supporting character from *The Fantastic Four* that Stan had so admired, the Silver Surfer. Working with the free hand provided by the presence of an artist as skilled and pliable as Buscema, the comic remains the best reflection of Stan's skill as a solo creative act. Lee credits Kirby with the character's creation. With Buscema, Lee created what he called the character's gestalt—essentially a fuller explanation of the Silver Surfer's motives and reasons for being. Lee's Surfer is a character trapped on Earth because he dared defy his master, Galactus, in order that the planet might be spared. The stories mixed every element of suffering heroism into irresistible story hooks. The Surfer was separated from his home planet and true love, he was completely (and literally) alienated from the planet on which he was now trapped, and he observed human mores and interactions without fully understanding anything about them except their often unjust nature. Lee made the Silver Surfer a poet, a street-corner Romeo tossing out pained commentary on mankind and his own miserable state. "Paradise unearned is but a land of shadows," the Surfer declares in one of the first issue's more upbeat moments. In traditional humanist fashion, Lee had taken a character with god-like abilities and made him noble but tragic. Lee's poetic quest to locate the heart of man's existence on Earth eventually led to a poem, "God Woke," that would take on a creative life of its own.

The Silver Surfer failed to find a sizable audience, partly because he appeared in a comic book that was directed toward older readers, with more pages and at a higher cover price. Lee remained enamored of the title for years, pointing to it as a career highlight. By mixing questions about the purpose of life with the sweeping landscapes and solid figure-drawing of John Buscema, Lee had replicated the jarring clash of light dialogue and heavy action that distinguished the early Marvels. For Jack Kirby, the Silver Surfer series carried another message entirely. Kirby had planned on introducing a backstory for the Surfer in an issue of *The Fantastic Four*, one very different in concept from what Lee and Buscema finally put together. The appearance of *The Silver Surfer* #1 was a pointed reminder that the characters Kirby worked on for Marvel were not his, and that others—Lee in particular—might be able to step on any long-term creative plans he might harbor.

There was no denying that Marvel's sustained excellence through the 1960s translated into increased sales and publicity. One figure reported by Marvel shows them expanding their comic-book sales from eighteen million copies per year at the time *The Fantastic Four* #1 was published, to thirty million less than four years later. Marvel also grew in influence. Although DC had been skeptical of Marvel's increasing sales, it was a source of frequent conversation in DC's offices and a subject of meetings from the very beginning. Writers such as Bob Haney had picked up on the effectiveness of the Lee–Kirby efforts even before the editors took notice. As early as March 1964, DC had its own take on Marvel's bold covers, cosmic villains, and "weird" heroes: a title called *Doom Patrol*. By 1968, a newer generation of writers had begun to transform the once-acknowledged market juggernaut from the inside out, all to better compete with the spreading influence and swelling sales percentages of Marvel. That same year, Lee reported that sales were up to forty-five million units. Marvel's growth had given them the credibility necessary for distributor Independent News to relax their restrictions; 1968 saw brand-new titles and shared books split into solo offerings, a freedom of format and pricing the company would expand upon in future deals. Superheroes had become viable again through the efforts of DC Comics, but it was Stan Lee who made them hot. Companies from Archie Publications to Tower to Charlton began to copy not just Stan's choice of genre, but his style—anything to catch the wave.

Lee remained focused on the content. Although he afforded certain artists almost complete control over their titles, even some that he scripted, Lee knew that his company was driven by what went between the covers. In a 1968 interview he ruminated on Marvel's goals and set his sights on a prize that was bigger than improved company sales. "[T]he thing that bothers me . . . corny as it may sound . . . we really are trying to make comics as good as comics can be made," Lee said. "We're trying to elevate the medium. We're trying to make them as respectable as possible. [O]ur goal is that someday an intelligent adult would not be embarrassed to walk down the street with a comic magazine. I don't know whether we can ever bring this off, but it's something to shoot for." Stan Lee had come a long way from the writer trying to leave comic books altogether, or the editor so concerned with trying to find the magic bullet his line could copy from another successful book.

By 1970, Stan Lee had proven himself to be a great comic-book editor, perhaps the most successful in the medium's history. Once dismissed as a hack writer and glorified production manager for a bottom-feeding trend follower, Lee had shown just what he could accomplish with a content-driven line. He got the best work out of artists who had been ignored by other companies. He rooted out the essence of what was appealing to the readers, distilled it, and communicated it successfully to a wide variety of artists and writers. He recruited new talent according to both short-term and long-term needs, and assigned them to roles suited to their particular skills. He also did the best writing of his career, both in service to ideas from other artists and working with artists whose creativity was subsumed into Lee's own. No pop-culture phenomenon has ever offered its readers more than Stan Lee's Marvel gave comic-book fans in the 1960s.

MOVING ON UP

Jim Shooter, Marvel's future editor in chief, made a brief appearance in the company's offices in 1969. Despite its unlikely success and sustained growth for the greater part of a decade, Marvel was still very much a small outfit. Shooter later said the office he entered as staff writer was made up of eleven people. Stan Lee and his trusted right-hand man Sol Brodsky enjoyed the only two formal offices in the space. Mimi Gold manned the reception desk, while an employee named Allyn Brodsky answered mail nearby. One partitioned area held artists John Romita, Marie Severin, and Tony Mortellaro. Another contained those doing more formal production work: Morrie Kuramoto, John Verpoorten, and Stu Schwartzberg. Shooter's desk was in that second grouping, and he noted the cluttered, "used" feel of the office and the lack of a dress code. "At Marvel, nobody cared what you wore." An overwhelmed and underpaid Shooter quit a few weeks later, but the frantic, highly tuned nature of the Stan Lee Marvel machine made an immediate, perhaps lasting, impression. Growing by millions of copies sold per year, Marvel was still the little office that could.

By the late 1960s, Marvel was experiencing the pains that came with making the transition from an editorial enterprise created on the run and fueled by a handful of artists and writers to one that could power a business and employ multiple talents. There was a significant change in the corporate makeup of the company. In the fall of 1968 Martin Goodman had sold his entire publishing business to Perfect Film and Chemical Corporation. Perfect became Cadence Industries soon after, and the publishing division, including comics, was consolidated on a business level as Magazine Management. Lee felt that the full swing of Marvel's comic-book renaissance had a definite bottom-line effect on a company sale that was in the $15-million range—adventure magazines took a hit in the Vietnam era, and the men's magazines seemed odd rather than salacious in the post-*Playboy* era. Further, Cadence wanted the comic-book line intact—Stan included—before the deal could be finalized. Goodman encouraged Lee to sign a three-year contract so that he could close the deal. Lee did so loyally, receiving a raise in base pay and a promise from Goodman: "I'll see to it that you and Joanie will never have to want for anything as long as you live." But when no reward beyond the pay raise made its way to Lee, he began to feel the promise had been frivolous. Goodman was still in charge of the Magazine Management division, still Lee's boss, but their relationship had changed.

The comic-book line was not as healthy as it may have appeared to the buyers at Cadence. Goodman was back in the volume business, having signed a distribution deal with Curtis Circulation Company that gave Marvel freedom to produce as many titles as it wanted, but the superhero line had begun to show the first signs of wear. Some titles were simply beyond hope. After a brief attempt to save *The X-Men* with art from fan favorite Neal Adams, the book went to reprint-only status in 1970. Despite Lee's lavish attention, *The Silver Surfer* was canceled in September of that same year. A similar fate befell the secret agent refashioning of Sgt. Fury, *Nick Fury, Agent of S.H.I.E.L.D.*, which faded away almost immediately after the departure of Jim Steranko, a vivid personality given to wild, formally innovative design on the comics page. It slipped into reprints and was gone by 1971. Marvel released several books that carried two features, a key format in the initial years of the superhero line. But this time there was no distribution deal to limit the number of titles Marvel could publish—these books had two features in an attempt to maximize sales. A number of titles slipped into a kind of half-life as second-tier books, perpetual candidates for cancellation, including such stalwarts as *The Incredible Hulk* and *Captain America*. By the end of the decade, Stan Lee was scripting just three ongoing titles that would outlast him: *Thor*, *The Fantastic Four*, and *The Amazing Spider-Man*. The rest of the titles were spread among a crew split between veterans and a growing assortment of creative people with backgrounds similar to that of Roy Thomas. One member of that group, Gerry Conway, had become a popular comic-book writer at age eighteen. Marvel was changing. The sole breakout hit of the period in no way owed its creation to Lee or any of the Marvel artists. It wasn't even a superhero. Roy Thomas and Barry Smith debuted their version of Conan the Barbarian in a comic cover-dated October 1970, kicking off a decade in which Marvel explored comic-book versions of pulp-novel heroes.

Jack Kirby quit Marvel in March 1970 via a phone call to Lee. Kirby had moved to California, partly for health reasons, and partly to be close to the entertainment industry in case an opportunity to work in Hollywood might present itself. His isolation from the New York creative community had only increased Kirby's resolve to find a better working relationship as he headed into the final stage of his long comic-book career. Kirby had suffered a number of humiliations at Marvel, a company largely fueled by his creative drive and ambition. He had watched Stan Lee's name be presented above his own on nearly every one of their joint credits. Kirby was greatly irritated by the overwhelming publicity that gave Lee the lion's share of credit for Marvel's surge in popularity; rumors abounded in the professional community that Kirby kept a file of articles about Lee. The first Marvel television cartoons, the 1966 effort *The Marvel Superheroes*, featured photostats of Kirby-drawn comic-book pages, with a bare amount of animation added to make the lips move, an insulting presentation and outright exploitation of his art. He had a good working relationship with Martin Goodman, which included a satisfactory number of incentive bonuses during his time in New York. But after Kirby testified on Marvel's behalf when former partner Joe Simon made a legal claim on the Captain America character, Goodman was a long time coming with Kirby's agreed-upon payments, or so those close to Kirby maintain, and he never matched, as he'd promised Kirby, the dollar amount that Simon might have received in settlement. When artist-turned-editorial-director Carmine Infantino began to court Kirby as part of a plan to revitalize DC Comics, Kirby was ready to be wooed. Kirby's departure was observed in fan magazines but hardly obsessed over; such was the status of his celebrity in comics relative to that of Lee. But Marvel and its professional community were thunderstruck. Lee had people such as Romita and Buscema to pick up where Kirby had left off as an artist, but as an animating presence, Kirby would be missed. Some illustrators thought Marvel might cancel *The Fantastic Four* rather than let it go on under a different voice after Kirby's 102-issue run.

One positive sign for Marvel's continued success was that recent trends in comic-book storytelling had moved away from Kirby's cosmic sagas. Comic-book readers wanted realism and relevance, depictions of social problems that reflected the world in which they lived rather than one that spawned superheroes. In many ways, this was an exaggerated conclusion to the Pandora's box opened by Lee and Kirby in *The Fantastic Four* #1. The early Marvel superhero books attempted to sustain an emotional honesty amid their wildly fantastic plots, through heroes who felt loneliness, fear, and alienation, and much of their creative energy came from the clash of the mundane and the fantastic. The Marvel style had proven such an unbeatable market force that fans were now using "realism" as a yardstick by which to measure a story's success. Many comic books of the late 1960s no longer used realism as simply a means by which to create narrative friction, but as an end unto itself. When in 1970 the DC superheroes Green Lantern and Green Arrow began to grapple with the role of the superhero in fighting racism and poverty, real-world events began to drive the stories, with some action thrown in to cut the tension.

Lee wrote the most famous story of this period. In three issues of *The Amazing Spider-Man* (#s 96–98, dated May–July 1971), Peter Parker's friend and roommate (and the boyfriend of the ironically named Mary Jane Watson) becomes addicted to tranquilizers. Pill-head Harry Osborn also happens to be the son of arch-villain the Green Goblin, which allows for a few fight scenes amid the domestic drama. The dialogue is sometimes less than convincing, such as Harry's testament to his bad habit in issue #97: "Here it is. This is all I'll need to make me feel on top of the world again." Gil Kane drew the issue with great aplomb and a seriousness that gave the blunt plot a measure of dignity. His depiction of Harry's meltdown is worthy of a Samuel Fuller movie. Yet, except for a final conflict where Spider-Man makes the Green Goblin quit fighting by forcing him to confront his hospitalized son, the story lacks the light-hearted self-awareness that originally sold Marvel to its fans. The real world worked much better as a way to undercut fantasy than fantasy worked as a way to shed light on real-world events. Still, all three special Spider-Man issues were a publicity-driven hit, and in the very next issue, Spider-Man was breaking up a prison riot.

Marvel published all three drug-story issues without the Comics Code Authority's stamp of approval, a calculated risk at the time. The CCA was clear that no depictions of drug use would appear in the comic books that received its approval. But Lee, who had been inspired to tackle the issue by a request from officials at the Department of Health, Education and Welfare, felt that he and Marvel could win against the code. The story was generally praised by fans and received a rash of positive press coverage. Lee and Marvel won their game of chicken with the CCA. A revised version of the code, which somewhat better reflected the more media-savvy times of the early 1970s, was issued on the heels of the Spider-Man drug storyline. In September 1972, Lee received a letter from the President's Special Action Office for Drug Abuse Prevention asking for help in coordinating other comic-book efforts in the growing antidrug campaign.

By the early 1970s, Lee's writing had become more competent than innovative. *Captain America* became the monthly most altered by explorations of realism, as the patriotic superhero gained a black partner named the Falcon and delved into issues of racism and violence from a street-level perspective. Cosmic adventures with high stakes in *The Fantastic Four* and *Thor* echoed similar lofty storylines that recalled Kirby's heyday. *The Amazing Spider-Man* kept up its mix of soap opera, soliloquies, and against-all-odds slugfests. But there was little Lee the writer could still do that Lee the editor hadn't already communicated to others. Roy Thomas pulled off multiple-issue, high-stakes sagas of his own in *The X-Men* and *The Avengers*. And even the youngest writers at Marvel's disposal could write a passable imitation of Lee's dialogue.

Stan Lee had his eye on a bigger prize: national celebrity. On Wednesday, January 5, 1972, at 8:00 P.M., Stan Lee found himself in his most curious position yet. He was standing on the stage at Carnegie Hall, hosting the first few minutes of a "Marvel-ous Evening with Stan Lee" before a full and eager crowd. The show had been organized by promoter Steve Lemberg, who had met Lee after entering into an early deal for media rights to Marvel characters. Although he had negotiated the deal with Chip Goodman, Martin Goodman's son, upon gaining the rights Lemberg almost immediately contacted Stan in order to translate the characters according to the Stan Lee style. "If you're going to produce things, you want them to be right. You'd have to be nuts not to utilize Stan, because he's the brains behind Marvel," Lemberg says. He soon became friendly with Lee, whom he liked quite a bit. "I thought he was wonderful."

Lemberg paid approximately $25,000 for the Carnegie Hall rental and the publicity, including an ad in the Sunday *New York Times* on December 12 that was as much a media push for the event as an attempt to put Marvel fans in seats. Lemberg hoped that a concert would help legitimize both Stan as a celebrity and the Marvel Comics success of the last decade as an entertainment comeback story. Barbara Gittler Lemberg, who went on to formally coproduce a Spider-Man album with Lee and Lemberg, says of the show, "We felt it was important to remove Stan from this hidden place he was in, where nobody in the outside world, except for people who were comic-book addicts, really knew who he was. We wanted him to be a celebrity." Even if the promoters had only been out to make money, it would have been impossible to fill the venue. With a seating capacity at Carnegie Hall of 2,800 and ticket prices of $3.50 in advance and $4.50 at the door, a sizable loss was guaranteed. The Stan Lee team hoped for some beneficial press coverage, however, the kind that could give a boost to Lemberg's plans for the Marvel characters in other media. On a personal note for Lee, Carnegie Hall was a long way from an apartment with a view of a brick wall—

it was a venue that carried an enormous amount of entertainment, New York, and Jewish cultural history, and as the lights came up Stan hoped to make good on the tremendous opportunity.

The show was a complete disaster.

"What a nightmare that show was," says Gerry Conway. "It brought out all the worst instincts of everybody involved, not knowing who your audience was." He adds that the show was a bigger disaster because of the anticipation it tried to elicit in the average Marvel fan. "This was a big deal. I remember, in New York, this was going to be the big thing in the comic-book fans' lives. Stan Lee at Carnegie Hall." The problem came in translating what Stan did to the stage. "Stan didn't sing, he didn't dance," says Conway. "He didn't really do anything. He could talk, but there really wasn't anything for him to do up there for two hours."

Promoter Steve Lemberg agrees. "It was a weird show, quite honestly. It's very difficult to do a Marvel evening with Stan Lee, because all the things you celebrated, except for Stan, are drawn characters."

According to Conway, the show suffered from a lack of creative direction, and was asking too much of the evening's genial host, no matter how enthusiastic he was about the event. "He didn't have a director for the show to speak of. They didn't have a script. The producer didn't know what he was doing. If Stan had someone to guide him through it, it may have been successful. Stan's strength and his weakness is his ability to improvise in the moment. Unfortunately, you can't improvise a two-hour show." Lemberg had decided that one way to bring color to an event was to have people on stage wearing "fabulous" costumes, which he had seen at conventions. Translating the sort of effort that went into character costumes was a little different for the Broadway stage, and the results were sometimes less than fabulous. "You know how the Spider-Man costume was made? We had a major designer for Broadway, they made Spider-Man's costume, it was the first time we'd ever seen Lycra, by taking magic markers and drawing spider webs on the costume," Lemberg says.

Instead of a focused event, fans were treated to an assortment of readings and performances involving many of Stan's professional colleagues and admirers. Roy Thomas and his rock band played. Secretaries dressed as the Invisible Girl danced in accompaniment to the music, while artists on stage drew as Stan Lee read aloud. It was a show anchored by entertainment figures reading aloud: actor Rene Auberjonois, who was involved with Lemberg's Spider-Man project; Tom Wolfe, the writer whose avowed love of Marvel Comics had greatly pleased Lee; and the French film director Alain Resnais, who was working with Lee on a potential film project and with whom Lee felt friendly. Lee's family also contributed to the show. "He had his wife and daughter reading a poem that Stan wrote called 'God Woke,'" says Conway. The loose nature of the show was exemplified by the inclusion of the *Guinness Book of World Records*' tallest man in the world, Eddie Carmel. Carmel was a great fan of Carnegie Hall, and asked to be included. Says Lemberg: "So I put him in the show. He was like eight feet tall, he was crippled, and he had this bag of candy bars to keep feeding. He stood there and read something and he cried. He was so moved by the fact that he was actually in Carnegie Hall. His whole life, he wanted to play Carnegie Hall."

The crowd became restless and eventually began to turn on the performers. The jazz player Chico Hamilton and his band performed a ten-minute set, during which bored fans ripped apart their comics and threw them at the musicians. "The kids got really antsy and angry after a while because things weren't happening," Conway recalls. "At one point, at the end of the show, Dr. Doom appears and supposedly takes Stan away. Then Stan's voice comes over the speakers: 'OK, everybody, if you want me to come back, you have to sing the Merry Marvel Marching song.' And there was deafening silence." At the show's conclusion, Conway was among the various comics people in attendance asked to come on stage to sing the Marching song to conclude the evening. "It was really pretty much a terrible show," admits Lemberg. "I feel very bad about the quality of the actual event. It's not what I would have wanted it to be." Even Lee admits the evening was a disappointment.

The show ran somewhere between an hour and a half and two hours. Afterward Conway slipped backstage to congratulate Stan: "He was sitting with this little kid, maybe of one of the people working at Marvel. The kid was talking to him, and Stan had this 'deer in the headlights' look on his face." Stan Lee's night at Carnegie Hall brought with it none of the cultural legitimacy Lemberg or Lee had hoped for—in fact, the event was covered by very few media outlets, and almost nothing written about it at the time or since has been favorable. One of the first major attempts to broaden Lee's horizons to that of a celebrity who transcended the four-color field was a failure. It wouldn't be the last.

PART V

"WITH GREAT POWER COMES GREAT RESPONSIBILITY"

FRIENDS OF NEW MARVEL

One day in the early 1970s, among his piles of fan mail and business correspondence, Stan Lee received a letter from the Middle East. The sender was Walid Jaafar, an executive with the Arabian Construction Company in Kuwait. Jaafar had heard about a possible TV project involving Captain America, Spider-Man, the Silver Surfer, and other Marvel characters. "As Kuwait is an expanding state, I think that it is time that the circle of expanding should be completed by showing your serials on our local TV station," Jaafar wrote.

Although the rumored TV show never materialized, the missive demonstrated how far the Marvel Comics brand had traveled and how big the once-struggling company had become. By 1972 Marvel and its foreign licensees were selling an estimated ninety million comics worldwide each year. Marvel titles were available everywhere from Rio de Janeiro to Osaka, Japan, with bootleg editions turning up in copyright-unfriendly zones such as Yugoslavia. In France, "L'Homme Araignée" battled "Le Bouffon Vert," while in Italy "I Fantastici Quattro" took on "Dottor Destino." Stan Lee's superheroes marched, swung, and flew across the globe, carrying with them the name of their cocreator and establishing him as a postmodern Walt Disney to an international readership of knowing high schoolers and college students.

Marvel's popularity continued to soar at home as well, with Spider-Man still the company's most visible and profitable character. In the fall of 1972, Spidey sparked a near-riot in a New York City department store during a promotional event for the release of *Amazing Spider-Man: From Beyond the Grave*, a rock album masterminded by Steve Lemberg, the producer of Lee's disastrous Carnegie Hall show. With an actor dressed as Spider-Man in tow, Lemberg arrived at the store to find a mob scene reminiscent of a mid-1960s Beatles record-signing event. Thousands of kids had shown up with their parents, packing the surrounding streets tight with bodies. The police were forced to close off several blocks from traffic. Spidey, clad in red-and-blue Lycra, had to "literally climb the walls" to make it inside to the autograph area. "I'd done a lot of rock 'n' roll concerts and events, and I'd never been to anything like this," Lemberg recalls. "Kids were falling down. The elevators were shut down. They trampled the department store. It was the scariest thing I'd ever encountered with any kind of celebrities." The Spider-Man record, which featured the cuts "Stronger the Man" and "Such a Groove to Be Free" and was performed by the Webspinners, went on to sell 84,000 copies in its first week.

Early that year, major changes had rattled the hallowed halls of Marvel. Stan's initial contract with Marvel's owner, Cadence Industries, was close to expiring, leaving his future with the company an open question. Lee was still smarting from having been left out of the $15-million bonanza that Martin Goodman had raked in when he sold his publishing empire in 1968. (Goodman had continued managing his former properties after the sale.)

The bad blood between the men was aggravated by the fact that Goodman was vying to have his youngest son, Chip, installed as the head of Marvel. Chip had been helping run his father's business operations for several years. Although he had a good head for financial matters, Chip, like Robbie Solomon at 1940s-era Timely, had become a figure of universal disdain among the artistic types in the bullpen. "You didn't want Chip to come around when Stan was not there," says Gerry Conway, who wrote *The Amazing Spider-Man* and other titles at the time. Even though Chip had limited comics experience, he would request editorial changes that were odd and sometimes bewildering. One of the more absurd examples concerned the cover of an issue of *Kid Colt Outlaw*, a long-running western title. The artwork depicted a typical cowboy action scene:

a horse-mounted hero, "the Bellows Mob" out to bushwhack him, and a thrilling shootout with bodies crouching, leaping, and tilting to form a concise loop of visual excitement. On a visit to the bullpen, Chip spied the illustration and found it wanting. "We've got to make it more interesting. Put animal masks on them," he ordered, referring to the outlaws. On the cover of the issue that shipped, one hombre, inexplicably, is wearing a gorilla mask, and another is disguised as a lion. "Chip was Martin's son," Conway says. "He was humored for many years."

Stan was Martin's relative, too, but as a cousin-in-law, he couldn't beat Chip in a nepotistic tug-of-war. Not that Lee needed to. Cadence's executives were in charge now. They, not Goodman, made the big decisions. As the public face of Marvel and the perceived architect of the company's creative triumphs, Lee found himself in an enviable negotiating position. The Cadence brass, stingy though they were, no doubt knew that letting Stan slip away was tantamount to commercial suicide. Nevertheless, as the negotiations dragged on, rumors abounded. *Stan's quitting Marvel. DC's courting Stan. Stan's going to Hollywood.* For a while, it seemed possible, even likely, that Lee would leave the company where he had made his career and his name. Lemberg, who then owned the movie and TV rights for the majority of Marvel's characters, including Spider-Man and the Fantastic Four, says he contacted Lee and offered to make him a partner in pitching big-budget movies to studios. Lemberg figured that since Lee had never been granted any ownership rights to his cocreations, he might be willing to move on. And besides, who was better qualified to sell Marvel characters to movie executives than Stan the Man, the original Marvel salesman?

In the end, Cadence trumped all other offers with a hefty raise and a promotion. Stan became Marvel's publisher in March 1972, shedding his regular writing and editing duties. While no longer responsible for the day-to-day production schedule, Lee would guide the company's line expansion and ventures into other media, such as television and movies. Stan had, in effect, supplanted Martin Goodman, and in doing so, he left Chip in the lurch. Pater Goodman was furious. As Lee recalled in his autobiography, "Martin actually had the gall to accuse me of disloyalty, of betraying him after all he had done for me. By then, I was beginning to realize that the fantasy tales I wrote might be more credible than some of the things that seemed to happen in my real life." Although Lee would be reluctant to admit it, the reality is that the situation had deteriorated into a power play with the man who had taken him in as a gangly teenager thirty years earlier. Over the course of their long relationship, Goodman had been many things to Stan: an employer, a mentor, a close friend. Their families had hosted each other at dinner parties. In the 1940s and '50s, whenever Goodman had scaled down his comics division, laying off dozens of employees, he always kept a job open for Stan, protecting his cousin-in-law from the vicissitudes of the freelance life. In light of all this, Goodman's sense of betrayal was understandable.

Under the circumstances, though, Cadence's executives made the smart choice. Goodman may have been the brains behind the company's financial success, but Lee was Marvel's soul. The tag line "Stan Lee Presents" was a far more precious commodity than even the sagest advice about paper supplies or newsstand distribution. Cadence had no shortage of business-minded individuals. They were less well-stocked with pop-culture icons whose outsized personalities could assemble a loyal fan following and headline at Carnegie Hall.

Soon after Lee's promotion, Goodman departed the firm that he had founded in 1932 and had built up over the course of a lifetime. Chip left the following year. The Goodmans would return to comics publishing for a brief period in 1974 before leaving the field for good.

With Lee firmly in control, accountable only to the Cadence money people, Marvel embarked on a tumultuous path that would see an explosion of new titles and the arrival and departure of five editors in chief within six years. Roy Thomas, Stan's former assistant, took the first turn as editor in chief. Lee and Thomas faced a tough road. The comic-book market was weakening due to rising production costs, paper shortages, and escalating competition from television and other media. And, despite their popularity, Marvel's superheroes were not selling as well as they had only a few years before. *The Amazing Spider-Man*, Marvel's number one title, sold 290,000 copies per month in 1972, compared with 370,000 monthly copies in 1968. Of the dozens of publishers who had tried to mine the comic-book business since the late 1930s, only six remained in operation. Marvel and DC, the leaders, were slugging it out for industry dominance. In a bid for the upper hand, Stan resorted to one of Martin Goodman's classic ploys: he flooded the market. DC responded in kind. From 1975 to 1978, the two companies would release 100 new titles, more than two-thirds of which were axed within two years. They lobbed genre after genre at their ever-shrinking readership, hoping something would stick.

The first wave brought horror. After the 1971 Spider-Man antidrug issues, the Comics Code Authority had relaxed its rules about scary subject matter, such as werewolves and vampires, so fright-inducing titles were acceptable again. Marvel's *Tomb of Dracula*, drawn by veteran artist Gene Colan, appeared in 1972. It was soon joined by *Man-Thing*, *Werewolf by Night*, *The Monster of Frankenstein*, and *Ghost Rider*, which featured a motorcycle-riding wraith with a flaming head. Books such as *Chamber of Chills* and *Dead of Night* reprinted stories from Marvel's 1950s horror heyday, when it was still known as Atlas.

Next came a succession of short-lived attempts to broaden the industry's audience, which by then had staked out a (mostly male) middle ground between a high-school Dungeons and Dragons club and a college fraternity. For a while, Lee had been trying to incorporate more minorities and female characters into Marvel's lineup, and now he saw an opportunity to give them leading roles. The Black Panther, who had originally appeared in the pages of *The Fantastic Four*, leapt into his own series, *Jungle Action*, in 1973. *Luke Cage, Hero for Hire* featured another African American superchampion, while the short-lived *Red Wolf* delved into American Indian culture. Meanwhile, *The Cat*, *Night Nurse*, and *Shanna the She-Devil* tried to carve out a crime-fighting niche for the fairer sex, but without much success. When Bruce Lee brought martial arts to the masses, Marvel came out with *Master of Kung Fu* and *Iron Fist*. "There was never a trend we wouldn't jump on," says Len Wein, a writer who also served a brief tenure as editor in chief.

Marvel also looked to what was working for other publishers. The Warren Publishing Company and its iconoclastic publisher, Jim Warren, had enjoyed years of modest success with black-and-white magazine-format comics such as *Creepy*, *Eerie*, and *Vampirella*. Stan hired Marv Wolfman, a former Warren editor, to create a line of similar titles for Marvel. Because they were published as magazines, the books were exempt from Comics Code Authority regulations on sex and violence. Although they never descended into outright nudity, titles such as *The Savage Sword of Conan* and *Dracula Lives!* boasted titillation and bloodshed that far exceeded what would have been acceptable in the company's four-color offerings. "We were experimenting with comics and the so-called Marvel formula that Stan had created in the early 1960s, and we were trying to take it to the next step," says Wolfman. "The new fans coming in wanted something stronger and better. This was a new generation and they needed their own approach while maintaining the things that worked at Marvel."

Without a doubt, Stan's oddest experiment in those days was *Comix Book*, a Marvel-financed black-and-white title that sought to capitalize on the trendiness of underground comics. By 1973 the undergrounds had lost economic steam due to a glut of product and declining interest from head shops, their primary market. Many of the artists who helped found the movement in the 1960s, such as Robert Crumb and Spain Rodriguez, were still active, but they were in danger of being buried under an avalanche of imitators. Editors of alternative newspapers and hip magazines still loved underground comics, though, particularly their radical politics and frank, unadulterated treatment of sex. If ever a comics-related article was published that didn't feature Stan Lee's Marvel Comics, chances are it was about the undergrounds. Stan and his potty-mouthed confreres were siblings in terms of media adoration, even if they took fundamentally different views of their shared art form.

Lee had seen some underground comics and he knew of their popularity. Thinking they might yield a profitable franchise for Marvel, he contacted Denis Kitchen, the Wisconsin-based publisher of Crumb's *Home Grown Funnies* and several other titles. Lee and Kitchen had been pen pals for a number of years, and the possibility of a job with Marvel had been floated before. Kitchen regularly sent Stan his books, to which the older man had typically responded with mocking shock at the vulgarity of the material. Soon enough, Lee came back with a question: *How can I tap into this?* "Stan wanted to be a part of anything that was exciting," Kitchen says. "He didn't quite understand what was going on, but he saw me as a conduit to it."

Until 1973 Kitchen had shown no interest in so-called "corporate comics." Now, though, he was newly married, he had a baby daughter, and his own company was on the ropes. "Suddenly, Marvel sounded a lot more attractive to me," Kitchen says. Lee suggested the creation of a national magazine aimed at adult readers, featuring comics that mixed the aesthetics of the undergrounds and Marvel. The magazine's print run would be in the neighborhood of 200,000 copies, ten times the circulation of the average underground. With Marvel's backing, the book would reach a mass market, bypassing the sketchy network of bong dealers and record peddlers upon which Kitchen normally relied. Sweetening the deal, Lee offered Kitchen an annual salary of $15,000 to edit the title. Kitchen accepted.

Almost immediately, there were problems. Some cartoonists, including Crumb and Jay Lynch, refused to work for Marvel. Crumb hated superheroes and the very notion of producing comics for a big company. Like many of the underground artists, Crumb looked to Harvey Kurtzman, the inventive visual stylist and creator of *Mad* magazine, as a role model. Crumb wasn't particularly impressed by Stan Lee, who was in many ways the embodiment of the fast-talking businessmen he satirized in his cartoons. On the other hand, several artists found Marvel's page rate—$100, compared with the standard $25 per page for undergrounds—an effective palliative for whatever pangs of guilt they felt for selling out.

Stan made it clear in the early stages of *Comix Book*'s development that, as much as he appreciated the unabashed approach of the underground artists, Marvel's book was going to be a comparatively tame enterprise. "It was constantly a battle over which swear words we could or couldn't use," Kitchen recalls. "Stan said no frontal nudity, and we broke that. At the same time, we understood if we pushed too far, we'd get slapped down for good." Kitchen found himself in the difficult position of having to negotiate between cartoonists accustomed to complete artistic freedom and a publisher who didn't want to alienate his distributor or offend his readership. To his credit, Lee tried to bend as far as he could, Kitchen adds.

"Stan wanted it to be outrageous to a point, and yet not too outrageous. It was never anything he was able to articulate."

When it came time to assemble the credits page for the first issue of *Comix Book*, the question arose of how to list Lee. Stan was concerned that such explicit material could be a source of embarrassment for him and his company. As it was, Marvel's name appeared nowhere in the magazine; the only clue to the company's association was a tiny cover logo of its distributor, Curtis Circulation Company. At the same time, Stan wanted his share of the kudos if the title turned out to be successful. His vacillation persisted until nearly the final moment. As Kitchen was finishing the pasteup for issue #1, he called his publisher and pressed him for a decision. "Here's what I'll do," Stan told him. "Call me 'instigator,' so if you get me in trouble, I can say, 'I'm not responsible, all I did was instigate it.' But if it's a big hit, then I can say, 'Hey, I *instigated* it!'" Here was a typical Stan Lee maneuver—politically safe, with a winking nod that preserved his hipster cachet.

"It was a quick way to escape and a quick way to get credit," Kitchen says.

Comix Book #1 appeared in 1974, with instigator Stan Lee leading the masthead. The title of Skip Williamson's contribution alone—"Super Sammy Smoot Battles to the Death with the Irrational Shithead"—announced that this was not typical Marvel fare. But it wasn't quite "underground" enough, either. Despite work by underground luminaries Art Spiegelman, Kim Deitch, and Justin Green, and a host of lesser lights, the Marvel-meets-the-underground-comics offering came off as watered-down and lacking bite. There were sexual situations and dirty words, but they seemed as authentic as a middle-aged man wearing bell-bottoms. The major appeal of the undergrounds was their rawness, the impression they gave of having been written, drawn, printed, and packed by a band of misfit virtuosos in a run-down warehouse somewhere. *Comix Book*, in contrast, smacked of corporate co-optation. In addition, Lee's estimate of the audience for underground comics had been overly optimistic. As it turned out, there weren't 200,000 hippies around who had the wherewithal or the interest to seek out *Comix Book* on newsstands.

Stanley M. Lieber, a.k.a. Stan Lee, in 1939, his senior year at the Bronx's DeWitt Clinton High School, also the alma mater of Batman cocreators Bob Kane and Bill Finger. Lieber was a member of the Law Society and the Ping-Pong Club, and served as a publicity director for the school's literary magazine. In his yearbook entry, he wrote that his life's ambition was to "Reach the Top—and STAY There." (COURTESY OF DEWITT CLINTON HIGH SCHOOL)

Martin Goodman, the original owner of Marvel Comics, started out in 1932 as a publisher of pulp magazines. Throughout his long and prosperous career, he was a relentless follower of trends. "If you get a title that catches on, then add a few more, you're in for a nice profit," Goodman once said. In late 1940, he brought in his wife's teenage cousin, Stanley Lieber, to work for his new comic-book division, Timely. © JASON GOODMAN (COURTESY OF JASON GOODMAN)

During the Golden Age of Comics, Timely, the comic-book outfit that would become Marvel, unleashed dozens of garishly clad supermen and -women. Its most popular heroes, Captain America, the Human Torch, and the Sub-Mariner, were featured together on this early-1940s cover of *All Select Comics*. © MARVEL CHARACTERS, INC.

Stan Lee (left) and Vince Fago in 1942. At nineteen, Lee had already been promoted to the post of Timely's editorial director. When Lee entered the army later that year, Fago, a former Fleischer Studios animator, ran the comics operation in his absence and guided Timely's expansion in the humor and funny-animal genres. © JOHN FAGO (COURTESY OF JOHN FAGO)

Splash panel from an installment of "The Ginch and Claude Pennygrabber," drawn by Jim Mooney and published in the August 1943 issue of *Terry-Toons*. Before Lee cocreated the Marvel superheroes that would make him famous, he wrote comics in every conceivable genre, ranging from western to horror to romance. In the 1940s, he scripted dozens of funny-animal features, including "The Ginch." © MARVEL CHARACTERS, INC. (COURTESY OF DR. MICHAEL J. VASSALLO)

In 1947, Lee wrote and self-published *Secrets Behind the Comics*, which he distributed out of his apartment. The volume offered a rare behind-the-scenes look at the comic-book production process and resonated with the jazzy, pitchman style that he would use to such great effect at Marvel in the 1960s. © STAN LEE

A Christmas card presented to Lee by several artists and production staffers during his early years as an editor. The illustration shows a closed-circuit broadcast of a bullpen, which suggests it dates back to a time before Timely's bullpen was dissolved in early 1950. Lee's lean frame, zany office antics, and joy he took in signing his name are all parodied here. (COURTESY OF STAN LEE COLLECTION, AMERICAN HERITAGE CENTER, UNIVERSITY OF WYOMING)

Three signature comic books from the early days of the Marvel superhero line. *The Fantastic Four*, created by Stan Lee and Jack Kirby, broke the mold for the superhero genre, showcasing conflicted characters struggling through mind-bending cosmic sagas. *The Incredible Hulk*, another Lee/Kirby production, featured the monster-as-hero, and became popular on college campuses for its focus on military excesses and inner demons. Spider-Man, who debuted in *Amazing Fantasy #15*, quickly moved into his own best-selling title, in which Lee and artist Steve Ditko gave fans a monthly soap opera about a normal high-school kid with out-of-the-ordinary responsibilities. © MARVEL CHARACTERS, INC.

Jack Kirby, the artist without whom there would never have been a Marvel Universe. Nicknamed "The King," Kirby was at the heart of American comic books from the early 1940s well into the 1970s, bringing to life entire genres for multiple publishers. With Lee, he co-created many of Marvel's most popular characters, including the Fantastic Four, the Hulk, Thor, and the X-Men. His expressive, powerful artwork also became the basis for the company's house style. Kirby's 1980s fight for the return of his original art pages and for proper credit as a creator altered the perception of Stan Lee in comic-book circles.

© THE ROSALIND KIRBY TRUST

(COURTESY OF ROBERT KATZ)

The mysterious Steve Ditko. The acclaimed comic-book artist who cocreated Spider-Man and suggested the character of Dr. Strange, his moody, sensitive art was the ideal counterpoint to Lee's playful writing. After drawing the first thirty-eight issues of *The Amazing Spider-Man*, which established the character's ongoing mythology, Ditko abruptly quit the book and Marvel in 1966. In later years, he chided Lee in print on the issue of creative title to Spider-Man. Ditko shuns publicity and hasn't given an interview in more than thirty-five years.

© BRITT STANTON (COURTESY OF BRITT STANTON)

Stan Lee in 1966 when the Marvel Age of Comics was in full swing. Lee excelled at publicity, and the story of Marvel's sales success and the increasing cultural relevance of its characters proved a popular topic for newspapers and magazines. As pictured here, Lee is recognizable as the comic-book editor who toiled in the industry without notice for more than two decades. A noteworthy change in his appearance was just around the corner. © MARVEL CHARACTERS, INC. (COURTESY OF STAN LEE COLLECTION, AMERICAN HERITAGE CENTER, UNIVERSITY OF WYOMING)

A cartoon depiction from a 1970s-era flyer advertising Lee as a speaker about Marvel Comics and youth culture. He lectured at dozens of college campuses every year, earning $1,000 or more per speech, providing a hefty annual bonus to his already considerable salary. Lee's time on the lecture trail solidified his position as the voice of Marvel Comics. © AMERICAN PROGRAM BUREAU (COURTESY OF STAN LEE COLLECTION, AMERICAN HERITAGE CENTER, UNIVERSITY OF WYOMING)

Stan Lee in 1976, four years after assuming the mantle of Marvel publisher. Lee began dressing to suit his well-crafted public image as the popular creator behind Marvel Comics, settling upon this laid-back, signature style—as well known among comic-book readers as any character's costume. © COMICS BUYER'S GUIDE (COURTESY OF COMICS BUYER'S GUIDE)

Denis Kitchen (left) and Lee in 1974 at Marvel's headquarters in New York City. Kitchen, who published underground comics by Robert Crumb and others, teamed with Lee to produce *Comix Book*, Marvel's short-lived attempt to cash in on the underground scene. "Stan wanted to be a part of anything that was exciting," Kitchen says. © 2003 DENIS KITCHEN

Denis Kitchen's "sort-of" introduction to the first issue of
Comix Book. © 2003 DENIS KITCHEN

PERSONNA DOUBLE II

30 Second TV Commercial

"Stan Lee"

LEE: You know, here at Marvel I've got Spider-man and all these characters and super villians like Dr. Doom to worry about.

I can't waste time worrying about things like shaving.

This guy calls me and he says

"try a Personna Double II." And I said "OK, I'll try it."

This Personna is beautifully designed.

Twin blades on each side. It's clean, it's got quality.

Like they told me,

"There's no finer shaving system made." I may create a whole new character . . .

Personna Man!

In 1976, Lee starred in a TV commercial for the Personna Double II shaving system. Through his ceaseless promotional efforts on behalf of Marvel and himself, he had attained the status of a celebrity. He hung out with film directors and rock stars, partied at the Playboy mansion, and rarely passed up the opportunity to mug for a camera.

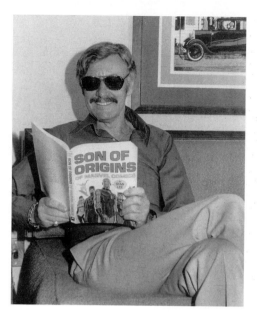

Stan Lee's deal with Simon and Schuster to write introductions and commentary for selections from Marvel reprints made him a published author at last. Together, *Origins of Marvel Comics* and several sequels promoted a version of Marvel's superhero success story with Stan Lee squarely its focus and prime mover. © MARVEL CHARACTERS, INC. (COURTESY OF STAN LEE COLLECTION, AMERICAN HERITAGE CENTER, UNIVERSITY OF WYOMING)

Stan Lee and Jack Kirby came together for the last time on this 1978 full-length adventure starring the Silver Surfer. It was an early, tentative step into publishing comic books in a longer, bookshelf-ready format called "graphic novels," and a rare comics scripting assignment for Lee, who by that time was concentrating his efforts on Hollywood. © SIMON AND SCHUSTER

Stan Lee in 1977. This photo first appeared in a book about the French new-wave director Alain Resnais, who befriended Lee and collaborated with him on a screenplay that was never filmed. Resnais was one of the first respected artists from another medium to seek out the creative voice behind Marvel Comics, and to ask for Stan Lee by name. © 1977 JAMES MONACO

Stan Lee (left) and Jim Shooter answering questions at a comic-book convention. After Marvel nearly hit bottom in the chaotic 1970s due to listless sales and changes in newsstand distribution, Shooter became the company's editor in chief. He led Marvel to renewed profits with an approach that stressed strict editorial control, publishing events such as crossovers and mini-series, and an aggressive pursuit of the hardcore fan audience through the emerging "direct market" of comic-book retailers. © *THE COMICS JOURNAL* (COURTESY OF *THE COMICS JOURNAL*)

Stan Lee with popular Marvel artists Rob Liefeld (left) and Todd McFarlane in 1991, a year before they left to help form Image Comics. Building on the same cult of personality that made Lee and other creators household names among comics fans, the artists quit Marvel and became millionaires publishing their own work. Image's lack of business discipline, and a brutal fight for market share among other publishers, eventually led to an industry-wide contraction. © ALBERT L. ORTEGA

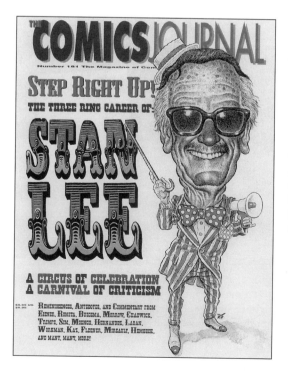

The cover of the 1995 Stan Lee issue of *The Comics Journal*, a snapshot of the industry's views in that era of the legendary writer-editor. Inside were critical articles and personal anecdotes that ranged from the laudatory to the outright vicious, reflecting Lee's controversial status in the comics field. The cover image was drawn by popular illustrator Drew Friedman. © DREW FRIEDMAN

Stan Lee and Peter Paul (right), with their wives, at the 1997 "Friends Helping Friends" Awards in Beverly Hills. Paul helped Lee become a popular fixture in the Hollywood community through charity work and celebrity-packed social events. Later, the two men cofounded an online media venture based around Lee's name and ability to attract investors—a company that became one of the most spectacular, sordid, crash-and-burn disasters of the Internet economy. © ALBERT L. ORTEGA

Stan Lee, his wife, Joan (right), and daughter, J.C., at the 1998 premiere of the comic-book movie adaptation *Blade*, starring Wesley Snipes. Blade was a minor character in the Marvel pantheon but a major hit at the multiplex. He was the first Marvel film success after decades of false starts, making the company's heroes attractive to the biggest producers in Hollywood. © ALBERT L. ORTEGA

David Lasky and Sam Henderson's short comics story about a chance encounter with Stan Lee on the weekend of a comic-book convention. Younger cartoonists like Lasky and Henderson, who work mostly outside the American mainstream comics industry, tend to view Lee less as a creative influence than as a nostalgic figure and outsized public personality. © DAVID LASKY (COURTESY OF DAVID LASKY)

Stan Lee signing autographs at a comics convention in 2002. Despite focusing his career on Hollywood for more than two decades, Lee has been careful not to cut ties to his comic-book past. Seated near Lee is artist John Romita, Jr., a talented industry veteran whose father helped ignite Spider-Man's rise to pop-culture fame in the late 1960s. © JORDAN RAPHAEL

Stan Lee with actors Tom Kenny (left) and Mark Hamill at a panel discussion during the 2002 San Diego Comic-Con. Lee has many fans in the entertainment industry, and he continues to strike movie and TV development deals as the head of POW! Entertainment, the production company he founded in late 2001. © GUS MASTRAPA

Stan Lee triumphant at the *Spider-Man* movie premiere in April 2002. Lee received an executive producer credit and had a cameo role in the film. Based largely on the soap-opera style of the comic-book series' early issues, *Spider-Man* was the year's box-office king. In November 2002, Lee filed a $10-million lawsuit against Marvel, claiming the company had cheated him out of his cut of the profits from the movie.
© ALBERT L. ORTEGA

Stan shut down the experiment after the third issue, citing poor sales figures. Kitchen, who says he never saw any sales reports for *Comix Book*, acknowledges that the title was probably selling poorly. But he suggests there might have been another reason for the book's cancellation. During Kitchen's initial negotiations with Marvel, one of the major sticking points centered on the issue of ownership of original art and copyrights. Kitchen's cartoonists had always retained control of their work. Indeed, the notion of artists' rights was an integral part of the underground-comics stance. The cartoonists used it to define themselves in opposition to the work-for-hire hacks in corporate comics. Lee and Marvel, however, operated under long-established rules that gave the company ownership of everything, including the drawn pages. Stan's first reaction was that these young upstarts would have to compromise. After much haggling, Lee began to yield. He gave back the original art. He agreed to let the cartoonists continue to own the trademarks on any preexisting characters they published in *Comix Book*. Finally, after the title was already on stands, the artists won full copyright to their work, with Marvel retaining limited reprint rights. This last concession came shortly before Stan terminated the book. The timing made Kitchen suspect that Lee, in ceding so many rights, had probably fomented a near-rebellion among Marvel's regular creators. The sentiment that filtered back to Kitchen from the bullpen was, *Why are these goddamn hippies getting all these breaks?* "Stan was in a difficult position," Kitchen says. "He was courting rebellion. I don't think he realized that there was this seething resentment among the [Marvel] creators about the way they were being treated."

In the coming years, mainstream artists such as Neal Adams would continue to push for expanded rights, eventually winning the return of original art from Marvel and DC. Both companies would also institute bonus and royalty plans that rewarded creators when their books sold well. In Stan's day as a young writer and editor—when, incidentally, comic-book sales were booming—concepts such as creators' rights and royalties were rarely, if ever, discussed. Even when Lee, as a seasoned pro, cocreated Marvel's most popular characters, including Spider-Man and the Incredible Hulk, neither he nor his artists received an ownership stake. By and large, the old-school comics creators accepted their page-rate serfdom. In the role of publisher, however, Stan became a company man with a vested interest in maintaining the ancient ways. After all, relegating the talent to work-for-hire status kept costs down and improved the company's bottom line. With *Comix Book,* Lee unwittingly tossed a wrench into the machine. The title didn't throw open the floodgates, but after its publication, fissures started to appear in the dam. What Stan viewed as a quaint side project—a short, strange trip through the counterculture—in the end added to the pressure to bring about substantial changes in the way comic-book companies dealt with their creators.

For all the creative experimentation and artistic enthusiasm that convulsed Marvel in the 1970s, the biggest catalyst for the company's rapid expansion was the competitive desire to trounce its main rival, DC Comics. In 1970 Marvel was publishing a dozen or so titles per month. By the mid-1970s, the lineup had swelled to fifty monthly titles, plus the black-and-white magazines. For an extended period, Marvel was adding one new book a month. The company's logic was simple: If Marvel could overwhelm DC on stands with a glut of product, it would capture a larger piece of the comic-book market. "We were always running to catch up," Len Wein notes. "It was really seat-of-the-pants cowboy publishing." One morning, an edict came down from Marvel's corporate bosses that four new titles needed to be added right away. The editorial staff went to lunch, hashed out the books, then returned to the office and assigned the creative teams. "The four first issues were in the works by the end of the day," Wein says.

The result of so much furious activity was chaos. Books shipped late. Some had to be filled in with reprint material at the last minute. Editors carved out their own creative fiefdoms and feuded with one another for control of creative talent and titles. The staff was demoralized. No one seemed to be in charge of the overall production schedule. As the line expanded, more writers were brought in, and that made top-down supervision increasingly difficult. "There were people working for the company who shouldn't have been writing anything," Gerry Conway says.

Although Marvel's overall business was growing slowly, individual title sales were slipping, meaning that the profit margin on any given book was getting slimmer. That led to cost-cutting measures, such as slashing page counts and reducing the physical size of pages commissioned from artists. At one point, Marvel instructed its artists to draw one story page per issue as a two-page spread, thus lightening their paychecks by a page's worth of compensation. When the company was still a family-run operation, with a sibling in charge of the coloring department and a cousin-in-law heading the comic-book line, these kinds of indignities would have been unthinkable. But now Marvel was part of Cadence, a publicly traded firm with fixed budgets and earnings targets. The interests of Spider-Man and the Avengers, and all their writers, artists, and readers, were subordinate to the greater corporate good. In the mid-1970s, there was even talk that Marvel, a profitable but relatively marginal holding in its parent company's portfolio, would either be shuttered or sold off to maintain Cadence's good standing on Wall Street. Not surprisingly, the bean counters at Cadence were, for many years, viewed with contempt by the creative-minded souls in the Marvel Bullpen. "Cadence was trying to get the most out of Marvel, and I don't think they were concerned with quality," Marv Wolfman says.

As the war between Marvel and DC intensified, Martin Goodman resurfaced with a new comic-book venture. Still bitter about his parting imbroglio with Cadence, Goodman and his son Chip formed a company called Seaboard Publications to publish magazines and a line of comic books. In a stab at his former business associates, Goodman named the comics division Atlas Comics, in reference to the pre-Marvel firm that he had operated with Lee in the 1950s.

Goodman's strategy was to tackle his old firm head-on with a flood of titles that mimicked Marvel's visual look and style. He began by hiring Larry Lieber, Lee's brother and former collaborator. At the time, Lieber—who was also Goodman's relative by marriage—was having trouble getting steady work from Marvel. The Atlas job offered a measure of security, and by all accounts, Stan didn't mind that his brother was working for a competitor. Goodman put Lieber in charge of several anthology titles and brought in a former Warren and DC editor, Jeff Rovin, to head up the main comics line.

Rovin began by trying to fashion a distinctive identity for the Atlas books, with characters that were more experimental and extreme than the superheroes being pumped out by the Big Two. That effort didn't last long. As Rovin later related in *The Comics Journal*, "Martin became more and more disgruntled as he read more and more of my comics. And what he decided, without having received a single sales report, was that they didn't look and read enough like Marvel Comics." Rovin protested, but his boss was insistent. Goodman had always been a follower of trends, and at the time, Marvel was the industry trendsetter. What's more, Goodman was determined to prove that he could re-create his prior success at Marvel without Stan Lee.

Backed by Goodman's significant cash reserves, Atlas mounted a raid on the talent pools of its competitors. Goodman offered creators higher page rates than were being paid by Marvel and DC, as well as a number of previously unheard-of incentives, such as the return of original artwork and an ownership share in the characters they invented. Several high-profile artists took the bait, including old-timers Wally Wood, Alex Toth, and Spider-Man cocreator Steve Ditko. A stream of younger freelance artists—Neal Adams, Howard Chaykin, and Walt Simonson, among them—signed on as well.

Carmine Infantino, the publisher of DC, countered Goodman's tactics with an offensive of his own—a compensation system that included rate increases, bonuses, reprint payments, and the return of artwork. Infantino's generosity, of course, extended only to those creators who agreed to work exclusively for DC. Defectors were frozen out of the company. At Marvel, the reaction was a bit more subdued. Stan was still on bad terms with Goodman, but he didn't view Atlas as a serious threat to Marvel. Nevertheless, Goodman's attempted incursion on the Marvel Bullpen had struck a nerve. In response, Stan drafted a letter to his staff.

"A situation has arisen in the comic-book field which I'd like to discuss with you," the letter began. "Recently, a number of smaller companies—some already established, some in the process of attempting a launch—have decided that the only way to match Marvel's success is to lure away as many of our people as possible.

"Unfortunately, the fact that we're big, the fact that we're solidly financed, and the fact that we're ethically responsible actually acts against us. It's like Nazi Germany and the Allies in World War Two. Hitler, being a dictator and having no one to answer to, could do as he wished whenever the mood struck him, and could make the most extravagant promises to his captive people, while being completely heedless to the consequences. The U.S., however, had to move slowly, following firmly established principles of law and government. Marvel, like the Allies, simply cannot counterreact with impetuous pie-in-the-sky offers and promises."

Having so elegantly drawn a distinction between the nobility of his cause and the fascistic disposition of his esteemed competitor, Lee went on to remind his freelancers about Marvel's medical benefits and life insurance program for those artisans "who do most or all of their work for us." In addition, Lee said, the current pay scale was under review and a number of bonus plans were in the works. As for original artwork, Marvel would look into helping artists sell their pages through in-house ads and galleries. "I might add," Lee sniped, "that years ago when I wanted to return original artwork to all artists, one of the very people in the field who is now making such extravagant offers was the very one who refused to allow me to do so!"

He closed with assurances about the "great and growing future here" and urged his staffers not to squander their own prospects by giving in to outside temptations. "Marvel has never lied to you. Marvel never will. Stay with us. You won't regret it."

Beyond shaking up DC's employment policies and causing Lee to respond as angrily as he ever had to an industry issue, Goodman's upstart company didn't make a significant impact on the comics world. Titles such as *Wulf the Barbarian, Tiger-Man,* and *The Brute,* a blatant knockoff of *The Incredible Hulk,* failed to find an audience. Goodman's creative differences with his editors, and his resolve to flood newsstands, eliminated any real chance the company may have had to be a contender. "Unfortunately, the demands on our time forced us to push out derivative, uninspired titles about every idiotic character we could invent, from the Son of Dracula to the Bog Beast to Man-Monster to Demon Hunter," Rovin recalled, adding that "the expansion of the line turned us into bonafide [*sic*] schlockmeisters."

With its powerful combination of weak properties and exorbitant pay rates, Atlas was soon bleeding money, forcing Goodman to close shop in mid-1975, ten months into the campaign. Goodman may have been motivated by anger, but he wasn't blinded by it. The desire for revenge evidently lost some of its appeal once the red ink started to flow.

After Atlas folded, Stan showed no apparent ill will toward any of his writers or artists who had gone over. He even hired his brother, Larry, back at Marvel. Lee's relationship with Goodman, however, disintegrated beyond repair; the Atlas Comics episode had driven a permanent wedge between the former friends and colleagues.

In 1978, an interviewer broached the subject with Lee: "Are you and Martin Goodman speaking any more?"

"No," Lee responded.

"It's reached that point?"

"Yeah," Lee said.

Martin Goodman retired to Palm Beach, Florida, where he died in 1992. Chip Goodman started a new company, which grew to encompass eighty magazines in a variety of genres, including softcore pornography, fitness, and home decoration. He died unexpectedly of pneumonia in 1996, at age fifty-five.

Amid all the turmoil both within and outside Marvel, the editor in chief position, after Stan's long tenure, entered a period of instability. Thomas quit in 1974. Wein moved in for nine months, and then turned the job over to Wolfman, who stayed on for a year. Next, Conway took a shot, but his reign lasted less than a month due to editorial infighting. Archie Goodwin, another former Warren editor, followed Conway and held on for a year and a half. Finally, in 1978, Jim Shooter, a twenty-six-year-old writer and editor, grabbed the reins and brought some much-needed stability to the company. "It was an insane job," Wein says. "I was technically responsible for sixty-five titles a month without any real editorial staff. It was overwhelming, far too much for one person."

Stan's role in the 1970s bullpen was similar to that of Martin Goodman's at the old Atlas and Timely. As publisher, Lee stayed largely out of the daily operations, although he would shepherd in some new titles and look over the monthly output, occasionally marking up an issue with notes. His main concern was that the most popular heroes—Spider-Man, the Fantastic Four, the Hulk, and Thor—were written and drawn by the company's best talent. "Stan was fairly hands-off," Conway says. "His strong suit has always been conceptualizing, in the sense that he would come up with the big idea and then send you on your way."

Lee became a creative advisor, someone the editors could lean on when their own wells ran dry. His office door was always open. Wein remembers a George Perez–drawn *Fantastic Four* cover that was so densely packed with figures, there was no room to place text. Perez went to see Stan and said, "Here's the cover. I'm stuck. I know it needs a blurb, but I can't figure out where to put it." Stan stared at the artwork briefly, and then pointed, "That man's raised arm. Bend it at the elbows." Immediately, the visual space opened up. "Stan was great for that sort of thing," Wein says.

Another time, in the mid-'70s, Conway was struggling with a character that he had created for *The Amazing Spider-Man*. Frank Castle was an ex-Marine whose family was gunned down by gangsters. His response to the tragedy was to embark on a jihad against crime, taking up arms of all calibers against drug lords, Mafia dons, and others who preyed on the weak and the innocent. Castle's costume, a tight-fitting black suit with a large white skull on the chest, looked fearsome enough, but the character lacked a suitable nom de guerre. Conway and Wein, who was then editor in chief, sought Stan's counsel.

"What does this guy do?" Stan asked.

"He's an ex-army guy whose family was killed by the Mob. He goes out and punishes the underworld," Wein responded.

Lee thought for a moment. "He's the Punisher."

Wein says that you could hear the sound of the two men slapping their foreheads—"Of course!"—at the flawless simplicity of the name. "All of Stan's characters' names told you exactly what they were and what they did," he observes. In the 1980s the Punisher would become one of Marvel's most popular characters, spawning several series and graphic novels, as well as a stunningly bad movie starring Dolph Lundgren.

Stan's leadership style, which was sometimes slack, entailed placing a lot of faith in the abilities of those who worked for him. He was quick to recognize talent in a new writer or artist, and he had no qualms about assigning important responsibilities to young staffers. Conway, for example, was twenty-three years old when he assumed the mantle of editor in chief. Given the turnover rate for that position, Lee arguably could have put more thought into some of his hires. But the majority of his employees respected and revered him, and, despite the sometimes crushing workload, they relished the freedom he gave them. "One of the signs of a good leader is the ability to delegate responsibility and step back, and Stan was good at that," Wein says.

On certain occasions Stan proved especially adept at shifting responsibility—for example, when facing down a crowd of incensed comics fans. Perhaps the most famous such incident involved the death of Spider-Man's early-'70s girlfriend, Gwen Stacy, who was knocked off a bridge by the Green Goblin. Lee has long maintained that he was out of town during the production of the issue that dispensed with Stacy in so callous a manner. He would say later that he was shocked—*shocked*—upon learning of her demise, and that he would certainly never have approved if he had known of it in advance.

But Conway, Spider-Man's writer at the time, and Thomas, who was then editor in chief, remember things differently. In their recollection, John Romita, the title's artist, suggested killing Gwen Stacy as a way to shake up the Spidey universe. Thomas then approached Lee and mentioned the idea, and Stan responded with great enthusiasm. "Stan said to make sure it's done in an intense and dramatic way, so the readers will feel it's well done," Conway says. *The Amazing Spider-Man* #121, "The Night Gwen Stacy Died," was released to near-unanimous fan condemnation. A short time later, Stan was at a public appearance, where his audience pummeled him with angry questions about the issue. "He immediately disavowed all knowledge," Conway says, laughing. "Stan is a guy who likes people to like him, and he doesn't want to take the heat for things. I'm sure in his mind, after a while, he didn't approve it. He certainly didn't approve the reaction he got."

While Stan was a capable creative leader, his business and administrative skills left something to be desired. He attended budget meetings, fretted over threats to his paper supply, and clashed with distributor Curtis Circulation over its inability to market Marvel products. But Stan wasn't really suited to the role of executive, and Marvel suffered growing pains in the early period of his tenure as publisher. The comic-book industry was struggling with flagging sales on newsstands and other mass-market outlets. Meanwhile, the fan culture that had coalesced around the 1960s Marvel canon was growing and establishing alternative venues for distribution, such as conventions and specialty stores. This shift demanded a more nuanced commercial strategy that seemed beyond Lee's abilities. The problem may have been with Cadence's management, who misconstrued Stan's editorial savvy as an infallible Midas touch. "Just because Stan Lee came up with the superheroes with angst doesn't make him a good businessman," says Joe Brancatelli, a business journalist who wrote a column about the comics industry in the 1970s. In a tacit acknowledgment of that fact, Stan eventually relinquished many of his corporate duties to focus more on his roles as Marvel's creative director and effervescent pitchman.

As a boss, Lee was easygoing and friendly. He exuded a relaxed confidence that, in part, reflected the stability of his home life. A few years earlier, Stan and Joan had moved back to New York City, where "Little Joan" was enrolled in acting school. After twenty-five years of marriage, the Lees were clearly still very much in love. "She could call at any time for anything, and he would take her call," says a former employee. "When she would come up, it was like an added light had entered onto his face. He adored her, and she adored him."

Around the office, Lee displayed a delight in the moment and a knack for making his recruits feel special. He was also prone to acts of exceptional kindness. One week, when his assistant, Carla Conway, was sick at home with the flu, he sent a messenger to her apartment every day to bring her groceries and hot chicken soup. "He just won me over with that," she says.

Lee often took the Marvel editors to lunch and regaled them with stories about the bygone days of comics. Stan was corny, but he had enough self-awareness to poke fun at his own persona. He wasn't above a little self-mockery, even about such ostensibly sensitive topics as his male-pattern baldness. Wein recalls that one day he was on his way to lunch with Lee and Wolfman when a huge gust of wind blew across the street. The younger men looked on with amusement as Stan grabbed for his toupee. "You think that's funny now," Lee snapped. "Not anywhere near as funny as watching a middle-aged man chase his hair down the street."

There were limits, however, to Stan's social side. Between his hectic speaking schedule, his publishing duties, and his attempts to launch Marvel into other media, he didn't have much free time to spend, say, loitering in bars. Nor was he really the kind of boss who liked to goof off with his employees after work hours. It was, perhaps, a generational thing. Stan turned fifty in 1972, while the bullpen was stocked mainly with twenty-somethings. He had a home, a wife, a grown daughter. With a few exceptions, the bullpenners lived in dingy New York apartments, produced comics in heady bursts of youthful exertion, and partied late into the night. Stan could seem downright ill at ease in the company of his young charges. Nevertheless, Lee wanted his staff to like him, so he made some halfhearted attempts to cross the generation gap.

In the early 1970s, DC publisher Carmine Infantino began taking his workers out for Friday dinners. It was a semiofficial gathering, a chance to mingle with the boss, and Infantino usually picked up the bill. A Marvel staffer who asked not to be identified recalls that Lee heard about the DC outings and decided he needed to do the same thing. "Of course, Stan had absolutely no real interest in hanging out with people," the staffer says, laughing. Regardless, the boss's order came down: We're going to the bar and we're all going to hang out. One evening after work, the staff dutifully followed Lee to a nearby watering hole and grabbed their drinks. "We're all sitting there looking at Stan," the staffer recalls, "and he's like, 'So, here we are, guys, we're hanging out.'" A long, awkward pause followed. Finally, after around ten minutes, Stan looked at his watch and stood up: "Well, gotta go." He left without paying the bar tab.

"Stan was a little more isolated from the rest of us than he would let you believe," the staffer remarks.

Like anyone in a position of authority, Lee sometimes got angry—for example, when an editor mistreated a veteran artist, or when a writer defected to DC. But those instances were uncommon. It took a major screwup to rile Stan, and even then, he rarely held a grudge. "If Stan got angry at something you did that day, it would be gone five minutes later," Wolfman says.

Lee was trying to act as a teacher to his brood of youthful writers and editors, Wolfman adds. Drawing on his three decades in the industry, Stan had plenty of lessons to impart: Every comic book is somebody's first. You can't assume that people have read the previous issue. Don't use the same background color on two issues in a row; readers will think they're the same issue. Letters columns and cover copy should be written in the snappy Marvel style; they need that Marvel zip. "Stan really understood the medium, and he had no problem explaining it, because he knew what he wanted," Wolfman notes.

Even if Stan had suddenly vanished from Marvel's offices in those days, he would have dominated the company's 1970s output by dint of his creative style and the lingering impact of his work from a decade earlier. Most of the writers and artists on staff, including Wein, Wolfman, and Conway, represented a fresh wave of creators who had been weaned on Lee's superhero collaborations with Jack Kirby and Steve Ditko. They knew how to write and draw Stan Lee's comic books because they grew up reading Stan Lee's comic books. While Lee and his peers from the Golden Age of Comics were inspired by everything from pulps to Shakespeare to film noir, the new guys claimed as their influences Lee and Kirby and Ditko. The American comic book, barely half a century old, had begun to feed on itself.

Conway's career path was typical: He started writing comics for DC at age fifteen. Eventually, after he had developed a more accomplished style, he moved over to Marvel. Despite its smaller size and lower pay rates, Marvel was the place to be. DC was a solid company, an institution, but Stan Lee's Marvel was hip, happening, cool. Everybody wanted to work for Stan. And those who did came

156 "WITH GREAT POWER COMES GREAT RESPONSIBILITY"

equipped with an ingrained "Stan Lee" sensibility to guide their work.

"Stan was the first writer to bring an ironic distance to the material, but he was unconscious of doing that," Conway says. "His models were the sitcoms and soap operas—their inherent silliness—rather than an intellectual awareness that what he was doing was self-referential." The next generation of writers, though, got the joke. And when they took over Marvel, self-reference became a standard stylistic trope rather than a mere by-product of zany storytelling. Conway and his peers filtered their imaginations through Stan's network of ironic knowingness, yielding a slightly removed, albeit more sophisticated, class of Marvel comics.

"When Lee was Marvel's head writer in the 1960s, he would have an ongoing dialogue with Kirby or Ditko about what a comic book should be, and that's how it would develop," Conway observes. "When I wrote *Spider-Man*, I was trying to do what Stan would have done. His impact was overwhelming.

"Everybody who worked at Marvel had Stan on his shoulder."

BUILDING THE BRAND

This was the itinerary for one of Stan Lee's weekend lecture tours in the early 1970s: on a Thursday at 7:00 P.M., he left LaGuardia Airport, stopped over in Chicago, and landed in Moline, Illinois, at 10:18 P.M. A representative from Augustana College met Stan at the airport and drove him to a nearby Sheraton. On Friday, Lee lectured at Augustana's Centennial Hall. By 6:00 P.M., he was back at the Moline airport, where he caught a flight to Chicago and stayed overnight at the Hyatt. Saturday morning, Lee flew to Lansing, Michigan, for a round of activities at Michigan State University. 12:00 P.M.: Brunch with faculty. 1:00 P.M.: Autograph session at a local bookshop. Then, back to campus for a lecture, dinner, and bed. On Sunday, Stan relaxed in Lansing. On Monday, he drove 120 miles northwest to Ferris State University for the final lecture of his tour. Tuesday morning, Stan departed Grand Rapids, Michigan, on North Central Airlines Flight 340. After a brief layover in Detroit, he arrived back at LaGuardia at 1:50 P.M.

In 1972, a decade into his reinvigorated life, Lee gave up the day-to-day management of a comic-book line and channeled his boundless energy into a vocation that suited him equally well, if not better—publicity. On college campuses, in newspaper and magazine articles, at fan conventions, and on television talk shows, Stan became the voice of Marvel, a one-man hype machine for a company and an art form that, recent successes notwithstanding, were still struggling for stability and respect. He was publisher, the creative head of Marvel, but now he sought to increase the empire's visibility, as well as his own. Lee's star had ascended on the strength of his writing and his connection to Marvel. Speech by speech, interview by interview, Lee would reinforce that connection and, in the process, complete his transformation from cultural unknown to cultural icon.

Lee took to his new role as if he had been rehearsing for it his whole life. Gone were his 1950s-era suits and ties, replaced by hip attire—open-neck shirts, casual slacks, Gucci shoes, a heavy-link silver bracelet. He bought hair, a toupee at first and later a transplant. He grew a mustache. He completed his look with the tinted prescription glasses that have since become his trademark prop. Following a trajectory begun in the late-1960s, Lee reinvented himself in the 1970s as a public figure every bit as colorful as his comic-book characters. Stanley Lieber was a distant memory. The skinny Jewish kid who once aspired to literary greatness had been shunted aside in favor of a persona that traded on showmanship and an endearing arrogance: Stan the Man. Lee never looked back. Even now, after three decades, he's older, grayer, a bit slower, but he still plays the part. Stan the Man has become Stan the Brand.

Lee didn't follow any premeditated master plan on his way to fame, but he certainly knew how to play the game. He hung out with film directors and rock stars. He joined the Friars Club, partied at the Playboy mansion, and starred in a TV commercial for the Personna Double II shaving system. He rarely, if ever, turned down an opportunity to hawk his wares or to mug for a camera. Stan welcomed all comers, from the *New York Times* and *Rolling Stone*, to *Canada AM* and *The Mike Douglas Show*, to public-radio programs and obscure European fanzines. When Marvel branched out to foreign markets, Lee went along for the ride. In October 1972, he flew to London to promote Marvel's British line with a week-long "Stan Lee" media blitz that included write-ups in the *Sunday Times*, lengthy chats on BBC-TV and Radio London, and a full-page profile in *Punch* magazine.

During the 1970s Lee conducted interviews with hundreds of newspapers, magazines, TV programs, and fan publications. For Stan, all press was good press. Journalists soaked up his splashy anecdotes and hyperbolic pronouncements, and regurgitated them in a flood of soft features about a long-forgotten corner of pop culture that was once again buzz-worthy: "Pow! Bam! Comics Aren't Just for Kids Anymore." "The Marvelous Stan Lee." "The Amazing Stan Lee." "Stan Lee, Superhero." Lee was the perfect interviewee. He was warm and sincere, enthusiastic and funny. Once, in response to a query about his motivation, Lee answered with a grin, "Greed. Sheer avarice." Half-truth, half-jest, the statement worked because it came from him. Marvel mania, his flashy personality—it was all a big joke that Stan was letting you in on.

There was no guile in Lee's demeanor. He was self-effacing, flattering. At a time when he was the highest-paid person in comics, Lee told a reporter, "I'm a salaried employee of Marvel—your average, humble little guy trying to stay afloat in the stormy sea of culture." To another reporter, he said deferentially, "I admire the Press [*sic*] and the rest of the media. Maybe I've been lucky but I don't think that in all the times I've been interviewed I've ever met one of the media men who didn't know his job. Now I'm not a personality. I'm not famous—and it makes me sort of humble in a way that people want to talk to me about my work and my business. It sure does."

Lee could pour it on. But, more important, he could tell a good story. After decades of writing origin tales for superheroes, villains, cowboys, and monsters, Stan crafted what was perhaps the greatest legend of all—his own. It was a story about the son of a poor dress cutter who, at a young age, wins a newspaper essay contest. Emboldened by the recognition of his talent, he endeavors to become a writer. But times are hard, he has a family to help support, there's no time for college. He joins a comic-book firm, goes to war, returns, and spends years laboring in a backwater industry where his gifts are squandered. Finally, at the prompting of his loving wife, our hero vows to shake up the status quo—to write comics his way. Dozens of new concepts and characters leap from his imagination, at last done right, revitalizing an ailing artistic medium. Children adore him, teenagers and college students think he's one hep cat. Stanley Lieber has risen from the ashes of poverty and inconsequence to become Stan Lee, purveyor of joy and wonder.

The media carried the story forward, presenting Lee as the author of the Marvel Universe. By decade's end, Stan Lee was known as "Mr. Marvel," the mastermind behind Spider-Man, the Fantastic Four, Iron Man, and all the rest. His collaborators, most notably Jack Kirby and Steve Ditko, had become obscure trivia items, revered by comics fans but relatively unknown among the general public. It's little wonder the two artists felt slighted. "I've had that problem all my life," Lee says. "I'm the guy that they invite to do the talk shows. I'm the guy who spent at least ten years going to every college in America, appearing on television shows, radio shows, boosting Marvel, promoting Marvel all I could. I began to get identified with Marvel. People thought of Marvel, they thought of me."

On a few occasions, Stan would correct an interviewer's false impressions—for example, regarding the invention of Captain America, in which he had no part. But in many more cases, Lee would let the misapprehensions stand, giving ammunition to the critics who would later accuse him of deliberately stealing the limelight from Kirby and Ditko. Lee would eventually respond to such criticism with mild indignation. He had no control over how an article or TV spot portrayed him. He had tried to set the record straight, to give Kirby and Ditko their rightful credit. What more could he do?

If only Lee could time-travel back to the 1970s and revise Marvel's press material. Because for all of Lee's good intentions, it seems that the company and its outspoken impresario were operating from different playbooks in that decade. While Lee was purportedly setting the record straight at every opportunity, Marvel was issuing press releases—the type sent to journalists as background information—that unequivocally credited Lee as the creator of Marvel and that conspicuously omitted the contributions of Kirby, Ditko, or any other artist. One release from that period leads with a brief synopsis of Lee's life: his fictional three-week winning spree in the *New York Herald Tribune* essay contest, his wartime record, and his prodigious writing resume ("no less than two complete comic magazines per week for a period of thirty years, which certainly must be a record"). The release goes on to give this account of the birth of the Marvel Universe:

"In 1960, Stan Lee innovated the new so-called Marvel Age of Comics, creating such now-legendary characters as Spider-Man, the

Hulk, the Fantastic Four, the Silver Surfer, Dr. Strange, and many others. He also brought new life to long-abandoned characters such as Captain Marvel, the Human Torch, Captain America, and the Sub-Mariner. Stan's new concepts revolutionized the comic-book industry by introducing a new type of theme—tales of superheroes that were both realistic and relevant. Marvel, and Stan Lee, have since become the 'in' thing, the most talked-about items in the 'now' market of the teenage and young adult world." It concludes: "Marvel Comics are a world-wide cult. Stan Lee is the head guru. And he's got the fan mail to prove it!"

What's left unsaid in this company missive is that Lee wasn't the head guru by default or by divine providence. It was a matter of company policy. If a university requested a Marvel representative to speak on a panel, the company sent Stan and only Stan. "The reason behind this policy," wrote Lee's secretary in response to a query from the University of Illinois, "is that as the innovator of what has now become known as the 'Marvel style,' Stan Lee is felt to be the one person who can best represent Marvel to the public." That may have been true. Lee was charismatic and entertaining, with a knack for sizing up a crowd. "I'm a real ham," Lee says of his ten-plus years on the college circuit. "I was never happier than when I was talking to an audience." But Marvel's policy also had a salutary effect on Stan's pocketbook, giving him a monopoly on a lucrative sideline business. He charged $1,000 per speech, plus travel expenses, increasing his fee to $3,000 by the early 1980s. He hired a lecture bureau to organize his schedule and to advertise him as Speaker-Man, "the king of the comic-books." With a reported forty to fifty engagements each year, Stan was pulling in a hefty annual bonus on the lecture circuit in addition to his already considerable salary from Marvel.

It wasn't all business, though. Marvel's main man also garnered his fair share of awards and accolades. The Popular Culture Association awarded Lee the Popular Culture Award of Excellence. He was the guest of honor at numerous comic-book festivals in Europe, such as the 1973 International Exhibition of Comics in Lucca, Italy. Comics were held in higher esteem outside the United States, and Stan was a folk hero of sorts in countries such as France and Japan. Lee took an interest in the nascent field of cultural studies, which was producing the majority of academic work about comic books. He kept up breezy correspondence with scholars such as Arthur Asa Berger, author of *The Comic-Stripped American*, and often discounted his speaking fee to appear at university symposiums. Berger and other emerging cultural critics played a key role in legitimizing Lee and his life's work. Stan, who never attended college, seemed to take a special pride in their interest, and he did his best to encourage it.

There were other things Lee did in the 1970s to weaken his later contention that he had always given his early-Marvel cocreators sufficient public recognition. Among them: he appeared in an advertisement for Hathaway shirts as the "originator of Marvel Comics." He wrote an essay titled "How I Invented Spider-Man." (Excerpt: "I've been asked to tell you something about the guy who reputedly started the whole thing—namely me.") He referred to Ditko not as a "collaborator" or a "partner," but instead as "the man I chose to illustrate the web-spinner's adventures." To be fair, Lee would bring up Kirby and Ditko once in a while, particularly when he was dealing with a comics-savvy reporter or convention audience. But on the whole, the available evidence indicates that in the 1970s Lee and Marvel were engaged in a spin campaign that placed Stan in the spotlight and gave short shrift to the artists on whose backs the company had been built.

Some historians have suggested that this might have come about as a preemptive measure on Marvel's part to stave off possible lawsuits by Lee's former colleagues. In 1966 Joe Simon had sued the company to reclaim his property rights to Captain America, which he had cocreated with Kirby in 1940. Although the suit was settled in the company's favor, it could easily have spooked Martin Goodman and Marvel's second owner, Cadence Industries. Kirby and Ditko had drawn for Marvel as de facto work-for-hire freelancers, but the terms of their employment had never been formalized, opening the door for future claims to the company's top characters. Putting Lee front and center, the theory goes, reinforced already prevalent notions that he had conceived everything by himself. Stan was also a well-paid employee of the company, and was therefore unlikely to cause trouble. Marvel had Lee on a golden leash, making him a safer bet to elevate in glory than two wild-card artists who might one day return looking for dividends from the billion-dollar franchises that they helped bring to life.

Whatever moral failings Lee may have exhibited in that time, he remained a well-loved figure by young and old readers alike. His early experience at Marvel had taught him the importance of maintaining strong ties with the faithful. Small though they were in number, the dedicated fans wielded enormous influence through informal networks, such as collectors clubs and mimeographed newsletters. Even as he chased the media spotlight, Stan carried on his efforts to build Marvel's readership one fan at a time, with frequent appearances at comic-book conventions, his "Stan's Soapbox" column, and company-endorsed fan ventures such as "Friends of Ol' Marvel" (F.O.O.M.). He also kept a vigilant eye on the mail.

Fans who wrote directly to Lee were sometimes rewarded with an autograph or a personal letter, or at least a form letter from his secretary on Marvel letterhead. Hundreds of letters poured in every month. Harry Mizutani, an eighth-grader from Toronto, Canada, wanted Stan to know that when he got depressed, he read comics to forget his troubles. High schooler Robert Berkey wrote to inquire about employment with Marvel. Ten-year-old Jason Palter had an idea for a "superheroe" [*sic*] called Norhawk, whose secret identity is Steve Action. Norhawk has powerful arms and legs, and can fly and move superfast. His ring gives him "very special powers," such as the ability to turn invisible and to speak various space languages. "Would you please let me know when you have decided if you will make Norhawk famous?" Palter wrote. Charlie Hutler, of Trenton, New Jersey, had a pressing question for Lee: "Why, in a cast of thousands of Marvel characters that try to parallel real life, is no one gay? Is it because your generation can't deal with the topic?" Carol Donovan's son Nelson, age ten-and-a-half, had created a character named Hot Fudge to fill his perceived need for black superhero women. Hot Fudge, who possessed magical melting powers and an ermine boa, had test-marketed well at Nelson's inner-city private school. Would Stan be interested in using her at Marvel?

And on and on. Entreaties, threats, avowals of admiration, business propositions, postcards, bar mitzvah invitations, requests for old comics, complaints, questions—Lee's office overflowed with mail. *The Fantastic Four suck. Bring back Godzilla. Give the Hulk a blood transfusion. My son's Spider-Man web shooter broke. Comics cost too much. Do you need a kid consultant? Here's a character: How about Skylark? Captain Terror? Nick Strider, Man of the Moon?* Lee tried to read as many letters as he could, but he only had time to respond to the ones that seemed urgent or that caught his interest. When Clint Higginbotham, of Fullerton, California, grumbled about Marvel writers taking God's name in vain, Lee responded that he would look into the matter. "My own feeling is that we should avoid doing anything, even if we are within our legal rights, if it offends a substantial portion of our readers—or even a small portion of our readers," Lee wrote back. Mother Flavia, a priestess with The Process: Church of the Final Judgement, sent Stan questions about the end of the world, which he dutifully answered: Mother Flavia: "When do you feel the end of the world will come about?" Lee: "Hopefully, not till after I'm long gone." "What would you like to see happen in the world today?" Lee: "Peace!" "How would you change the world?" Lee: "If I were God, I'd make everyone live according to the concept 'Do unto others etc.' No one could ever really do anything wrong or harmful if he followed that precept. Everything else could remain as is and we'd still have a Paradise here."

Lee's secretaries dispatched form letters in response to common queries, such as artwork evaluations, job applications, and autograph requests. Occasionally, Stan reviewed the text of the form letters to make them more personable. He hated to disappoint anyone who had taken the time to put pen to paper. At the same time, he was reluctant to invite more interaction. "Never say 'keep in touch' unless I specifically request it," Lee advised one of his secretaries in a memo. "Although I make it a policy to answer every letter I can, I hate writing unnecessary letters, and I'm never anxious to encourage additional correspondence. The important thing is—try to be pleasant, courteous, appreciative of their interest, but in no way indicate that I'm breathlessly waiting for their next letter!"

Stan also used the mail to court famous names of the day. In 1972, after hearing that Bobby Fischer was an avid comic-book fan, Lee sent him a package of Marvel books, care of Reykjavik, Iceland, where the chess phenom was in the middle of a grueling match against Russian grand master Boris Spassky. In late 1976, Lee spotted a newspaper photo of Amy Carter, the nine-year-old daughter of President-elect Jimmy Carter, reading a copy of *Spidey Super Stories*. "We, here at Marvel Comics, are delighted to number you amongst our many readers," Lee wrote to her, "and we thought you might like to have an original copy of the cover of the magazine you were reading—with our compliments."

One of Lee's greatest strengths was that he played well to many different audiences. If you were a kid, Stan the Man was everything you wanted in an adult friend. He was lively and cheerful, eternally smiling, uncomplicated. Lee's comics had shades of gray, but they weren't preachy. "I think the only message I have ever tried to get across is for Christsake, don't be bigoted," Lee said in a 1971 *Rolling Stone* article. "Don't be intolerant. If you're a radical, don't think that all of the conservatives have horns. Just like if you're a John Bircher, don't think that every radical wants to blow up the nation and rape your daughter." He continued: "I try not to make my villains all bad. Like Dr. Doom is a lovable villain. He thinks of himself as a guy who wants to rule the world 'cause he thinks he can do a better job than anyone else. And he is amazed that people try to stop him. There's no law against wanting to take over the world. You can be arrested for being a litterbug, but you're not breaking the law if you try to take over mankind."

Stan didn't play favorites. Despite his obvious fondness for a few characters, such as the Silver Surfer, he never publicly expressed a preference for any of the spandex-clad do-gooders in Marvel's pantheon. Spidey, the Hulk, the Fantastic Four, the Avengers—Stan loved them all. His favorite character, he would say, was whichever character he was working on at the moment. Like a politician campaigning for office, Lee strenuously avoided giving offense to any of his constituents. He favored some artists in the Marvel Bullpen, but he would never name them for fear of insulting an artist he left out. As for his political and philosophical leanings, they, too, were a mystery. "I'm not a hippie, I'm not a conservative, I don't know what the hell I am," Lee told *Rolling Stone*. "I don't think labels are that important because, boy, I'll tell you, I've been with guys whose hair is down to their ankles and would scare anybody, they just looked so weird, and they were the greatest guys in the world. And some of my friends are real establishment people. One of my best friends is the chairman of the board of one of the most respectable companies in the world and he's the greatest guy living. And I just don't think it matters what kind of philosophy you have as long as you're a good guy within that philosophy. I belong to all worlds, am comfortable in all worlds."

To the older set, Stan was an object of nostalgic devotion, a gratifying whiff of those long-ago nights spent hiding under a blanket with a flashlight and a pile of ten-centers. For the grown-ups still obsessed with the four-color treasures of their youth, the lawyers and teachers and stock brokers who felt a twinge of embarrassment reading *The X-Men* on the subway, Lee brought a stirring message: It's OK for adults to read comic books. Peter Parker's roommate is addicted to drugs. Ben Grimm is a lovelorn freak. Bruce Banner can't catch a break. Marvel's heroes are real people with real problems. Comic books are more than just collector's items, they're literature. "If Shakespeare and Michelangelo were alive today, and if they decided to collaborate on a comic strip. . . . Think of what a work of art that would be," Lee said in 1977. "It would be more important creatively than most any book or anything else you could think of. Comics are as valid as any other art form." Remarkably, Lee has been working the "comics are for adults, too" angle since nearly the beginning of his public visibility. Every five to ten years, like a herd of cultural amnesiacs, reporters trot him out for yet another round of articles about the "new maturity" of comics. Newspapers have been "discovering" that comic books are all grown up since at least 1965.

Even in down times for Marvel and the comics industry, Lee was an indefatigable cheerleader for both. "I think the future of comics is growing every day," he said in an interview conducted in the mid-1970s, when individual title sales had fallen to historic lows. "Not only will they always be here but they'll be bigger and better."

Stan put forth an unshakable optimism that was refreshing and appealing in a culture increasingly marked by jadedness and distrust. Could anyone else in comics have shilled as well? It's doubtful. Chip Goodman, who was then a vice president at Marvel, made a weak attempt in a 1971 interview with *Rolling Stone* about the drug-abuse storyline in *The Amazing Spider-Man*, which he characterized as "a realistic put-down of the use of narcotics." Goodman told the reporter, "We're not crusaders, we're publishers. It's our job to turn out the best fictionalized, interesting material we can. It's become an impossible task to do this without touching on some of the things people are interested in, whether it be violence, race relations, drugs, or whatever."

A while later, Lee gave a more lively account in an interview with *Oui* magazine: "Years ago I got a letter from the Department of Health, Education and Welfare saying, 'Your books have such great influence, and drug addiction is such a problem, that it would be great if one of your stories pointed up the dangers.' I felt that was a worthwhile project. So I did a Spider-Man series, a story that ran for three issues. The drug-addiction theme was peripheral. I don't like to hit a kid over the head with a lecture. Spider-Man was fighting the Green Goblin, and one of his friends was taking an overdose. Spider-Man ended up giving his friend a lecture on what an idiot he was to take the drugs."

Lee was a natural storyteller, and through his stories he fashioned himself into a star. His hubris, which would become the basis for his later vilification, only magnified his allure in the 1970s, a decade dominated by such idols as Evel Knievel and Muhammad Ali, for whom rabid self-promotion was part of the shtick. "Stan Lee is uniquely Stan Lee. There's only been one," says Len Wein, the former Marvel writer and editor. "You couldn't hire someone to be him. He created himself. Stan Lee is famous for being Stan Lee. He's an extraordinarily talented man. He's earned the right to do that. The industry would not be where it is today if it weren't for him."

PART VI

"FLAME ON!"

STAN LEE, AUTHOR

Western Union international cablegram, sent May 14, 1974:

> MR ALAIN RESNAIS 55 RUE TELEGRAPHE PARIS (FRANCE)
>
> I SENT YOU XXX A LETTER TELLING YOU NOT TO CONTACT STEVE KRANTZ AT CANNES BECAUSE COLUMBIA PICTURES MIGHT PRODUCE SPIDERMAN INSTEAD. HOWEVER, SINCE THAT LETTER EVERYTHING HAS BEEN SETTLED AND WE WILL REPEAT WE WILL HAVE STEVE KRANTZ PRODUCE SPIDERMAN. SO PLEASE BE SURE TO CONTACT STEVE KRANTZ AT HOTEL MAJESTIC AT CANNES AS PER MY FIRST LETTER IF XXXXX THERE'S A CHANCE YOU MIGHT BE ABLE TO DIRECT SPIDERMAN.
>
> WE'LL BE THERE MAY 17TH TO 20TH.
>
> SORRY FOR ALL THE CONFUSION MUCH LUCK AND LOVE FROM JOAN AND MYSELF
>
> STAN LEE

Long before a spandex-clad Tobey Maguire swung across the New York City skyline in 2002's *Spider-Man*, bringing in $400 million at

U.S. theaters for Sony's Columbia Pictures; before Wesley Snipes exterminated vampires in two installments of *Blade* that collectively grossed $150 million; and before *X-Men* made its $160-million mark in 2000, becoming the first bona fide movie hit based on a Marvel Comics property after decades of company missteps and failures; long before any of these things, there was Stan Lee, pop-culture icon, literary wannabe, and Hollywood player in the making.

When Lee became Marvel's publisher in 1972, his professional career took a major turn. After three decades of near-continuous toil in the four-color salt mines, he stopped writing comics. No more stories for *The Amazing Spider-Man* or *Thor* or *The Fantastic Four*. No more collaborations with "Big" John Buscema or "Happy" Herb Trimpe. Lee quit cold turkey, and a new generation of scripters seized the reins of Marvel's expanding mythology. From his managerial position, Lee continued to guide the company creatively. Through his relentless promotional efforts in the media and at colleges and fan conventions, Marvel's fame kept growing—as did his own. Few people noticed that Lee was no longer the plotter of the Marvel Universe. And if they did notice, they didn't care. His jazzy, energetic style still permeated the company's titles. The phrase "Stan Lee Presents" appeared on the splash page of nearly every Marvel comic book. To the minds of most readers, Marvel *was* Stan Lee, regardless of who did the actual writing.

By his own admission, Lee didn't especially miss making comic books. "You only miss things if you're not busy," he says. He might have felt a sense of closure if he had quit Marvel and moved into another field. But he had simply moved up the ranks, carrying on with business as usual.

True to his depression-era work ethic, Lee did more than just keep busy. In addition to his day job, he conceived, pitched, and wrote numerous side projects in an apparent attempt to raise his standing. For all that he had accomplished in comics, and his expanding renown, Stan still hadn't written the Great American Novel or a Hollywood movie or a Broadway musical. In the 1950s, before Spider-Man and the Hulk legitimized him as a creative force, Lee had tried to escape the lowly world of comics through newspaper strips and schlocky magazine ventures. "In those days, anything else was considered more prestigious than comics," Lee says. In the

1970s, despite his celebrity, Stan retained some of that sentiment. His work and tireless stumping on behalf of the comics medium had brought him recognition. But prestige? Not really. Although comics had made some inroads among academics and the tastemakers of cool, they still lacked the sustained intellectual output and the critical vocabulary of a true art form. There were few comic-book works of serious merit being produced, and even fewer individuals with the interest or ability to provide the critical judgment necessary to evaluate the medium in a literary framework. There was no Pauline Kael of comics to bestow distinction upon Lee or anyone else. He would have to find it in another field. Now, though, he was well positioned to parlay his reputation into more dignified pursuits. His name opened doors. Prominent movie directors befriended him. Journalists and literati celebrated him. Lee could credibly ask for $50,000 to write a film script, as he did in response to a query from a British producer in June 1972.

As Stan might have put it, with great power comes great opportunity. From the time he became publisher, Lee expended a great deal of effort to take advantage of those opportunities—in books, newspaper strips, movies, and other non-comic-book venues. With some of those labors—mainly the ones related to his Marvel oeuvre and persona—Lee would enjoy success. But in his attempts to strike out alone, apart from Marvel, he would find only disappointment. In time, it would become clear that just as Marvel was Stan Lee, Stan Lee was Marvel. He couldn't evade the shadow of his most public achievement. Marvel's comic-book empire was the foundation of Lee's fame and cachet, and as hard as he tried to elevate himself above the field, the comics would remain his artistic legacy.

In 1974 Lee published *Origins of Marvel Comics*, the first in a line of Marvel-themed mass-market books put out by Simon and Schuster. To call *Origins* a book is a bit of an overstatement. It was a collection of Marvel Comics reprints fronted by colorful Lee-written reminiscences about the genesis of the company's major heroes. The selling proposition was Stan Lee meets Marvel in a mainstream format. While it was hardly the novel that he once dreamed of writing, *Origins* was produced by a major publishing house and Lee's name appeared on the cover. It also sold more than 150,000 copies, making Stan, by some standards, a best-selling writer.

Lee's contribution, roughly forty pages of stock company history, is sufficiently entertaining. It certainly bears his stamp. "Ah, but this was not to be merely another of the hundreds of comic-strip features I had concocted in my long and lachrymose career," he writes in reference to the 1961 creation of the Fantastic Four. "No, this was to be something different—something special—something to stupefy my publisher, startle my public, and satisfy my wife's desire for me to 'prove myself' in my own little sphere."

At the same time, Lee's flashy tone and abridged—some would call it self-serving—version of events make it difficult to treat *Origins* as a serious work. In the book, he seems more interested in turning a clever phrase than in revealing any significant details about the creation of the Marvel Universe. In some cases, he fudges the timeline to make later Marvel innovations part of the original plan: "[T]he characters would be the kind of characters I could personally relate to; they'd be flesh and blood, they'd have their faults and foibles, they'd be fallible and feisty, and—most important of all—inside their colorful, costumed booties they'd still have feet of clay." At other points, he plays down the contributions of his cocreators Jack Kirby and Steve Ditko, setting the stage for years of withering criticism from both men, as well as from comics fans and historians. Credibility issues notwithstanding, *Origins* accomplished a number of things. It made for a fun read. It got Marvel into bookstores. For young superhero fans with no memory of the 1960s, it put Stan Lee front and center as the source for their own Marvel experience. It also spawned several sequels, written by Lee, including *Son of Origins of Marvel Comics* and *Bring on the Bad Guys*. And, despite all its shortcomings, it made Stan an author.

Lee took pride in *Origins* and his subsequent books, hyping them to the assembled minions of Marvel and trumpeting his status as a best-selling author in his press material. He also took exception when his book publisher's enthusiasm showed signs of waning. In late 1976, perceiving a "woeful lack of advertising" for his literary works, Lee dashed off a letter to his editor. "In the past two years, we did have some ads, small though they were," Lee wrote. "This year, however, Simon & Shuster [*sic*] seems convinced that the public will learn about our new title, and the two preceding titles, through some special form of telepathy." Sales for Lee's skewed histories declined steadily thereafter.

In the same period that Stan was making the transition from newsstand racks to bookstore shelves, he was also dipping a toe into less savory waters—pornography. In numerous interviews, Lee has professed a dislike for what he calls "dirty stuff." Even during his mid-1970s experiment with the underground *Comix Book*, he showed no particular affinity for the title's edgy language or frank sexuality. That's what makes *Thomas Swift*, a soft-core pornographic strip that Lee cooked up with longtime *The Amazing Spider-Man* artist John Romita, such an oddity. The feature, which spoofed *Flash Gordon* and the *Tom Swift* series of children's books, was pitched to *Playboy* magazine in 1975 and rejected. Stan Lee's pornography was too bizarre, disturbing even, to be taken seriously.

"Thomas Swift is as American as apple pie, the stars and stripes, baseball, and Sunday lynchings," Lee wrote in the strip proposal. "While still in college . . . Thomas Swift became an All-American quarterback, won a Pulitzer prize in nuclear physics, and was the first heterosexual to receive the coveted Al Goldstein Golden Sperm Award for paranormal sexual proclivities." The pitch continues in this peculiar, overblown style with a litany of nonsensical story twists and awkward double entendres. Swift wins the state lottery. His bunkmate, Margo Tender, is "a long-legged, fun-loving bundle of blue-eyed mischief who had come to sell him a box of Girl Scout cookies some time before, and decided to stay on, the better to personally service the account."

The strip's style, Lee wrote, would be a "somewhat original one"—a typical superhero yarn populated by characters engaged in "all sorts of highly gratifying, non-comic-code-approved activities." He added: "We'll seek low-key, eminently respectable means of describing the most sordid sexual activities. As for the artwork, that should be lush and horny, with a beauty and a sensuality that will transcend the earthy subject matter."

To demonstrate the promised lushness and horniness, Lee and Romita enclosed a sample illustration with their pitch. The splash page of their proposed first storyline, "Thomas Swift and His Eclectic Sauna," is set in a futuristic Ming the Merciless–style throne room adorned with a bevy of naked, big-breasted women lounging in various states of sexual arousal. A brawny, evil-looking man with a head shaped like the tip of a penis sits on a throne that resembles two giant testicles. He is Magnificus the Mighty, and he rules the world of the future. To his right stands the High Priestess Clitanna, a dominatrix with malevolent eyes and large, exposed breasts.

"Let all lips be silent! Let all gaiety cease!" Clitanna intones. "Hark to his studship—Magnificus speaks!"

"Lord Peckerton! Approach you my throne!" Magnificus commands an underling. "I await your report. How goes the new time probe?"

"All is in readiness, your studship," responds Lord Peckerton, bowing his veiny, pecker-shaped head. "We shall send the time-travel globule further into the past than ever before!"

'Nuff said.

There aren't many Stan Lee-written proposals around that contain the phrases "evasive erection" and "man-eating lesbians." Which is probably a good thing. Despite his obvious knowledge of the mysteries and pleasures of sex, Lee made for a bad pornographer. For *Playboy* at least, his jaunty Marvel style was a poor fit. Michelle Urry, the magazine's cartoon editor, sent Lee and Romita a critique of their proposal, in which she counseled them to sketch a wider variety of body types for their characters. "Though Mr. Hefner likes the pecker-heads very much, perhaps Magnificus could be more like Ming the Merciless, and the girls not all like Amazons," Urry wrote. She suggested the addition of sex monsters and costumes with ornate dildos, as well as more sharply delineated characters, such as an evil black stud or a gay foil. Furthermore, the names "Thomas Swift" and "Margo Tender" are too obvious, Urry said. Porn names should work on two levels.

It's unclear how much of this advice Lee took to heart. *Thomas Swift* never saw print. And Lee now says he cannot recall his long-ago attempt at pornography, adding that it was most likely motivated by money. "It would have been nice to have something in *Playboy*," Lee says. "It probably paid well."

With tamer comic-strip ventures—most notably, a newspaper version of *The Amazing Spider-Man*—Lee had more luck. Like most comic-book creators of his generation, Stan had long aspired to produce a regular newspaper strip. Comic-strip artists were admired as professionals, political commentators, and philosophers. The purveyors of comic books, on the other hand, were viewed as one step removed from pornographers. In the 1950s, when comic-book makers like Jack Kirby and Gil Kane were scrambling for work as their business collapsed around them, "Pogo" strip creator Walt Kelly was being celebrated for his social conscience and attacks on demagoguery. "Every comic-book artist wished he had a newspaper strip," Lee says. Along with respect, a strip offered financial stability—and a great deal more if a concept generated a bounty of licensing deals. Earlier in his career, Lee had tried to launch several strips, including the short-lived "Mrs. Lyon's Cubs" in 1957 with Joe Maneely. None of those efforts panned out. By the 1970s, he could be assured of greater success because he was backed by two popular brand names—Marvel and Stan Lee. So he tried again.

Lee developed a strip based on *The Incredible Hulk*, which ran from 1978 to 1982. A by-product of the hype from the *Hulk* TV show, the green-skinned Goliath's newspaper exploits were largely forgettable. With veteran cartoonist Frank Springer, Lee produced "The Virtue of Vera Valiant," a soap-opera feature about a "typical American librarian" who bounces between two suitors. "Valiant" began syndication in 1976 and lasted only a year.

In late 1976, Lee created "Says Who!", a photo-realistic strip similar to his early-1960s *You Don't Say!* magazine series. Instead of conventionally drawn art, "Says Who!" used photographs of famous personalities laid out in a series of panels, accompanied by word balloons written by Lee. One installment featured four identical images of outgoing President Gerald Ford, who is presumably speaking to an off-camera Jimmy Carter:

Panel 1: "Yes, Jimmy, I understand your dilemma."
Panel 2: "You can't absorb everything at once."
Panel 3: "But in time, you'll learn . . ."
Panel 4: "It's the little door marked 'his.' "

"Says Who!" was the ideal format for Lee, requiring no artist and playing to his strengths as a dialogue writer. But it was also labored and corny, and its premise got old fast. The strip was canceled after a few months due to technical and logistical problems. Many newspapers were unable to reproduce the photographs, and few celebrities would permit the use of their pictures in the strip. Stan had been relying on photos of public officials, and, as the Gerald Ford gag demonstrates, he didn't quite have the gift for political satire.

By far, Lee's most successful strip endeavor was "The Amazing Spider-Man," which, after a few aborted attempts, debuted in 1977. Originally drawn by John Romita, the strip went on to appear in 500 newspapers worldwide. As of late 2002, "The Amazing Spider-Man" was still ongoing, drawn by Lee's brother, Larry Lieber, and scripted by a ghostwriter, although Stan's name remained in the credits.

Creatively, the strip has accomplished little of note in its 9,000-plus daily installments: the writing and artwork have never stood out, and the plots have seldom been the topic of watercooler conversation. The strip has brought Stan extra income, however, and it has enjoyed a long run during a period when the newspaper adventure strip, once a staple of the funny pages, was in sharp decline.

The Spider-Man strip hasn't changed much since its inception. In slow-moving storylines, Spider-Man still battles run-of-the-mill thugs and supervillains while struggling to hold things together on the home front with Mary Jane. There's value in sticking to a formula, especially when it comes to maintaining the core appeal of a popular character like Spider-Man. Over the past quarter century, the comic-strip Spidey has stayed more or less the same. Meanwhile, in the Marvel Comics universe, the character's life is a mess, the result of forty years of convoluted storylines crafted by multiple scripters in up to five titles a month. Comic-book Spidey has swapped costumes, he's grown extra arms, he's been separated from Mary Jane, he's visited faraway planets, he's been replaced by a clone, he's even died and come back to life. To a casual reader picking up a comic book for the first time in twenty years, the current webhead would be largely unfamiliar. But in the strip, which runs seven days a week, it's as if Spider-Man were frozen in 1968. This is the source of the strip's durability. The newspaper Spidey is a comforting figure, classically rendered in red and blue. Like Dagwood Bumstead, the webbed wallcrawler is a familiar face in the morning paper, forever wisecracking, forever worrying.

If there were a high point to Lee's writing career after his retirement from active comic-book scripting duty, it would be his 1978 collaboration with Jack Kirby on *The Silver Surfer* graphic novel. The book, a lavish 114-page production published by Simon and Schuster, was a badge of distinction for the former cocreators and a chance to bring some of the old Lee–Kirby magic to the mainstream. It held additional significance because it came on the heels of a brief, demeaning homecoming for Kirby at Marvel.

After his breakup with Stan in 1970, Kirby had gone over to DC, where publisher Carmine Infantino had promised him artistic and editorial freedom. Kirby created several titles for the company, including the acclaimed Fourth World line—*The New Gods, Superman's Pal Jimmy Olsen, The Forever People*, and *Mister Miracle*. However, it soon became apparent that Kirby, for all his mastery of plots and pencils, needed an editor, someone to restrain his more outlandish impulses and to clean up his clunky dialogue. At Marvel, Stan had fulfilled this function in what had been a near-perfect arrangement for both men until their later difficulties. On their own, neither creator would ever again match the specific, accessible brilliance of their combined efforts during the formative years of the Marvel Age. Kirby's early-1970s DC work—raw, frenzied, laden with metaphor but occasionally baffling—underscored that point. Increasingly, DC's editors meddled with Kirby's titles, rankling the veteran artist to the point that when it came time to re-up his contract in 1975, he was already headed back to his former employer.

In the first years after his departure from Marvel, Kirby had been on bad terms with Stan. "If only Jack wouldn't hang up on me, I'm sure something could be worked out," Lee reportedly told a mutual friend at the time. Eventually, there was a reconciliation, the details of which have never fully been revealed, but it was enough to persuade Kirby to try another stint at Marvel. This time around, though, there were ground rules: Kirby would write, draw, and edit his own stories, with no interference from the company. Some have suggested that this was his way of guaranteeing that no one, Stan included, would be able to diminish or erase his credit in the future. If Kirby worked alone, there could be no doubt that the characters issuing forth from his pencil were his and his alone. From Lee's perspective, Kirby's return was extremely advantageous. Having Kirby back was a boon for Marvel, and it assuaged any lingering guilt that Lee may have felt about their original skirmish. Also, since Lee was no longer Marvel's chief writer and editor, and with the rest of the bullpen in chaos due to an increased workload brought on by the company's mid-1970s publishing strategies, it was fairly easy to leave Kirby to his own devices.

From his home in Thousand Oaks, California, Kirby started working again for Marvel in spring 1975. He returned to *Captain America*, the character he had cocreated with Joe Simon during the Golden Age of Comics. Kirby also created several new titles, including *The Eternals*, which featured superpowered beings inspired by Greek mythology, and *Machine Man*, a science-fiction series spun off from a comic-book version of *2001: A Space Odyssey*. Kirby's output from that period contained some of the most evocative art of his career. Two decades later, critics would write admiringly of Kirby's second Marvel run, citing its mix of realism, action, and outright psychedelia. But these positives were largely lost on readers of the 1970s. For them, some of the new Kirby books came across like second-rate rehashes of earlier career high points, and others as the kind of undesirable assignments that typically went to veterans past their prime. In the context of the increasingly slick soap operas and portentous cosmic odysseys favored by Marvel's second generation, Kirby's rough-and-tumble dynamism seemed quaint and out of touch.

For his part, Lee stayed mostly on the sidelines, giving Kirby his space. Stan approached his old partner just once, for perhaps the only project worthy of a Lee–Kirby reunion—a Silver Surfer graphic novel, to be released by a major book publisher. Given the potential payoff and the prestige, it would have been hard for Kirby to decline. Stan and Jack, the original architects of Marvel, teamed up for what would turn out to be the last time.

The dealings between Lee and Kirby were, by all accounts, cordial. In fact, their reestablished bond stood in direct contrast to Kirby's deteriorating relationship with the new guard at Marvel. Bullpen editors fiddled with his dialogue, sometimes rewriting it completely. Staffers seeded the letters columns of Kirby's books with negative comments—some of which were fake—in a seeming attempt to spite him. They referred to him as "Jack the Hack." Some editors scrawled derisive comments on copies of Kirby's pages and posted them on their office doors. Artist John Byrne, who witnessed some of this behavior, said in a 2000 interview that he wasn't surprised by any of it: "[T]he industry is notorious for not taking care of its own. We eat our young and abandon our old." On more than a few occasions, Kirby was aggravated by the ingratitude of the company he had helped build. Stan had to step in to smooth things over.

In January 1977 Lee met with Kirby on the West Coast and sent him a follow-up letter a few weeks later. "Just a line to tell you how much I enjoyed seeing you in Los Angeles," Lee wrote. "I am sorry we didn't have more time to spend together, but at least we did have a chance to talk awhile. I hope everything we discussed is clear and agreeable with you and that all will work out well. Keep rolling along on the SURFER—it is bound to be the 'All the President's Men' of 1977!"

Kirby quit Marvel the following year to work full-time in the animation industry. *The Silver Surfer* would serve as an epitaph for both his 1970s stint at Marvel and his relationship with Stan. From the early 1980s until Kirby's death in 1994, there would be mainly bitterness between the two men: angry accusations, hurt feelings, revised accounts of who created what and when. A tidal wave of criticism would arise against Lee, and some of that negativity would splash back on Kirby. Both creators would be left poorer for the experience.

Before everything fell apart, though, there was *The Silver Surfer*, a nostalgia buff's dream project, a farewell kiss to the faithful who had long ago made theirs Marvel. As one reviewer put it, "It's like 1967 all over again." The graphic novel reworks the story of the space-faring philosopher's arrival on Earth, as originally told in the celebrated Lee–Kirby run of *The Fantastic Four* #s 48–50. Reed Richards and his teammates are conspicuously absent; in this version, the focus is squarely on the Surfer, his trials and revelations.

The Silver Surfer is the herald for a world-eating, godlike being known as Galactus. Riding a cosmic-powered surfboard, the Surfer scours the galaxy, searching for planets to target for destruction in service to his master's insatiable appetite. On one such mission, he finds Earth. Our planet intrigues him; he is taken with its beauty and the compassion of its inhabitants. "There is energy here—there is spirit—there is vitality such as I have never known!" he observes. Seeking to protect humanity, the Surfer rebels against Galactus and is beaten down. In a fit of pique, Galactus imprisons the Surfer on our green-and-blue world and leaves.

Soon, though, Galactus's fury gets the better of him and he returns with a new plan. He sends an emissary, a golden-skinned girl named Ardina, to convince the Surfer that mankind is not worth the effort. Ardina presents her case: humans are evil. Crime, violence, and intolerance fester in their midst. "Humanity is sense-less, sick, and savage. In the name of reason—let it perish!" she declares. But the Surfer is steadfast. He admires humans for their spirit and courage, their capacity for kindness. He loves humanity, sins and all. Through the force of his goodness and his conviction, the Surfer converts Ardina to his point of view. They fall in love. Galactus destroys her and presents the Surfer with a final choice: He will leave Earth alone if the Surfer rejoins him. To save mankind, the Surfer must make the ultimate sacrifice. At the story's end, the Silver Surfer soars back into the grasp of Galactus, a god and his adopted son reunited once more.

The Silver Surfer graphic novel was a far cry from vintage Lee and Kirby. But the trademark touches were there: Kirby's grand cosmic vision laid out in his bold, dynamic style; Lee's introspective dialogue, grounding the tale with illuminating truths about love and faith. Even *The Comics Journal*, a magazine known for its hostility toward mainstream comics, found a kind word for the creative team's final curtain call. "If you've ever wondered why you still read comics, this book will give you an answer," wrote a *Journal* reviewer. "And if you ever have to deal with some idiot who calls Lee a con-man [*sic*] or Kirby a hack, just shove this book in his face. It will shut him up for the rest of his life."

By the late 1970s, Stan Lee was at the center of a whirlwind. He was Marvel's publisher and traveling salesman, the writer of a daily newspaper strip, an author, a father, and a husband. As he settled into his mid-fifties, he could look back with pride at his many accomplishments. He had cocreated dozens of fictional characters who were known the world over. He had guided a failing company to the top of its industry. He was famous—not Robert Redford famous, but famous enough to be accosted for autographs in restaurants. He had an annual income of $150,000, a fourteenth-floor condominium in Manhattan, and a house in the Hamptons.

Stan had always been an avid, fast walker who once boasted that he could average a block per minute. It was an apt metaphor for his life. He seemed to be going everywhere quickly. And yet, sometimes he went nowhere at all. In 1978 Lee signed a contract with Harper & Row to write an autobiography. The publisher gave him $12,500 and five years to turn in a 60,000-word manuscript. Lee wrote an outline, then ran out of time and had to return the advance. Possibly, it was the size of the project that deterred him. Stan had written comic books, strips, a script or two, but never a "real" book. He didn't have the patience. He had too many projects on the go, too many opportunities coming his way.

Stan worked long hours, sometimes late into the night, and never took vacations. He was successful and comfortable, but he kept pushing himself. "It's not work, it's fun," Lee would say. Vacations were like prison. He needed to stay busy. But there was something else: a vague sense of discontent that slipped through his veil of exuberance in rare, unguarded moments; a kernel of disappointment that his life hadn't started rolling earlier, that he was still stuck in comics.

Lee hinted at his unrest in a 1978 article in *Circus*, a rock 'n' roll magazine. The reporter posed a question: Any regrets?

Stan sighed. "I wish I made my move at Marvel twenty years ago, had done the different things earlier. I was stupid—for my first twenty years, I did what my publisher wanted."

Lee paused, then sighed again. "And I think I should have gotten out of this business twenty years ago. I would have liked to make movies, to be a director or a screenwriter, to have a job like [TV producer] Norm Lear or [network programmer] Freddie Silverman.

"I'd like to be doing what I'm doing here, but in a bigger arena."

STAN IN HOLLYWOOD

In May 1979, while Stan Lee and his wife, Joan, were in Los Angeles on a long-term business trip, their Manhattan condo was robbed. The thieves made off with $100,000 worth of Joan's jewelry, none of which was insured or ever recovered. "We try not to think about it, but it's the most depressing and distressing thing imaginable," Lee wrote soon afterward to the French director Alain Resnais. "It's one of the reasons we'd like to pull up stakes and come out to Los Angeles permanently, if we can. I've met a lot of people here and hope to meet lots more. With luck, I may be able to infiltrate into the tv [*sic*] and movie business yet."

The West Coast had been on Stan's mind for a long time. Since the early 1970s, he had been managing Marvel's Hollywood dealings from New York with middling success. Except for the live-action TV series *The Incredible Hulk* and a few cartoon shows, the company's multimedia ventures had all either crash-landed or collapsed in the hangar. At one point, Lee asked veteran comic-book artist Will Eisner to take over his post as Marvel's publisher so that he could head west. Eisner declined, because, he says, "I felt it was a suicide mission." In the late 1970s, it must have looked that way. Comic-book sales were slipping. Marvel's editorial operation was in disarray. In 1978 the company generated a significant portion of its $23.1 million in sales from licensing. The future, it seemed, lay in Spider-Man bath towels, Captain America bedsheets, Hulk Underoos, and toys, with films and TV shows driving the merchandising behemoth forward. To make the strategy work, the company needed to place someone close to the action, and Stan was the logical choice.

When Lee finally got his chance to relocate permanently to Los Angeles in 1980, he was all too happy to go. He loved L.A.—the climate, the lifestyle, the culture. He was a celebrity, and these were his people. What's more, he had several non-Marvel pitches to shop around, including some cowritten with Resnais. Stan was a pop-culture icon for his comics work, but what he really wanted to do was make—or at least sell—movies and TV pilots. "I have the sense that he wants to be like Walt Disney," observed a Marvel writer in a 1979 article in the *New York Times*. "Comics are sort of beneath him." That may have been so, but Lee would find in the years to come that, in many ways, he was also beneath Hollywood.

By April 1980, Stan and Joan were living in a luxury condo near Beverly Hills. They eventually settled into a large, vine-covered two-story home—complete with a pool and guest house—in the hills above the Sunset Strip. Lee was on the verge of signing a new employment contract that included a profit-sharing arrangement for all Marvel-related TV and movie projects. His college-speaking schedule had slowed considerably, which meant he could devote most of his time to wheeling and dealing. He was already talking to Henry Winkler, "Fonzie" from *Happy Days*, about playing Spider-Man in a big-budget movie. Winkler was excited, but he still had to reach an agreement with Marvel. (He never did.) Lee hoped to persuade Resnais to direct. Yet despite all that star wattage, Stan was only guardedly optimistic that the movie would come together at all. As he noted in a letter to Resnais, "I'm learning (as you've always said) nothing is ever definate [*sic*] out here, and it takes forever to come to any agreement on anything between any two parties." Lee would learn many more lessons while navigating Hollywood's harsh terrain. It would take at least eighteen years of missteps, false starts, and outright failures for Marvel to establish a foothold in the film industry, and by then, Stan would be largely out of the picture. He would be similarly stymied in his extracurricular cinematic endeavors, landing a few low-level deals that quickly fizzled but otherwise failing to transcend the confines of his comic-book fame.

In the wake of *Spider-Man*'s phenomenal box-office success and the impressive screen performances of *X-Men* and *Blade*, it's hard to remember a time when Marvel's characters weren't in demand. But way back in the mid-1960s, as the Marvel Age was gathering steam, the company's heroes were a tough sell. One of the first people to buy in was Steve Krantz, a former executive with Columbia Pictures Television. Krantz, who had recently started his own production company, was casting about for an animation property when he ran across some Marvel comic books. "I was knocked out by them," Krantz recalls. He immediately flew to New York and acquired the animation rights for several of the company's characters, including Captain America, Iron Man, and Thor. That deal resulted in the 1966 cartoon series *The Marvel Superheroes*. To save time and money, the animators filmed panels from the comic books and strung them together, giving the episodes a peculiar stilted quality. *Superheroes* wasn't very good, but die-hard Marvel fans came to appreciate its kitschy elements, and it sold well in international syndication. Krantz also financed a series based on *The Amazing Spider-Man*, which ran from 1967 to 1970 and was written and directed by animation rebel Ralph Bakshi. Working with a bigger production budget, the animators graced the webbed wallcrawler's first TV adventures with a more fluid style; its heavy shadows and quirky storylines evoked the tone of Lee's run with Steve Ditko on *The Amazing Spider-Man*. The final Marvel TV series from the 1960s was *The Fantastic Four*, which ran for two seasons. Produced by animation house Hanna-Barbera (*The Flintstones*), the show was most notable for its character designs by renowned comic-book artist Alex Toth.

On all the cartoon shows, Stan provided editorial advice and direction, but he was clearly dissatisfied with how they turned out. "From an aesthetic point of view I think it's horrible, because we try to do *Spider-Man* for an older audience and on television they do it for the six-year-olds," Lee told a crowd at Vanderbilt University in 1972. He continued: "I was very interested in the television series in the beginning. I flew out to the coast and I discussed these things with Hanna-Barbera and Krantz Films and so forth, until I realized discussing it meant nothing because all they're interested in doing is pleasing the sponsor. Not the network, not us, but the sponsor." Marvel's owners, Martin Goodman and, later, Cadence Industries, were significantly more bullish about the cartoons. The company had secured a percentage of the gross revenue from the shows, which enjoyed long lives in syndication. "Marvel made a great deal of money on the basis of the shows I produced," Krantz says.

Of course, animation was an easy and natural progression for a comic-book company. The real challenge was in live action. Despite the success of the *Batman* TV show in the 1960s, there wasn't much interest in translating Marvel's superchampions to the celluloid world of flesh and blood. Lee's brush with Hollywood in Marvel's mid-1960s salad days was limited to a 1965 visit from Federico Fellini, which yielded a lifetime's worth of anecdotes but little else of note. Stan's big break, if it could be called that, came a few years later when another foreign director showed up at the Marvel offices. Alain Resnais, whose films included *Last Year at Marienbad* and *Hiroshima, Mon Amour*, was a student of American culture who had learned much of his English from comic books. He was a huge admirer of the Marvel Universe and of Lee; at their first meeting, Resnais snapped photos of Stan as the two men talked. They soon became friends, often meeting for lunches at a Third Avenue coffee shop and for dinners in Chinatown. Resnais cast Lee as a narrator in his 1973 movie *L'An 01*. The French director also proposed a collaboration. "I want my first movie in English to be written by you," Resnais told him. "I have dreamed that when I finally do a movie in English that you will write my first one."

Their first project was *The Monster Maker*, a pop-art parody about a frustrated movie producer who seeks creative and spiritual redemption by making a film about pollution. With gentle direction from Resnais, Lee wrote a full script, the first—and last—time he would invest so much effort in a movie project. From then on, Stan would stick with story treatments and outlines, which are quicker and easier to generate. "I'm a very fast writer," Lee told author James Monaco. "Working with Alain, I had to go against the grain. All my life I had written just for myself. Now I was trying to please somebody else as well."

The Monster Maker's protagonist, Larry Morgan, is an apparent stand-in for Lee himself. Morgan produces schlocky horror pictures that make money and are popular with kids, but he can't help but feel that he's reached a dead end. He is despondent about his life and his job, and what he craves more than anything is recognition from an adult audience. Through a series of story twists, Morgan embarks on a "serious" film project to expose the evils of pollution. There's some violence, a fire, and then a climactic montage sequence in which a monstrous wave of pollution descends upon New York City, choking the sky, the waterways, and the streets. The true horror, it is revealed in less-than-subtle fashion, is the accumulation of garbage that we so callously resign to landfills, mindless of the terrible price that we might pay in the future. The movie closes with a voice-over: "We deserve no pity, for we have done this to ourselves. We were placed on this Earth, this veritable Eden, with all we could ask for, all we could desire, ours for the taking. We were warmed by the sun, nurtured by the soil, and sheltered by the trees. The life-giving waters flowed pure and clear, and the air that sustained us would sustain us forever. Or, so we thought. So we thought. . . . "

If, as they say, all art is autobiographical, then Lee's dialogue offers insight into the inner turmoil he had experienced in an earlier stage of his career. At one point in the movie, Larry Morgan tells his ex-wife, Catherine, about his new, meaningful work. She glows with pride: "Larry, you must have known how I always felt about those shallow horror films of yours. I always wondered how you could bring yourself to keep grinding out such juvenile, unintellectual pablum. But now, to think of you tackling a worthwhile theme like pollution—to think of you turning your back on commercialism in order to say something that must be said—Oh, Larry—I can't tell you how thrilled—how proud of you I am."

Unlike Morgan, Lee wasn't exactly turning *his* back on commercialism. He and Resnais sold *The Monster Maker* in 1971 for $25,000. The script gathered dust and was never made. In 1976, they put together an outline for a film called *The Inmates*, a romantic comedy set against the backdrop of an imminent alien invasion of Earth. By that point, Lee was either too busy or too disconcerted to attempt a full script again. "Personally, I'd like to sell the treatment (when complete) for lots of money and a percentage, and have someone else do the screenplay, although Alain says he'd prefer me to write it," Lee wrote in a letter to Steve Krantz. *The Inmates* bounced from producer to producer for several years, but never went anywhere.

While Stan was dabbling with the French New Wave, he also teamed up with Lloyd Kaufman, a young filmmaker whose credits in later life would include Troma Entertainment's *The Toxic Avenger* and *Tales from the Crapper*. Kaufman had attended Yale University in the mid-1960s, where, he says, he double-majored in recreational drugs and Marvel comics. Upon graduation, he struck up a friendship with Lee that bloomed into a partnership. They worked in Lee's condo, surrounded by Joan's collection of sculptures and antiques, with Stan spouting his cinematic brainstorms and Kaufman scribbling away furiously. For 1971's *Night of the Witch*, about a witch in Salem who kills only evildoers, Lee dictated his vision onto a quarter-inch tape, which Kaufman dutifully converted into a script. "As a writing partner, he knew what he wanted," Kaufman recalls. "He would create the basic story and rely on me to put the sense of humor in." Among the half-dozen or so film projects that they concocted, *Night of the Witch* went the furthest. It was optioned for $500 and then forgotten. Lee let Kaufman keep all the money.

In what may not have been a wise move, Stan also brought Kaufman, a self-described "LSD-brain idiot," on board for a pitch to Resnais. Lee had an idea for a movie about a man who talks to God. He relayed the concept to Kaufman, who speedily turned around a first draft for a film called *The Man Who Talked to God*. "My guess is Resnais said, '*Merci beaucoup*, I go back to France.' That was the end of that," Kaufman says. "I think Stan was too polite to tell me it sucked."

Lee took several meetings with agents and producers to pitch their projects, and sometimes he brought his young associate along. The Hollywood folks were always enthusiastic, even reverential, but the discussions would lead nowhere. "We'd keep going to these meetings, and it was always the same thing. 'We love this! Everybody loves this! The kids will love it.' And then, nobody ever called," says Kaufman, adding that he found the stream of rejections mystifying. "Stan is a saint. He's a good, talented, kind person.

What idiots are they? How stupid are they? The guy is just foaming at the mouth with brilliant ideas, with mainstream inexpensive characters and plots. It's an absolute puzzlement."

During the 1970s Marvel's heroes had their own bumpy ride into showbiz. A particularly inadvisable deal struck by Chip Goodman while his father, Martin, was out of town got the company off to a bad start. In 1971 rock promoter Steve Lemberg sat down with Chip to negotiate for the radio rights to several Marvel characters. Lemberg was only interested in radio serials, but then a strange thing happened. "I just kept asking for more rights," Lemberg recalls. "Every time I asked for something, they gave it to me. I'd say, 'Does anyone have the rights to do movies?' They'd say, 'No,' because at the time no one really wanted to do movies. And I'd say, 'OK, I'll give you a few hundred dollars . . . for those rights too.'" Lemberg says he walked away with an exclusive option to license the majority of the company's heroes—including Spider-Man, the Hulk, and the Fantastic Four—for motion pictures, television, *and* radio. The total price: $2,500, plus an annual fee to renew his option. "Chip really thought this was found money," says Gerry Conway, who was then writing for Marvel.

Lemberg was young, in his late twenties, but he had big dreams for the Marvel pantheon, encompassing all of the major entertainment industries. He wanted to create an ice show with the Silver Surfer, a Thor radio program, and a film starring Spider-Man. Through his music-industry connections, he was able to set up appointments in Hollywood. And what he found mainly was resistance. "It was too expensive to make these things," Lemberg says. "The technology didn't exist. In order to produce that kind of film and try to do it as a real thing, it would have been unimaginable." In the end, Lemberg produced only the Spider-Man rock album and Lee's Carnegie Hall show, both in 1972.

From Marvel's perspective, there was another problem: Lemberg's contract didn't include a performance clause, which meant that, technically, he could renew his licensing option indefinitely without ever accomplishing anything. After some legal wrangling in 1973, the company extricated itself from the exclusivity of that agreement, forcing Lemberg to show results in order to maintain his standing. He eventually let his options lapse.

That entire ordeal set Marvel's timeline back a few years, but Lee soldiered on. He worked every angle to get his superheroes off the page and into just about anything else. "I'd like us to be involved in every form, shape, and type of media," Lee told an interviewer in 1977. "I'd love for us to do movies, television, stage shows—everything. We ought to have a Marvel Land, like Disneyland." When *Tommy* hit big in 1975, Lee wrote a treatment for a Fantastic Four rock opera. Other rock operas were proposed, featuring Thor, Captain America—even one for Spider-Man, with Elton John and Mick Jagger as possible leads. None of them was ever mounted or filmed.

In 1978 Marvel's fortunes perked up when *The Incredible Hulk* live-action TV show debuted on CBS. Starring Bill Bixby as David Banner—"Bruce Banner" sounded too homosexual to network execs—and Lou Ferrigno as his green-skinned alter ego, the weekly one-hour series caused a mild sensation and was a solid ratings performer. Eschewing the campy conventions of the 1960s *Batman* show in favor of a pastiche on the *Fugitive* series, *The Incredible Hulk* reflected a more serious approach. Banner wandered the country in search of a cure for his "Hulk-outs," helping the random troubled souls that he met along the way. The Hulk showed up for a few minutes each episode to knock around the bad guys and to destroy cars and property. Lee acted as a creative consultant, for which he received $1,250 per episode. The show ran for five seasons.

Another live-action series, *The Amazing Spider-Man*, didn't fare as well, despite Lee's more direct involvement. In preproduction, he attended several meetings with the show's executives where he felt he sold them on his fantasy-humanistic approach for making Spidey sparkle in prime time. But when the show arrived, it resembled nothing more than a run-of-the-mill action show. The boob-tube Spider-Man, played by the wooden Nicholas Hammond, didn't run or jump or swing like the comic-book Spider-Man. He was Starsky in a red-and-blue jumpsuit. The Spider-Man series became legendary in comic-book circles for its awfulness. Stan registered his complaints while the program was still in its first season. "The people doing the Spider-Man show keep writing one bad script after another," Lee lamented in a 1978 interview with *SunStorm Magazine*. "So we're either going to have to drop the show or go with bad scripts—I don't know which is worse." He went on, "The writers are all a bunch of hacks—the best of them—used to writing TV series with interchangeable plots. The problem is, our characters need specialized plots—they're unique."

The 1978 release of *Superman: The Movie*, with Marlon Brando and Christopher Reeve, accelerated the pace of Marvel's deal-making and was probably the catalyst for finally sending Lee to Los Angeles. *Superman* grossed $300 million worldwide, which was remarkable considering that the DC character's comic books were then languishing on newsstands. It also spawned several sequels and a host of lucrative merchandising licenses. More important, it proved the concept of a live-action superhero movie. By 1982 Lee, firmly rooted in Los Angeles, could boast of dozens of Marvel-related projects in the works—Broadway shows featuring Captain America and Thor, live-action TV pilots based on Daredevil and the Black Widow, and motion-picture vehicles for characters including Ghost Rider, the Dazzler, Howard the Duck, and the Sub-Mariner. Lee Kramer, Olivia Newton-John's former boyfriend and manager, was moving forward on a proposed $20-million *Silver Surfer* production. Paul McCartney had been approached about the score, and a levitation device was being built at the Imperial College in London. Even *Kid Colt Outlaw*, the 1950s-era Atlas title, had been optioned for the big screen. Marvel was on the move. And Stan was pedaling as fast as he could.

In the span of five or six years, he wrote outlines for dozens of projects that never saw the light of day. *Ragnarok*, starring Thor, was an off-Broadway musical in the vein of *Godspell*. A Silver Surfer treatment contained elements of early-1970s blaxploitation movies. In Lee's proposed storyline, the Surfer races across the Earth on his board. As he swoops down over New York, a "tall, overdressed black man" enters the picture: "It's Sweet-Daddy Wisdom, leader of New York's Black Mafia. He aims a hand gun at the Surfer. He commands the Surfer to land gently and get off the board. He says that everyone's been trying to get a line on him. And now he belongs to Sweet-Daddy Wisdom. Ol' Sweet-Daddy's gone and caught himself the world's choice prize. He's captured the ultimate honky."

Lee tailored his Marvel visions from a previous era to the tenor of the times, even if it meant taking his characters in strange directions. This was how he described Thor in one outline: "If Arnold

Schwarznegger [*sic*] had Robert Redford's face and Richard Burton's voice! Thor is surely the handsomest, most heroic, most powerful, most dutiful son any doting super-God ever had. The poor guy doesn't lie, doesn't cheat, doesn't do drugs, and fights his fool head off for truth, justice, and the Asgardian way of life. One thing though—he's great in the hay." In the comic books, Thor's sexual prowess had never really come up.

In a way, Lee had returned to the trend-following, scattershot sales methods of his days at Timely and Atlas, except now he was flooding the market with movie ideas. Nowhere was this more obvious than in his non-Marvel undertakings. His treatment for a Buck Rogers script was a dead ringer for *Logan's Run*. *Decathlon 2020*, about a futuristic world where a violent bloodsport reigns supreme, smacked of Roger Corman's *Death Race 2000*. And there were others: *Shockers*, *The Last Unicorn*, *The Menace of the Mandroid*, *Mighty Man*. When a concept exploded into his brain, he would jot it down in his large, printed handwriting. "Mafia takes over govt!" read one note. "Now what? Now they're legit—they have to worry about crime!" In another note, he scrawled: "Pacifist gets frozen to escape death. Wakes up years later. War outlawed—but life is terrible. He becomes warlike in order to save world." And another note, this one typewritten: "Write screen play [*sic*] or story re: guy on subway seeing innocent person being assaulted and afraid to help." Lee was bursting with inspiration. "People out here are starved for ideas and concepts," he said in a 1979 interview with *The Ambassador*. "I've always found that the easiest thing—as long as someone else does the tiresome work of writing the actual script. It's very nice: the things I do best are the things in demand."

Ultimately, it was the Marvel characters that were in demand—and those only on a limited basis. When Lee stepped outside of the Marvel arena and proposed a new heroic concept or science-fiction premise, he invariably got shot down. It was an odd dilemma: Stan was well loved and respected, particularly among the young producers and agents who grew up reading Marvel comics. He could land appointments at any studio or agency in town. But when it came right down to it—show-him-the-money time—things inevitably fell apart. "Loving Stan doesn't mean that they're going to give a green light automatically," says Don Kopaloff, who was

Marvel's film agent during the mid-1980s. Lee's non-Marvel projects were hard to unload, Kopaloff adds, because "it was like Laurel and Hardy without Laurel." Hollywood may have been hungry for innovation, but Stan's brainstorms—many of which were warmed-over, gimmicky, and underdeveloped—weren't even on the menu. Age may also have played a factor. L.A. is a youth-obsessed town, and not the most forgiving place for a sixty-year-old man vying for his big break. Lee acknowledged as much in late 1979 when he told a reporter that he was sorry he hadn't come out to the West Coast thirty years earlier. "I've achieved some measure of success in comic books, but out here maybe I could have been a success making movies," Lee said. "An equal success in the movies would have made me a multimillionaire, and the work would have been a lot easier."

Jason Squire, a producer who tried unsuccessfully to organize deals for *The Inmates* and *The Menace of the Mandroid* in the early 1980s, says that Lee was dismayed by the lack of progress, but that he was always encouraging. "He was realistic," Squire recalls. "He was well familiar with the attitude, but it seemed to never really get him down for long." For his part, Lee says he leavened his frustration by keeping busy. "I was still doing things at Marvel. It's not like I gave up everything to do that stuff."

Marvel, meanwhile, continued to do well with animation, and in 1980 it established an L.A.-based division that went on to produce dozens of successful cartoon shows including *Spider-Man and His Amazing Friends*, *G.I. Joe*, and Jim Henson's *Muppet Babies*. In the realm of live action, however, the company seemed cursed. Of the dozens of deals, great and small, that Stan helped bring together in the 1970s and '80s, only four resulted in movies, and all of them were embarrassments. There was *Howard the Duck*, based on a comic book written by Steve Gerber, which landed in theaters with a heavy thud and has since become a punch line for cinematic dreadfulness. A $9-million film based on the Punisher, the gun-toting hero-executioner that Lee had named in the mid-1970s, went straight to video in 1989. *Captain America*, starring Matt Salinger, squirmed to life in 1991 and quickly died—it was completely unwatchable. And *The Fantastic Four*, possibly the worst of the lot, was made in 1994 but never released. It came about as the result of a legal maneuver by Bernd Eichinger, a German producer and director who held the rights to the superhero team. Eichinger was in danger of losing his option if he didn't start principal photography within a given time frame. As the deadline loomed, he still didn't have a satisfactory script, so he hired schlockmeister Roger Corman to churn out a cheapie production. That enabled Eichinger to exercise a contractual clause to make a sequel, the *Fantastic Four* movie that is currently slated for a 2005 release. The Corman version was never meant for human consumption, but it seeped into the public domain through bootleg copies sold at fan conventions and on the Internet.

In recent years, Lee has blamed Marvel's extended losing streak during his tenure as Hollywood honcho on ill-advised business choices by the company's management. "The people back in New York who made these decisions—these contracts—gave the rights to do the movies to the wrong people," Lee said in an interview with the Web site FilmForce. "I mean, they took a valuable character like Captain America and they allowed a company to do it as a low-budget, quickie movie. They took *The Punisher*—which could have been good—and again, it was a low-budget movie. It was just a thing that was batted out. The only time we had a bigger budget movie [*Howard the Duck*], we were just unfortunate."

But Kopaloff remembers matters a bit differently. In his recollection, when he made the rounds of the major studios with Marvel's characters in the 1980s, no one was buying. "You couldn't give them away," he says. "The industry was not yet tuned in. I got a lot of interest from the younger people, but the older people, who were in charge, they didn't bite." Having struck out with the big players, Kopaloff was forced to deal with minor-league companies such as Menahem Golan's Cannon Films, which specialized in low-budget action pictures such as *Missing in Action* and *American Ninja*. "I would never have gone to [Cannon] as a first choice," he notes. "I went to them after I couldn't get Captain America or Spider-Man sold." In other words, Marvel got stuck with second-rate movies because it was dealing with second-rate production companies.

The winding, tortuous path that Spider-Man took from page to screen exemplified the problems that were facing the entire Marvel franchise. After Steve Lemberg's multimedia run in the early 1970s,

Steve Krantz tried to arrange a deal. His first notion was for a musical-fantasy picture starring Spidey, but he later settled on a more conventional approach. A 1976 story outline that Krantz shopped to the studios featured a college-age Spider-Man battling a 100-foot robot and Nazis, plus the death of Gwen Stacy.

By 1982 Roger Corman had bought the rights to Spider-Man and was planning a movie based on a Lee-written treatment. That version also placed Peter Parker in college, but the supervillain this time was Dr. Otto Octavious, also known as Dr. Octopus. Lee's film proposal contained all the familiar elements: the radioactive spider, the mechanical web shooters, Uncle Ben's murder, and several love interests, including a Russian KGB agent and Mary Jane. But Stan was far too ambitious, especially considering the anemic budget that Corman was likely to pony up. The climactic battle scene Lee envisioned was set atop the United Nations building with vertiginous action sequences of Spidey swinging, sticking to walls, leaping, jumping, falling—all the while battling the murderous tentacles of Doc Ock. There was also a subplot about a possible nuclear war with Russia, which Spidey narrowly averts by defeating his superpowered nemesis.

In 1985 Cannon Films acquired the Spider-Man movie rights for $225,000. From that point on, there would be no fewer than eight different scripts. In one of them, Peter Parker was transformed into a giant eight-legged tarantula. In another, an in-depth treatment by *The Terminator* director James Cameron, Spider-Man was dark and violent, and his enemy was Electro, the master of electricity. Cameron also came up with the concept of Spidey shooting webs directly from his wrists rather than through any kind of device. Cannon chief Golan hit rough financial waters in the late 1980s, and sold off Spider-Man's theatrical, TV, and home-video rights to separate companies. By the time Marvel declared bankruptcy in 1996, MGM, Viacom, and Columbia were battling in court over ownership of the character. In March 1999, after years of litigation, Columbia emerged with the exclusive film rights, setting the stage for the triumphant 2002 release of Sam Raimi's *Spider-Man*.

Lee basked in the reflected glory of his cocreation's big-screen debut, attending fan conventions and conducting yet another round of media interviews. Because of a 1998 employment contract, he appeared in the movie's credits as executive producer and was due for a cut of the profits. But Stan was no longer Marvel's Hollywood point man; that duty had fallen to Avi Arad, a former toy designer who had helped navigate the company out of bankruptcy. Arad, the head of Marvel Studios, orchestrated the deals for *Spider-Man*, *X-Men*, *Daredevil*, and *The Hulk*, and, on the strength of their successes, became one of the film industry's hottest producers. Lee faded from view, restricting his Marvel-related activities to promotion and the Spider-Man newspaper strip. "I take great pleasure in the successes at Marvel," Lee said in 2000. "But I can't claim to be responsible for all of them right now. The only responsibility I can perhaps claim is that I was the cocreator of so many of these characters."

Stan Lee got the ball rolling for Marvel in Tinseltown. Someone else would get the credit for its eventual success.

PART VII

"THIS MAN,
THIS MONSTER"

THE EVIL EMPIRE

The comic-book world that Stan Lee left behind in the late 1970s was a dismal place compared with the vibrant, booming industry he had entered three decades before. Where once there had been dozens of scrappy firms competing for control of a burgeoning mass medium, now there were only a few companies scuffling over a dwindling marketplace. In the early 1950s, annual comic-book sales totaled 600 million copies; by 1980 that number had fallen to 150 million. Comics were no longer a mass medium. The decline brought on by television had been exacerbated by the disappearance of traditional distribution outlets, such as soda shops and "mom and pop" stores, as well as rising cover prices, which dissuaded young buyers. Comic books now attracted an audience of older collectors and nostalgia buffs, but they were losing ground among children and teens, two groups essential to the medium's long-term survival.

Writers and artists, meanwhile, were agitating for greater rights and creative freedom. It was a battle that had been brewing since the industry's first decade, but it gained special fervor after a public-relations victory on behalf of Superman's inventors, Jerry Siegel and Joe Shuster. Cartoonist Neal Adams lobbied DC Comics for recognition of the two men and, aided by the publicity surrounding the 1978 release of *Superman: The Movie*, won a pension for Siegel and Shuster and the restoration of their names to the Man of Steel's titles. Thus emboldened, the fight for creators' rights continued at the grassroots level, almost on a contract-by-contract basis. Publishers had already conceded reprint payments and the ongoing return of original art pages, but creators wanted more: royalties, ownership stakes in their characters, copyrights. They were also chafing at the restrictions of the superhero genre and sought to push the boundaries with complex, epic-length storylines.

Much of this—the dire sales figures, the artistic demands—sat poorly with Lee. "Comics are in bad shape right now," he said at the 1978 Atlanta Comics and Fantasy Fair, "because there are too many self-indulgent writers and artists in the business today. They're the people who grew up in the '50s and mostly '60s, and they've succeeded in destroying it. They haven't analyzed the market. What they're doing is books that please them, and obviously that's not the market." Standing in front of a comics-convention crowd of devoted—and mostly grown-up—Marvel fans, Lee went on to argue that the market was, as it had always been, made up of twelve-year-olds, and that comic books should continue to appeal to that demographic. In retrospect, it's clear that Stan couldn't sense the tremors that were shifting the ground beneath his feet. Even he didn't know where the market was heading. What he viewed as self-indulgence would play a much greater part in the industry's future than he could have anticipated. While Lee spent the next decade ingratiating himself with Hollywood, a fresh crop of young, independent-minded creators would appear to kick-start the comic-book medium with their singular creative visions and to provide a brief revival for the entire business.

But first, there was more hardship. In the late 1970s, Marvel Comics, the leader with a nearly 50 percent market share, reversed the course of its earlier rapid expansion and pared its monthly output to some thirty titles. Its closest competitor, DC Comics, cut back even more drastically, in what came to be known as the "DC Implosion." Despite its sales woes, Marvel continued to report a modest operating income on the strength of its ballooning licensing revenue. But internally, the bullpen was churning with discontent. Writers and artists groused that Cadence's managers were more interested in exploiting Marvel's characters as toys and TV shows than in putting out good books. Acrimonious working circumstances led to the departure of several longtime staffers, including Marv Wolfman and Roy Thomas. "There is a feeling among most of the people I know that Marvel has become more callous and inhuman," Thomas lamented in a 1979 article in the *New York Times*. The catalyst for much of this turmoil was Jim Shooter, Marvel's new editor in chief.

Shooter, who was tall and had a stern face marked by deep scars, began his comics career as a teenage writing prodigy. He sold his first script in 1966, at the age of fourteen, to DC honcho Mort Weisinger, the archetype of the vindictive, egomaniacal comic-book editor. Weisinger was renowned for terrorizing his employees and for backstabbing writers by stealing their plot ideas and forcing them to make unnecessary rewrites. He was also responsible for DC's cautious publishing strategy, which made the company vulnerable to a revitalized Marvel. Weisinger took Shooter under his wing, and, through a process of bullying and belittlement, taught his young protégé the mechanics of comics writing. Shooter eventually made his way to Stan Lee's Marvel, the source of his original inspiration to enter comics, only to take an extended leave from the field in 1969. He resurfaced in 1976 as an associate editor at Marvel, where he wrote *Daredevil* and *The Avengers*, and assisted the revolving cast of editors in chief, including Marv Wolfman, Gerry Conway, and Archie Goodwin. Shooter ascended to the top job himself in 1978 and stayed on until 1987, longer than any editor in chief except Lee. His tenure was fraught with ill will and controversy, but it also brought a measure of stability and prosperity to the company.

When Stan was running the show, Marvel was a relatively simple operation, consisting of himself, a team of freelance artists, and a few assistants and production people. In the early 1970s, when the company's lineup exploded and dozens of new staffers came aboard, the bullpen devolved into a collection of fiefdoms, each under the control of a separate writer-editor. The editor in chief found himself in the tricky position of managing all of these different factions while juggling the near-impossible task of keeping several dozen titles on schedule. Shooter saw the flaws in the system and stepped in with some changes. He hired several editors to work directly under him, eliminating the writer-editor positions that had been held by former editors in chief such as Wolfman and Thomas. He established a streamlined, top-down structure that gave him greater influence over the editorial and production flow. After the chaos of the post-Lee era, many on Marvel's staff saw the changes as necessary and desirable. With Shooter at the helm, the company completed its transformation from a family-run hack shop to a corporate publishing house where scores of editors directed the fates of Spider-Man, the X-Men, and their legion of spandex-clad brethren from a suite of clean, airy offices on Park Avenue.

But for all his organizational strengths, Shooter also developed a reputation as a tyrant. He had apparently picked up something else from his old DC mentor Weisinger—a knack for making enemies and alienating employees. One Marvel staffer whom he fired called Shooter a "moral coward" and decried his hard-line tactics. Another, Marv Wolfman, defected to DC after Shooter revoked his writer-editor status and meddled with his other writing assignments. "Human beings don't do that to each other," Wolfman reportedly fumed at the time. Thomas, the writer who had contributed more to the Marvel Universe than anyone except Stan Lee, soon followed. "I was willing to accept [Shooter's] authority as editor in chief, of course, but could see little to be gained by knuckling under to the rest of the mostly uninspired and uninspiring lot he has hired as editors the past year or so," Thomas wrote in his April 1980 letter of resignation.

Shooter righted the Marvel ship and boosted the firm's profitability, but in the process he became the most reviled figure in comics. In manner and temperament, Shooter was the anti-Stan. Although he shared Lee's market instincts, he lacked the older man's grace and charm. In his heyday, Stan could criticize a script, ask for a rewrite, and still make the writer feel as if he had won the lottery. Shooter, by contrast, was brusque and patronizing. He returned comic-book proof sheets marked with harsh notes and grades, as in, "C-minus. See me." The negative sentiment toward Shooter would reach a fever pitch in the mid-1980s during a prolonged battle with Jack Kirby over Marvel's refusal to return thousands of the artist's original art pages. A few weeks before Shooter left Marvel in early 1987, the staffers gathered to burn him in effigy. He remains a pariah in the comics industry to this day.

From a creative standpoint, Jim Shooter's Marvel was, by and large, a wasteland of formulaic self-imitation and blatant profit-seeking. Securely on top as a result of the superhero trend instigated by Lee, Kirby, and Ditko, Marvel became less innovative and experimental. To maintain its leadership position, the company adopted a conservative publishing strategy that basically amounted to more of the same—more far-out powers, more colorful costumes, more angst-ridden characters. Before 1961 and *The Fantastic Four*, superheroes were only one of an array of comic-book genres that included westerns, horror, and romance, and not a particularly successful genre at that. After 1961, superheroes dominated the landscape so completely that, by 1980, it was almost impossible to distinguish the medium from the material.

Stan Lee's heroes had made a lasting impression. By the time of Shooter's reign, however, Spider-Man and his superpowered pals were running out of narrative juice. There were only so many personal crises and supervillains bent on world domination to go around. The majority of Marvel's books began to look like lifeless retreads of the original Lee-Kirby and Lee-Ditko runs that had spawned them. And so, like a TV series entering its tenth season, Marvel rolled out the gimmicks: guest appearances, fake deaths, new costumes, female counterparts—whatever they could come up with to goose sales. In the span of six years, from 1981 to 1987, Spidey became a criminal and was exonerated; received visits from Moon Knight, the Black Cat, the Avengers, and an omnipotent being known as the Beyonder; fought extended battles against the Vulture, the Sandman, Kraven the Hunter, and the Hobgoblin; switched to an inky-black outfit and back again to his classic red-and-blues; and, finally, married his longtime sweetheart, Mary Jane. He did all of that in the pages of one title, *The Amazing Spider-Man*, which, incidentally, was selling roughly the same number of copies on both ends of that time period.

Some of the company's efforts were driven entirely by commercial considerations. When TV executives proposed shows for female versions of Spider-Man and the Hulk, Marvel came out with the titles *Spider-Woman* and *The Savage She-Hulk*, mainly to secure the copyrights to those characters. Popular heroes and concepts were spun off into multiple series. *The Amazing Spider-Man* was joined by *Peter Parker, The Spectacular Spider-Man* and *Web of Spider-Man*, giving the webhead three books per month in which he could toss around baddies and fret about Aunt May. After *The X-Men* became a hit in the early '80s, Marvel released *The New Mutants*, *X-Factor*, and a stream of limited-run series starring Wolverine and other mutant-powered heroes. It was a logical form of brand extension: if Marvel couldn't bring in enough twelve-year-olds to spur revenue growth, then it would have to soak the readers it already had by making them buy more product. Since collectors are by nature completists, the plan worked for a while. But it didn't generally make for very good comics.

The ultimate cross-marketing scheme was 1984's *Marvel Super Heroes Secret Wars*, a twelve-part series that featured nearly all of Marvel's major heroes and villains locked in deadly combat on a far-off planet. Written by Shooter and drawn by dependable workhorse Mike Zeck, *Secret Wars* originated as a tie-in for a line of Mattel action figures. The economics of the book were easy enough to discern: teaming up two heroes always gave a bump to sales, so throwing together the whole Marvel pantheon was a guaranteed slam dunk. The comics sold phenomenally well, but Shooter and Zeck were not the kind of fan-favorite creators that comics junkies gushed over, and many longtime readers felt gypped. The *Secret Wars* storyline resembled little more than a Worldwide Wrestling Federation battle royale, and nearly every Marvel title had been interrupted for the cosmic dust-up. Predictably, Marvel rushed a sequel, *Secret Wars II*, out the door, but it met with considerably less success.

Licensing played another big role in the Marvel lineup, with a batch of titles based on entertainment and toy properties, including *Raiders of the Lost Ark*, *Battlestar Galactica*, *Shogun Warriors*, and *The Transformers*. The long-running *Star Wars* series was Marvel's biggest hit in this arena, with record-setting sales that were later credited with having saved the company from crippling financial difficulty in the late 1970s. Although some of the licensing-driven comics, such as *Micronauts*, enjoyed longer lives than their non-comics tie-ins, none of them broke any artistic barriers. They were money-making ventures, pure and simple, and part of Marvel's overall strategy of expanding into more profitable fields. Comic books were a fine calling card, but the company's directors realized there were better ways to unlock the value of the Marvel brand—through movies, television, cartoon shows, and merchandising. In recognition of this fact, the company renamed itself the Marvel Entertainment Group. "My idea is that Marvel should be the company that people think of when they think of kids," said then Marvel President Jim Galton in a 1983 interview. "Marvel should be thought of as the prime supplier of entertainment for kids from ages six to sixty."

Of course, it wasn't all bad on the Marvel end of the rack. Amid the piles of rehashed superhero smackdowns and toy-related comics, there were a few standouts. Writer Chris Claremont and artist John Byrne turned the marginal *X-Men*, which for five years in the early 1970s consisted of reprints of earlier editions, into the company's most consistently engaging title. Their seminal, much-copied run set a new standard for superhero soap opera and high adventure, and it was perfectly pitched to the misunderstood, put-upon, and ultimately romantic teenagers and teenagers-at-heart that made up Marvel's core audience. Claremont's noble and relentlessly verbose mutants evolved into Marvel's best-loved characters, and he became the most popular writer since Lee. *The Uncanny X-Men*, as the book was later known, was the industry's top seller for much of the 1980s. It also became an attractive licensing property to Hollywood, based less on Stan and Jack's original creation than on Claremont's cagey revamp.

Daredevil, another second-string title, received a boost from a young writer-artist named Frank Miller, who stripped the blind superhero to his film-noir essentials and created some of the most visually inventive mainstream comics of the 1980s. "The Man Without Fear," as *Daredevil*'s tagline described him, was the 1964 brainchild of Stan Lee and Bill Everett. The character went through the hands of several creators, including a long run by comic-book stylist Gene Colan. But it was Miller's Daredevil—a dark, brooding crimefighter who metes out street justice with a seriousness more evocative of Bruce Lee than Superman—that became the definitive version and inspired the big-budget 2003 movie starring Ben Affleck and Jennifer Garner. It also launched Miller's comics career, the majority of which would be spent making money for companies other than Marvel. He wouldn't be the last big-name creator to leave the so-called House of Ideas.

Behind the scenes at Marvel, working conditions improved for the creative types who kept the four-color dream factory running. In 1982 Marvel introduced Epic Comics, a mature-audiences line spun off from its fantasy and science-fiction newsstand magazine *Epic Illustrated*. Epic, under the guiding hand of respected industry veteran Archie Goodwin, allowed creators to retain the copyright to their work and to explore more sophisticated thematic and subject matter. On the regular titles, Marvel began paying royalties to writers and artists who reached specific sales targets, in effect tying their pay to their popularity. Several marquee creators, including Miller and Byrne, had become so popular that they could sell a book based on their names alone. That drawing power greatly improved their position in negotiations for projects and page rates. The Marvel incentive plan came about, in part, as a result of a more enlightened management, which saw the benefits, both tangible and intangible, of letting the talent share in the rewards of their labors. But it was also very much a reaction to a changed comic-book marketplace where buyers hunted down back issues drawn by their favorite artists and fan tastes ruled.

In the 1980s comic-book readers ditched newsstands and shifted their dollars to specialty stores that focused more or less exclusively on comic books and related items, such as protective plastic bags and backing boards. These hundreds, and eventually thousands, of shops constituted a new distribution network for Marvel and its competitors, one that gave them direct access to their customers. With sales drying up on the stands, the new market was a welcome boon for the industry. The owners of comic-book stores were typically devoted fans, which made them ideal marketers for the product. And the comic books they ordered were nonreturnable, in exchange for a higher discount than the newsstands received, enabling publishers to stabilize their print runs and to minimize their losses from returns. By 1982 Marvel was logging half its sales from comic shops, and it was producing titles exclusively for them. Ultimately, however, the system ended up weakening Marvel's overall position. As the 1980s progressed, the company abandoned mass-market appeal for an increasing dependence on this loose confederacy of fans-turned-merchants. The system was profitable in the short term, but it was a fragile base on which to build an empire. Today, 80 percent of the company's books are sold through that market.

Another effect of the system was that it lowered the barriers of entry for new publishers. It was no longer just Marvel and DC duking it out for dominance of a large, unwieldy, newsstand-based market. Anyone with a few thousand bucks and some basic writing and drawing skills could gain access to the growing network of comic-book stores, and perhaps steal a piece of the pie from the Big Two. At first there were only a few entrants, among them *Cerebus the Aardvark*, by Canadian self-publisher Dave Sim, and *Raw*, an anthology of art comics edited by underground comix legend Art Spiegelman and eventual *New Yorker* art director Francoise Mouly. Then, in 1981, Pacific Comics published *Captain Victory and the Galactic Rangers* by Jack Kirby, and a slew of companies came tumbling in. Eclipse Comics, Comico, Fantagraphics, Dark Horse Comics—some of these firms mimicked the formula of costumed superchampions and their arch-nemeses, but others took the opportunity to reintroduce old genres and to test new ones. Most companies were financed by fans, and although they rarely posted the sales numbers of Marvel or DC, some of them managed to make a solid return and to eventually compete for creators and market share.

When two young, unknown artists named Kevin Eastman and Peter Laird hit it big with *Teenage Mutant Ninja Turtles*, a self-published black-and-white book whose greatest virtue was a catchy title, the publishing floodgates swung wide open. Dozens of tiny companies sprouted into existence to fulfill the seemingly insatiable demand of comic-shop owners for a piece of the Next Big Thing. Collectors rushed to scoop up the hundreds of titles glutting the market, on the assumption that even the lousiest of the lot would be worth a premium some day. As was inevitable, the bubble burst, in 1987, and most of the small companies were driven out of business, taking many a comic shop with them.

On the whole, though, the emergence of new independent companies benefited the medium by bringing in fresh perspectives and demonstrating the viability of publishing outside the auspices of the

Big Two. When the dust cleared, there were still a dozen or so active publishers, and comics were in the throes of a creative renaissance. In 1986, DC released two ambitious, creator-driven works to tremendous critical acclaim: Miller's stylish *Batman: The Dark Knight Returns*, which radically reinvented the titular hero, and Alan Moore's and Dave Gibbons's *Watchmen*, a sprawling superhero series that was heavy on narrative and literary symbolism. That same year, Art Spiegelman published *Maus: A Survivor's Tale*, the story of his father's experiences during the Holocaust, for which he was later awarded a special Pulitzer Prize. Once more, magazines and academic journals wrote about comics as literature, a discussion that Stan Lee's Marvel had been at the center of twenty years before. Comic books were buzz-worthy again, but Marvel was generating none of the noise.

Lee watched everything unfold from his comfortable perch in Los Angeles. The business had changed dramatically. When he started out, the comic-book audience consisted of dime-carrying kids whose biggest worries were how the garishly garbed hero would win the day. Now, the average comic-book buyer was a twenty-three-year-old male who viewed *West Coast Avengers* #1 as a sound investment. He liked the story well enough, but he was much more concerned with preserving his treasure, maybe getting it signed, and sealing it away in a specially designed, acid-free box for the future.

The medium, too, was skewing older, becoming grittier, racier, and more violent. This awkward stumble toward maturity caused Lee concern about the possibility of alienating kids. "I think a lot of this stuff is good for the older readers," Lee told an interviewer in 1983. "I think that we are probably losing or confusing—maybe not losing, but we are confusing—some of the younger ones. Now, there's a great effort to get older readers in comics and whether it's worth it, I don't know."

At Marvel, the most popular characters at the end of the 1980s were the claw-wielding Wolverine and the gun-toting Punisher, neither of whom was a Lee creation in fact or spirit. Spidey was still the company's flagship character, but sales-wise, Spider-Man's books were eclipsed by *The Uncanny X-Men*, a title that had departed significantly from Lee and Kirby's original conception. In 1986 Jim Shooter attempted to duplicate Lee's original act of creation by inventing a new batch of titles that were separate from the traditional Marvel continuity. The New Universe, as it was called, featured superpowered characters in more thoroughly pedestrian, real-world settings, eschewing the traditional flights of fancy that pitted superheroes against space aliens and mythological creatures. These were Marvel Comics without Stan's sense of humor or Jack Kirby's sense of imagination. Lee said at the time that he didn't resent the fact that the company was moving on without him. "I might feel differently if I were still writing the books, and suddenly somebody came along and started bringing out new things, and I thought they were better than what I'm doing," he said in a 1986 article in *Variety*. "But I think what they're doing is a good idea, and I hope it works." Stan's good wishes notwithstanding, the New Universe turned out to be a very *bad* idea. It was a spectacular failure on comic-book racks and a black mark on Shooter's resume.

Lee continued his Hollywood life, hobnobbing with celebrities and attending functions at the Friars Club. He returned to New York to officiate at the staged wedding of Spider-Man and Mary Jane before a crowd of 55,000 baseball fans at Shea Stadium. He met President Reagan. By 1986 Stan was the publisher of Marvel and also the vice president of creative affairs for its animation production arm, which then made up more than half of the overall company. Several live-action projects were in development, including one for a Lee-created character called the Protector.

It would be several years before any big-screen sensations would materialize, but so far Marvel's cross-media efforts had served it well. Bolstered by the success of its animation division, Marvel Entertainment was generating $73 million in annual revenue. That same year, Cadence Industries sold Marvel to New World Pictures, a producer and distributor of low-budget movies, for $50 million. New World saw the acquisition as a way to achieve synergy, giving the combined operations a presence in movies, television, animation, and comics. Lee barely had time to settle into his New World office when Marvel was sold again, this time to financier Ron Perelman for $82.5 million. In what was perhaps the only benevolent move Perelman made as Marvel's owner, he raised Lee's salary substantially, to a reported $375,000 per year.

On the face of it, Lee's life was playing out more grandly than he could have imagined back when he was Stanley Lieber. But beneath the surface, trouble was brewing. Former artistic collaborators were speaking out against him. Fans and cultural critics were taking another look at the record. The dismantling of Stan Lee's legend had begun.

STEP RIGHT UP!

Stan Lee has long been the feature writer's dream. Always available and ceaselessly quotable, Lee parlayed his personality and the success of Marvel into a second career as the public face of American comic books. Few modern creative personalities have been as successful at keeping themselves in the public eye for so long. When Lee and the early Marvel artists revolutionized their little corner of pop culture, Stan was there to talk to reporters and lecture on college campuses. When Marvel emerged as the top comics publisher in the 1970s and began to garner mild interest from Hollywood, Lee was there to help translate comic books for movies and television, and to distill Marvel's essence for audiences who might not quite get it. In the 1980s and '90s, as Marvel experienced the massive growing pains that came with being the fulcrum for several visions of an entertainment conglomerate, Lee was there to provide a nostalgic connection to the company's past. Throughout his more than thirty-five-year career as an active spokesman, Lee has vigorously promoted comic books regardless of the nature of his relationship to them: comics he cocreated, comics he helped midwife as an editor, and comics he never saw or heard about until after they were published. Where resentment for Stan Lee exists, it is within the industry that bore him, and the chasm between Lee's creative output and the public credit he's received is its root cause.

Much of the early criticism leveled at Lee was the kind directed at anyone in a position of authority. When he was a young editor and writer dealing with the various incarnations of Martin Goodman's comic-book line, Lee seemed generally well liked. Coworkers and subordinates recall Lee's constantly smiling, upbeat presence. His artists drew him Christmas cards and cartoons that affectionately spotlighted his eccentricities. Joe Maneely, in particular, seemed gifted at depicting Lee's impossibly long figure and cherubic face. But the flip side of Lee's devil-may-care attitude toward his accidental profession was the reputation he'd picked up in some circles as a creative lightweight. Lee was youthful, he was the boss's relative, and he held court like a cutup at the local Rotary club—he was, in other words, the slightly older embodiment of the annoying kid that Joe Simon and Jack Kirby remembered from their early days at Timely. Stan's combination of lightheartedness and profit-seeking was reflected in a line of titles that never quite reached the commercial heights of DC Comics and its well-managed properties, or of EC Comics and its groundbreaking artists. Many in the comics field didn't view their medium as an art form, but those who did condemned the masters of volume publishing such as Lee. Artist Bernard Krigstein, who worked at 1950s-era Atlas, summed up this position in 1965 in response to Lee's then-recent success. "I was delighted to learn that Lee has attained the status of an authority in the comics field," Krigstein said. "Twenty years of unrelenting editorial effort to suppress the artistic effort, encourage miserable taste, flood the field with degraded imitations and polluted non-stories, treating artists and writers like cattle, and failure on his part to make an independent success as a cartoonist have certainly qualified him for this respected position."

The Stan Lee of the Marvel era also suffered from the expected workplace grumbling. The Marvel Method, which played a large part in distinguishing the new comic books from their competition was not without a certain level of controversy. Artists were being asked to shoulder the additional responsibility of breaking the story down into its visual components without a corresponding increase in pay. Steve Ditko eventually received credit as a co-plotter of his books, while the efforts of Jack Kirby were occasionally noted in a give-and-take "Stan and Jack" credit, but these were special cases that had more to do with the nature of the plotting sessions than a recognition of the extra work that Marvel artists did. Kirby in particular chafed at Lee's editorial changes. "Jack made up all these stories, and I'm positive he'd made up practically all the characters, too," artist Gil Kane said in 1996. "When he brought those things in, Stan would look over them and very often be critical of the material. He would ask him to change some of it. Jack would be totally accommodating and accept the notations for a change, and he'd change it. But when we would go out to lunch, you'd have to almost tie him to the seat—he would just be raging!"

As the line became more entrenched, Lee encountered some resistance from artists who were not just asked to work using this specific method, but were called on more and more to adopt the visual storytelling style of Jack Kirby as a de facto house approach. Unlike the slick commercial styles that had dominated some publishers in the past, from artists such as Alex Toth or Dan Barry, Kirby's work was one of a kind, tailored to his particular abilities and sensibilities. Being asked to draw like Jack Kirby was similar to being asked to sing like Louis Armstrong. Don Heck, who had so admirably served as an artist on the genre books of the late 1950s and early '60s, was an artist who chafed at drawing in the Marvel style, once quipping that if Lee wanted it drawn like Kirby would draw it, he should hire Kirby. John Buscema told other artists he nearly quit over criticisms of the *Silver Surfer* material. Even John Romita, a staunch supporter of Lee who had found a fruitful place for his own style in drawing Spider-Man and Captain America, admitted to some professional frustration due to the crushing workload given top artists. Romita referred to late-night work sessions on the various Marvel books as work done "when somebody else had already cashed the check."

Lee's success as a promotional agent for Marvel also stirred up resentment. Stan was making additional money as the sole representative of what many artists considered a group effort, and solidifying his place in the minds of the wider public as the sole agent responsible for Marvel's success. Lee would sometimes, if given opportunity, mention the role of the various artists, as well as the support staff in the bullpen. But no amount of deference could make up for the fact that Lee was a staple of the college lecture hall, pulling in tens of thousands of dollars per year, or on the phone with media interviews, while the artists did neither. Jack Kirby's resentment over his unflattering portrayal in Nat Freedland's 1966 article for *New York* covering the early Marvel phenomenon made him suspicious of Lee and eventually, many felt, helped lead to his departure in 1970. "The King is a middle-aged man with baggy eyes and a baggy Roger Hall-ish suit," Freedland wrote. "He is sucking a huge green cigar, and if you stood next to him on the subway you would peg him for the assistant foreman in a girdle factory." As early as the mid-1960s, Lee had gained a reputation as a gloryhound, something that, to a lesser degree, had always dogged him. Professionals at DC poked fun at Lee for his tendency to sign all of his work before it was common practice in comic books. Now the criticism took on a more unsavory feel.

The growing differences between Lee and younger cartoonists who saw the field differently than he did initially emerged during his time with the early-1970s organization the Academy of Comic Book Arts. The idea behind the ACBA was simple—a booster organization along the lines of the Motion Picture Academy of Arts and Sciences, with an awards program that would spotlight the industry's best and brightest. Nearly every potential member lived in the New York area, making meetings and banquets possible. Early membership drives proved extremely successful. Lee served as the first president, while the young, talented artist Neal Adams served as vice president.

The pair worked together well in some regards. Adams says that Lee kept him close because he had trouble putting names to faces. "Come over here, Neal," Lee once said. "I don't remember the names of half the people in this room."

"Stan, you're the editor in chief."

"I'm really not that good at remembering names," Lee replied. "Who is that coming towards us?"

"That's your best penciler, John Buscema."

The group quickly split along the lines of those who simply wanted a promotional organization, like Lee, and those, like Adams and Archie Goodwin, who believed that the ACBA should agitate for creators' rights on behalf of its membership. Adams spent the first meeting disclosing his page rate to various pencilers in attendance, causing a minor ruckus when many of them went to their editors the next Monday and asked for a raise. Lee believed that what Adams really wanted was a union, and that however lofty the goals a union might have, such issues were out of place in the ACBA. But Adams and the younger artists weren't going anywhere, and soon it was Lee who appeared slightly out of place. Lee saw himself as a freelance writer, but many members saw him as management, and they were happy when Dick Giordano took over the lead role in the group's second year. "I think Stan did sense that people felt funny about him being president," Adams says. "But he felt like a freelancer rather than an officer of Marvel, because that's how he made his money." Although the ACBA's Shazam Awards recognized some of the newer talent in mainstream comic books, the organization never came close to having the televised awards and media focus Lee wished for it. By mid-decade, the ACBA had given out its last Shazam and disbanded.

It was harder for Stan to step away from the criticism that came in the 1970s when he increased his presence as a promoter at the expense of continued work on the comic books. Promoting comics through other media was a dicey proposition, especially at first, and Lee suffered a gauntlet of snickers and trivialization based solely on preconceptions about the material. Comic-book fans may have greeted Lee's promotional work with enthusiasm and a contextual appreciation of what Marvel had accomplished, but some adult audiences and talk-show hosts were a bit more skeptical of the "relevant superhero." After suggesting to Dick Cavett in the late 1960s that many fans continued to read Marvel books into their college years, Lee was asked by a fellow panelist if pacifiers were also to be given out. Even into the 1980s, sitcom star and theme-song writer Alan Thicke seemed much more fascinated by denigrating the level of material he was looking at in the comic books on his desk than speaking directly to Lee during his appearance on the short-lived *Thicke of the Night* chat show. Lee's image as a suddenly "with-it" entertainment figure also rubbed some observers the wrong way. Of a late-1970s Lee appearance at his university campus, cartoonist Steve Lafler said: "[H]e just seemed like the biggest, krinkled-up bullshit-artist hustler I'd ever seen in my life. He just seemed like a real huckster, he seemed like a used-car salesman or something. We still enjoyed him and admired him, but it was kind of like, 'Oh my God, this guy is a sleazeball.' It was good for laughs. It didn't take anything away from the enjoyment that we felt as kids, but we just saw the guy for what he was."

The most intense criticism came from within the comic-book field. In 1972 Jack Kirby used a character in his DC escape-artist title *Mister Miracle* for a considered vivisection of his old creative partner. Funky Flashman was a promoter extraordinaire, more than willing to put someone else's life and effort on the line in the quest for profit. Kirby depicted Flashman slipping into a toupee, and even gave him a second-in-command, a Roy Thomas stand-in named House-Roy. "So he breaks a leg or dies!!" declares the exploitative Flashman. "I'll just sip my martini by the ocean—and wait for the next fish to jump." The depiction worked within the inflated universe of Kirby's New Gods, but for the comic-book readers who puzzled out the target, the criticism was blunt and severe, like Jerry Lewis doing twenty minutes of sketch comedy painting Dean Martin in as unflattering a light as possible. Lee's generous nature and admiration for Kirby was enough to later bring the artist back to the Marvel fold, but the criticism itself lingered in the air.

The most damaging episode in terms of Lee's public reputation was also Kirby-related. In the 1980s, Kirby launched himself into a pitched battle with Marvel Comics for the return of his original art pages, the pieces of art from which the comic books were shot and published. The traditional policy regarding original art in the American comic-book industry was that there was no traditional policy regarding original art. Comic books were considered by the overwhelming majority of readers and practitioners to be a disposable art form, and thus the components used to assemble those books were equally disposable. In most cases, only artists who made an issue of getting their art back were likely to see it again. Originals were stored in the worst locations in buildings, offered to visiting businessmen as souvenirs or given away as freebies to interested children who wrote letters. But as the nostalgia-fueled market for comic books grew in the late 1960s alongside the graying of the first generation of comic-book fans, original art began to acquire a significant market value. The return of original art to the pencilers and inkers became part of the improving conditions for comic-book creators. By 1974 both Marvel and DC had acknowledged the desirability of returning art to creators, and soon afterward both companies instituted policies that returned current artwork to their creators on a monthly basis. When Jack Kirby penciled a series of books for Marvel in the middle 1970s, the art pages he submitted were returned.

DC made the issue a greater priority than did Marvel, and it instituted a more progressive policy. In its 1978 freelancer contracts, DC acknowledged the artist's right to his or her original art as a legal obligation. DC also assumed the role of caretaker for the art while it was in its custody. The contracts stated that if DC lost any original art, the artist due its return would be paid for the value of the pages commensurate to what the company had paid for the pages originally—even if they were later discovered and returned to the artist. In contrast, Marvel took several years just to take stock of its backlog, and did not immediately return any older art. The job of finding out what art was on hand proved too big to handle for the production department. In 1975, Marvel assigned an employee named Irene Vartanoff to sort through the backstock, which was warehoused in New Jersey. Her initial cataloging effort took a full year, and she remained in charge of the facilities until 1980. Vartanoff later said that the backstock on hand stretched all the way back to the early 1960s, and that in the late 1970s Marvel was still using pages of art as a business giveaway.

Jack Kirby wanted his art back, both for its remunerative value and as a signifier of his legacy to American comic books. A few persistent Marvel artists had received old art back, including Kirby's longtime *Fantastic Four* inker Joe Sinnott. In May 1978 Kirby's second run at Marvel ended when his contract expired. He was not interested in renewing, and with Jim Shooter the new editor in chief at the company, it seemed a perfect time to settle any long-standing difficulties, including original art returns. Yet by 1978 there existed a massively complicating factor: new copyright law. Congress passed copyright legislation in 1976 that went into effect at the beginning of 1978 and had a direct effect on work for hire. Work for hire was the basic building block of corporate comic-book America. Under work-for-hire agreements, both independent contractors working at home and company employees working in a bullpen were considered to have created their characters for the publisher, who retained all future rights. The new law called for written contracts defining work-for-hire arrangements, casting into doubt years of doing business through assumed standard practices and the signing of the occasional release.

Kirby did not feel that the issue of copyright was a battle he could win, and according to friend Mark Evanier, he held this opinion for most of the 1970s. Kirby later claimed never to have broached the topic, although Jim Shooter recalled in 1999 that Marvel's lawyers at the very least thought he had. "I guess his contract ended in the summer," Shooter said. "Shortly thereafter, I was called into a meeting with upstairs management and lawyers, and told Jack was at least intimating that he might do a number of legal strategies to recapture ownership of characters he'd been creator or cocreator of." It was not an unheard-of strategy. In 1978, writer Steve Gerber had been removed in 1978 from the newspaper strip "Howard the Duck," which featured a character he had created for Marvel, when he threatened a lawsuit seeking ownership of the character. He eventually sued Marvel, and the case was settled out of court in 1983.

In 1979 Marvel issued new contracts that contained work-for-hire language. Artist Mike Ploog left Marvel mid-assignment rather than sign one, while Neal Adams once again took a strong pro-creator advocacy stance and called for a general refusal to sign the contracts. Kirby received a copy, and after reading it, did not feel encouraged about returning to Marvel. He continued to seek employment elsewhere and eventually did work for a number of small comic-book companies and animation production houses. His negotiations with Marvel for original art continued into the 1980s, starting up again in earnest in 1982. Kirby wanted the art more than ever, particularly because stories continued to circulate throughout the industry about vandalized storage facilities and stolen pages. Shooter said later that fears of legal fallout far outweighed any benefit Marvel could see in returning art. At one point, Marvel's legal team told Shooter that giving away original art would be tantamount to giving away corporate assets; at another time, they feared it could be interpreted as legitimizing any assertion Kirby might make of copyright ownership.

In 1984, Marvel made a widespread effort to return art to its creators, sending documents detailing how much of their art was available and providing them with a one-page release form to sign. By signing the release, an artist acknowledged that a work-for-hire relationship existed, and forfeited all copyrights to characters he might have had a hand in creating. It was basically a reiteration of the new standards set out in the 1979 contracts, but this time it was applied to all of the older art as well. Marvel was doing its best to coerce its creators into signing away their rights. "Anybody who signs that form is crazy," declared Neal Adams.

Kirby said he would have been willing to sign such a document, but he hadn't received one. Instead, in August 1984, Kirby was offered a much longer, four-page document that asked him to explicitly give up more rights and oblige Marvel more completely than any other artist. He would not be allowed to sell the art, display the art, transfer ownership of the art to a member of his family, or profit in any way through ownership of the art. Marvel could take the art back at any time for any purpose to make copies or pursue business with the art, and could even have the art modified if it wished. It was, in effect, a contract assigning Kirby to act as Marvel's storage facility. Further, Marvel claimed to have found only 88 of the approximately 8,000 pages of art that Kirby had created for the company. Kirby tried to negotiate with Marvel, even offering to send an assistant to help locate more art. But in a letter Jim Shooter sent to Kirby in January 1985, the artist was rebuffed. In response, the Kirby team sent its toughest letter to date, formally broaching the subject of a copyright challenge to Marvel's characters. The negotiations between Marvel and Kirby had reached an impasse.

The wider comic-book industry learned of Kirby's mistreatment through news coverage in the trade magazine *The Comics Journal* in July 1985. Letters flooded into the magazine overwhelmingly in support of the artist, including a letter from DC Comics chiding its longtime rival, as well as a missive from the man who had once been offered Stan Lee's job, Will Eisner. Although the national media failed to pick up on the story, the industry press and convention circuit talked of little else for over a year. In February 1986, *The Comics*

Journal devoted an entire issue to the matter, including an extensive interview with Kirby about his career. Even those who felt Kirby had little to no case for ownership of the copyrights were hard-pressed to defend Marvel's actions concerning the return of original art. It was a public relations disaster for Marvel from every angle. While it did not lead to a significant sales decrease for the company's titles, it forever altered the industry's perception of Marvel, Jim Shooter, and finally, Stan Lee, who endured criticism for not publicly fighting for the return of Kirby's art. Although Lee was in California, and Jim Shooter was firmly in charge of the New York publishing division, a strong statement of support by Lee could have had a positive effect on publicity surrounding the case.

After a contentious 1986 convention season, Marvel and Kirby agreed to a settlement. Marvel's lawyers had in April responded to the hints of a copyright challenge by unearthing those releases that Kirby had already signed, in which he'd abdicated his claims to the copyrights—one from 1969, believed to relate only to Captain America, and one from 1972. Kirby backed away from his stronger statements demanding public credit for various Marvel characters. By August approximately 150 professionals had signed a petition demanding Kirby's art be returned, hastening Marvel's desire to see the issue put to rest. In October, Kirby received a new inventory of his art in Marvel's storage that listed almost 1,900 pages, a vast improvement over the original 88 he was told existed. To have his art returned, Kirby had to sign a smaller, two-page document confirming that he had earlier disclaimed any and all copyrights. He signed it in 1987.

The fallout was enormous. Kirby could claim a practical victory—a sizable amount of art for his wife, Roz, to sell if his health problems proved fatal. In the eyes of many artists and writers, Marvel had become the evil empire, and not only for their dominant market share. Issues of creators' rights in the comic-book industry now enjoyed an immediate currency that would bring changes in publishing contracts and arrangements for the next decade. Jim Shooter was ousted from Marvel in early 1987, making the Kirby art conflict one of his major and longest-lasting legacies. The biggest casualty, however, may have been Stan Lee's reputation in the comic-book industry. And the worst was yet to come.

"Stan Lee and I never collaborated on anything!" Jack Kirby declared to Gary Groth in a 1989 interview for *The Comics Journal* that served as a follow-up to the art imbroglio and a deeper exploration of the artist's creative legacy. In their massive talk, in which Kirby was accompanied and occasionally corrected by his wife, Roz, the artist claimed that Lee was an office functionary whose job was to act as an intermediary for Martin Goodman. Kirby asserted that he not only created the stories by making a narrative of the art, as was the case with the ballyhooed Marvel Method, but that he also had been creating the characters beforehand and writing out the dialogue in the margins of the art he turned in to Lee. He even claimed never to have seen the detailed synopsis for *The Fantastic Four* #1 that Lee later found and had published. Kirby gave his own explanations for the origins of various Marvel characters—a panicked mother who lifted a car to save a baby was the genesis for the Hulk, his readings in Norse mythology inspired Thor, and an article in the newspaper about kids surfing in California coalesced into the Silver Surfer. Kirby described a Marvel universe that was created out of artistic and financial necessity from the same mind that helped create Captain America and the Challengers of the Unknown before the 1960s, and the Fourth World universe a decade later.

Kirby had claimed sole creatorship of the Marvel Universe as early as 1970. He consistently repeated this assertion throughout the 1980s, most notably in a 1982 interview with fellow comics great Will Eisner in *Spirit Magazine* #39. In the interview, Kirby described Lee as his conduit to the ear of Martin Goodman, claimed that he created Spider-Man, and firmly declared, "Stan Lee was not writing. I was doing the writing," stressing that his words on the penciled art constituted the actual scripting of the book, but that Lee kept him from filling in the word balloons. "Stan Lee wrote the credits. I never wrote the credits." The suggestion of improper credit was a jaw-dropping moment for many who had bought wholeheartedly the legend that had grown up around Stan Lee and Marvel. Lee denied the claims as strongly as possible. Admitting that Kirby had drawn a few pages of Spider-Man that hadn't seen print, Lee maintained that "in no way, shape, manner, or means did Jack Kirby create Spider-Man. I don't even know how he can dare to say that." What had changed in the years between the interviews by Eisner and Groth was that the original-art controversy had turned Kirby into an icon for the mistreated comic-book artist. The comic-book industry had developed a raw nerve when it came to Kirby and Marvel. Kirby's insistence on receiving full credit had the force of a beloved comics-industry personality calling a slightly disfavored one onto the carpet, forever casting into doubt where Kirby's contributions to the comics stopped and Lee's trumpeted contributions began.

According to Shooter, Lee and Kirby eventually settled their differences during a meeting he arranged between the two former creative partners. Lee says that Kirby approached him at a convention and absolved him of any past crimes he may have done the artist. Even at the height of the art dispute, Kirby had been reluctant to lay direct blame at the feet of his former creative partner. "There was never a conflict between me and Stan," Kirby said in a 1986 interview. "I understand Stan very well." But on the issue of credit, Kirby was unyielding. "I would not call it a 'reconciliation' in any sense of that word," says comics historian and former Kirby confidant Mark Evanier of the relationship between Lee and Kirby late in Kirby's life. "Jack never really wavered in his view of who had done what, or what he felt was owed to him. What he did do was to turn loose of certain angers and regrets. Part of this was, I believe, due to the knowledge that his health was failing."

Jack Kirby died on February 6, 1994. A rumor quickly spread that Lee would not be welcome at the memorial services, and that the family wanted him "banned." Lee cautiously reached out to the family and to family advisor Evanier through mutual friends such as writer Harlan Ellison. With Roz's assent, Stan Lee attended Jack Kirby's funeral. "I stayed in the back," says Lee. "I didn't want anyone to see me, and make a fuss and start talking about Jack and me and our relationship." A reconciliation between the Kirbys and Lee failed to transpire that day. "At the funeral, when I told Roz that Stan was seated in the back, she asked me to make certain that she got to speak to him after," says Evanier. "She wanted to make sure that he understood, and that others saw, that the family had no 'issues' with him. Unfortunately, at the end, Stan left before that could be choreographed. I ran out to the parking lot to try and bring him back but saw him speeding off in his car." Lee recalls hearing someone call for him, but says, "I thought I was imagining it." A week or two after the funeral, Evanier arranged for a phone conversation between Stan and Roz. Lee was later instrumental in securing from Marvel a modest pension for Roz, which was paid out a year or so before she passed away in 1997.

The boldness of Kirby's repeated claims to perpetuating the entirety of the early Marvel creative effort has lingered, however. The artist's interview with Eisner was republished in book form in 2001, the Groth interview under different cover in 2002. Stan Lee says he seriously considered suing *The Comics Journal* for the comments made within its pages, and he bitterly decried the comments Jack made there and elsewhere as being motivated by frustration. Some industry observers who support Lee claim that Kirby made such a strong case because he was being directed to do so by the interviewer, Gary Groth, a charge Groth firmly denies. "I thought he was absolutely lucid during our interview," Groth says. "If anything, my experience with Kirby was that he could be a bit political, cautious."

More significant, Kirby's claims led to a more equitable examination of the early Marvels and a greater appreciation for the role of the artist—particularly Kirby. Evanier says that the outpouring of support convinced Kirby that "he would not be forgotten; that the history of comics would not be written with Stan Lee receiving sole credit for creating all those characters." Additional evidence surfaced to support the thrust of Kirby's contention that the artists were deeply, if not primarily, responsible for the Marvel superhero revolution. Fellow professionals such as Gil Kane stepped forward to confirm the extreme level of input and control that Kirby and Ditko enjoyed on their signature books. And yet, on closer examination, Lee's presence as a writer on Kirby's books was rediscovered as well. Kirby's original art revealed proposed captions in many of the margins, but only rarely did Kirby's words match perfectly those found in the final published comic book. Further testimony from those around both Lee and Kirby during Marvel's most fertile period indicates that both contributed story ideas during long verbal arguments, neither necessarily listening to the other. The greatest casualty, perhaps, was the bombastic claims that Lee sometimes made as a promoter. Stan the comic-book creator gained slightly at the expense of Stan the Man.

Another party had yet to be heard from, one with specific insight into Stan Lee, the early Marvel Bullpen, and the issue of creative credit: Spider-Man cocreator and artist Steve Ditko. Unlike Kirby, Ditko had not gone on to become an uncle figure and positive role model for a new generation of comics professionals. He was a far more difficult personality. He was distant, withdrawn, and ultimately reluctant to attend any of the comic-book conventions or social gatherings at which industry professionals mingled, grew fond of one another, and made public cases for each other's relevance. He was also not as sorely missed as Kirby was upon their respective initial departures from Marvel. Ditko was a one- or two-book artist at his most productive, while Kirby practically defined the Marvel line through his prodigious page rate and ability to knock out covers. John Romita's *Spider-Man* was prettier and sold better than Ditko's, and his artwork provided such a distinctive break from Ditko's style, that Romita's approach is what many of the character's fans recognized as the feature's seminal look. While Kirby went on to do his Fourth World work, which was admired by many of his fellow professionals even as it failed to connect with fans the way his 1960s work had, Ditko divided his time between low-level genre work and his increasingly odd and sometimes unpleasant moralist comics. According to fellow professional Gil Kane, Ditko had long been a believer in the writings and philosophies of Ayn Rand, even as an artist at Marvel. After leaving Spider-Man, he began to put those ideas more directly into his comics. Ditko's occasional superheroes were no longer struggling teens but terrifyingly grim avengers driven by rigid ideas given concrete application. Much of Ditko's later work consisted of little more than outright editorializing about various concepts, drawn as abstractly as possible—cartoon polemics. By the time Kirby began fighting with Marvel over the return of original art, Ditko had achieved notoriety not only for his considerable artistic legacy, but also as an object of intrigue. He had never been extensively interviewed about the early days at Marvel, nor about the turns his career had taken since leaving the company.

Ditko attracted a small but extremely dedicated fan base, many of whom considered him a brave artist who pursued his own creative path at great personal cost. This provided Ditko with an audience not just for his comics lectures, such as "The Blabber Mouth vs. First-Hand Experience," but for his writing as well. Ditko contributed a series of essays that were published in Robin Snyder's newsletter *The Comics* and later collected in a book called *Avenging World*. While much of Ditko's writing is concerned with jargon and examining philosophical concepts in an attempt to gauge their accuracy and relevance, a few speak clearly and directly to various matters of public contention concerning Stan Lee. In his essay "Jack Kirby's Spider-Man," Ditko sets out the most levelheaded explication of the early Marvel process to date. He suggests that Lee probably came up with the character's name, but that the creative back-and-forth between writer and artist was such that the general narrative of the first story and Spider-Man's visual look were his own creations. Ditko gives Kirby credit for the few pages of art that he did for the project, notes that Kirby penciled the cover that was used, and cites similar work from the Simon/Kirby team in the past. But Ditko also explains how little of Kirby's conception made it into his own breakdown of the story, and informs the reader that the cover was done after the story's completion and Ditko's rejected attempt at a first cover.

Ditko's view provides a fundamental shift away from the argument in which Lee and Kirby had engaged since the 1960s. Ditko sees the published comic books as the primary creation, not some sense of the character's personality that precedes and informs the creative work that follows. He cites the comics industry's history of borrowing and reimaging, stretching back to Superman, as proof of the difficulties in trying to figure out where an original idea might have come from. Published ideas, particularly the kind turned out by comic-book companies, are so fluid that those who concretely participate in the final product are the only creators who matter. "A valid comic book creation (character, hero, costume, etc.) is that which is actually brought into existence, finished whole, a complete creation," Ditko wrote in one of his typical booming conclusions. Ditko's testimony weakens Kirby's claim to any significant contri-

bution to the published Spider-Man, but strengthens both artists'
standings as creative forces across the Marvel line. Using Ditko's
guidelines, Kirby may have overstated his case in the midst of his
disagreements with Marvel over returned art, particularly with
regard to the genesis of Spider-Man. But Stan Lee fashioned an
entire career out of such overstatements. In some ways, Ditko has
become Lee's watchdog on the issue of creative ownership. He's
quick to point out when Lee reinforces his public stance in something as unassuming as a comment in an editorial note. He has also
remained consistent in his views about Lee's efforts to restore Ditko
to cocreator status: that status is not Lee's to confer.

By the mid-1990s, Lee's image had gone through the wringer
and was now being inspected on the other side. Many professionals
and industry observers considered Lee a silent partner in the Kirby
art fiasco. Others simply viewed him as the public image for a company that was now more corporate bully than underdog pop-art
hero. An emerging generation of artists and writers had less history
with Lee or mainstream comics than those who had emerged from
organized fandom years before. They saw Marvel Comics, and Stan
Lee himself, as either irrelevant to where comics were heading, a
hazily remembered icon of childhood nostalgia, or as a symbol for
the sometimes hostile business relationship between Marvel and
smaller publishers. In 1990 cartoonist Dan Clowes produced a series
of stories in his award-winning title *Eightball* featuring the rise and
fall of a generic mainstream comic-book artist named Dan Pussey.
Pussey starts out as a fan artist who goes to work for a thinly veiled
version of Stan Lee, named Dr. Infinity, in a setup reminiscent of
the original Marvel Bullpen. Clowes takes shots at Lee's publicity
patter and his image-conscious salesmanship, throwing in various
horror stories about working in mainstream comics that had been
batted around the industry for years with little corroboration,
including one about an editor who demeaned artists looking for
work. Clowes also deftly tracks the employment cycle of a typical
mainstream superstar artist, from working stiff to dealmaker and
back to faceless company drone. When a peek into the future
reveals that Dr. Infinity is remembered more than any single, more
deserving artist who worked in comic books, the message transforms into a critique of Lee's relentless publicity-seeking. Stan Lee,

through the character of Dr. Infinity, becomes "The Man" not in the sense of an emergent, authoritative voice, but as a representative of a status quo that threatens divergent artistic voices.

Clowes wasn't the only cartoonist of the 1990s to struggle with Lee and his work. In *Hicksville*, a fictional story about comic-book culture by New Zealand–based cartoonist Dylan Horrocks, Lee makes a brief appearance, desperately asking an entertainment mogul about his untouched proposal before snapping back into public-relations mode. Other artists paid kinder tribute to the work Lee did with Kirby, Ditko, and the other early Marvel illustrators. Writer Alan Moore and a group of artists, many of whom had been vocal in decrying Marvel's mistreatment of Jack Kirby, put together the purposefully nostalgic series *1963*, published by Image Comics. Their homage included language that closely approximated Lee's own, plus takeoffs on Marvel's "Bullpen Bulletins" pages and early letters sections. In 1997, a group of East Coast artists published a comic featuring Marvel characters in underground comix styles— the cover featured the X-Men drawn in a style reminiscent of early *New Yorker* illustrations—and handed out the book at conventions. The book, *Coober Skeeber*, gave a curious energy to many of Lee's creations that hadn't been seen in the Marvel comic books for decades. A version of Spider-Man, drawn by artist Ron Rege, Jr., seethed with the energy of the early Steve Ditko version, his thought balloons expressing rage with a few dirty words thrown in for emphasis. By the decade's end, a wider variety of artists and writers were brought in to work on Lee's creations by Marvel, from crime-comic cartoonist Brian Bendis to filmmaker Kevin Smith to comic-book auteur James Sturm. Peter Bagge, an underground-style cartoonist whose work deals with adult social satire, created a Spider-Man story for 2002 that portrayed Peter Parker as torn between the kind of corporate success that was enjoyed by Stan Lee and the freedom that came with the reclusivity of Steve Ditko. In terms of his contribution to comic-book content and as an industry figure, Stan Lee's legacy was poised to enter the twenty-first century splintered across hundreds of four-color panels.

The conflict in the professional ranks was most clearly seen in the October 1995 issue of *The Comics Journal*, the magazine that had forcefully made the case against Stan Lee in the Jack Kirby art imbroglio ten years earlier. The cover was adorned with an unflattering portrayal of Lee as an aged circus huckster, complete with the headline "Step Right Up!" Inside, a number of essays and industry tributes took Lee to task on the issues of creator credit and the image that he portrays on behalf of Marvel Comics. In a typical broadside, writer Paul Wardle declared, "I'm not much of a Kirby fan, but it's pretty clear that *Origins of Marvel Comics* and its two sequels are about as accurate a record of the creation of the Marvel Universe as *Hee Haw* is an accurate record of life on a farm." Another artist simply and brutally stated, "Stan Lee should have died thirty years ago."

Yet many of the articles and reminiscences were also complimentary. Essayist Greg Cwiklik decried Lee for taking too much public credit as a writer when the artists were constructing their own narratives, and for promoting house styles over innovation in texts such as *How to Draw Comics the Marvel Way*. But he also allowed, "Stan Lee's creative contributions were very real and substantial during the time he presided as editor, writer, and ringmaster at Marvel during its heyday in the heady period of the 1960s. In fact, his role was crucial: without him, Marvel Comics would never have achieved either the critical or commercial success that it did." Critic Earl Wells clarified Lee's creative presence in the early Marvels by contrasting their themes with those explored by Kirby in his solo work at DC. Many of the contributions from industry professionals expressed admiration for Lee personally, or at least paid grudging tribute to his skills as a public presence. The rehabilitation of Stan Lee had begun, largely outside the eyes of a public that knew him vaguely or not at all.

PART VIII

"IT'S CLOBBERIN' TIME!"

IN STAN'S IMAGE

In 1991, comic-book historian Les Daniels published *Marvel: Five Fabulous Decades of the World's Greatest Comics,* an official company history complete with illustrations, hero profiles, and a section of reprinted comic-book stories. Daniels's amiable look back drew on interviews with dozens of Marvel employees past and present, from former editor in chief Roy Thomas to longtime Spider-Man artist John Romita to late-'80s comics "It" boy Todd McFarlane. As the longest-tenured employee by a wide margin, Stan Lee is all over the Daniels tome, his comic-book scripting profiled and his memory plumbed for quotes applicable to all decades and on all subjects. Yet beyond a characteristically hyperbolic introduction, in which he crows that the intro writer gets first crack at the still-happy reader and promises that the pages to come will boggle our minds, Lee's writing does not appear in the book. For the first time, custodianship of Marvel's story had passed from his hands.

Lee had actually been working on an earlier incarnation of the book for several years, crafting the history of Marvel from his own point of view. He even prepared a manuscript containing several chapters that were never used. "I remember how impressive it was when Joe and Jack produced a comic-book panel that took up an entire page in *Captain America* #4," Lee wrote in one of them, positioning himself as a witness to a pivotal event in comic-book history when he couldn't claim it for his own. But Lee's book never saw print; the publisher, dissatisfied with his written material up to that point, removed him from the project in late 1988. Even though he wasn't in full control of the Daniels book, Lee was ably and amply represented in it, making it the perfect metaphor for the way Stan Lee related to the comic-book field in the 1990s. Although ostensibly still involved with comics, Lee was a minimal presence. The changes he had instituted at Marvel in the 1960s, however, were now spread throughout the industry. During the 1990s, the American comic-book field reflected Stan Lee's influence more than it had at any time in its history—sometimes with disastrous results.

On a late December evening in 1991, a trio of Marvel's most popular comic book artists visited the office of then company president Terry Stewart. Rob Liefeld, Jim Lee, and Todd McFarlane were three of the highest-paid artists in the industry's history. The twenty-one-year-old Liefeld, who drew a popular spin-off of the X-Men comics called *X-Force*, enjoyed a healthy following of teenage boys excited by the manic crudeness of his art and his frat-boy swagger. Jim Lee—no relation to Stan—drew the company's best-selling title *X-Men*. Lee took the energy and exaggerated figure drawing many fans equated with Japanese adventure comics and applied them to Marvel's best-selling characters, pushing the company's top franchise onto another sales plateau. Todd McFarlane was a hardworking industry pro who had toiled on secondary titles at DC and Marvel before putting Stan Lee's favorite wallcrawler back on the sales map with a splashy new title simply named *Spider-Man*. Fans embraced his appealingly rounded, intricately rendered art.

All three professionals were creations of the Marvel machine, with Lee to thank in large part for their industry celebrity. Through his prodigious efforts at self-promotion begun in the 1960s, and by convincing Marvel's readers to identify not just with the costumed heroes but also with the men and women creating them, Lee had set Marvel on the slow but inevitable road to a star system. The "Jolly Jack" and "Jazzy John" references of the early Marvel days gave way to a second generation of creators who were lauded on their merits distinct from the characters they worked on—writers and artists who earned healthy six-figure salaries and commanded long autograph lines at comic-book store signings and conventions. In the early 1980s the general public might not have known who the

X-Men were, let alone creators like Dave Cockrum, John Byrne, and Chris Claremont. But for comics fans, successful creators who worked on popular characters were the subculture's equivalent of rock stars.

The emerging generation of Liefeld, McFarlane, and Jim Lee benefited even further from this focus on creators, as Marvel perfected a strategy designed to increase sales through the exploitation of "hot" artists and writers. Young creators were groomed on books featuring minor-selling or new characters. Anyone who made an impression was moved to one of Marvel's top titles, such as one of the "mutant" books. If successful there, editors conceived a fresh project built around the artist's particular creative gifts, perhaps a spin-off of a high-selling brand or an additional title featuring a popular character. Those titles profited from an increase in readership that came when fans followed the creator to the new work, while the established franchise titles were freed up for the next generation of stars-to-be. Thus Todd McFarlane went from the moderately popular *The Incredible Hulk* to the venerable *The Amazing Spider-Man* to the re-launched *Spider-Man*.

Most artists were happy to follow the cycle from beginning to end. By 1991 Marvel was rewarding some of its more popular artists to an extent that industry veterans never would have believed possible. Five- and six-figure royalties on a single issue were reported with increasing regularity, with rumors of seven-figure royalties for the launch of Jim Lee's new *X-Men* title. But as much as they had benefited from the system, Liefeld, McFarlane, and Jim Lee were suspicious of the process. Liefeld, his family's sole provider, wanted to extend his commercial viability as an artist for longer than Marvel and its revolving-door policies allowed. McFarlane, a naturally sharp and perceptive businessman, was horrified by the field's traditional economic exploitation of its artists and writers, particularly the abuses that developed during Marvel's relationship with Jack Kirby. He believed that the time had come for artists to make demands on issues of compensation and creative control. Marvel might have considered them replaceable—Liefeld later claimed that Terry Stewart compared the artists to faceless field hands recruited to pick cotton on a plantation, perhaps the most indelicate description of the role of creative people in the history of the arts—but their status within the industry as hitmakers gave them a tremendous amount of capital with which to start up their own venture if negotiations collapsed.

The 1991 meeting with Marvel president Stewart went poorly, as did all subsequent overtures between the parties. Jim Lee, Liefeld, and McFarlane were pushing for a radical studio setup within Marvel's larger framework, and Stewart's only serious counteroffer was control of the weakened and historically ineffectual Epic imprint. Unable to strike a deal to their liking, the three men staged a mass defection from Marvel, taking with them several other popular artists including Erik Larsen, Marc Silvestri, and Jim Valentino. In August 1992, the group of expatriate artists formed Image Comics, a new comic-book imprint built upon their cachet with fans. Between Image and Marvel, it was as if the two sides of Stan Lee's model for comics success were gearing up for battle: the flamboyant creators (Image and its big-name artists doing new characters) versus the larger-than-life creations (Marvel and its established characters drawn by the next group of artists).

The results surprised everyone in comics, even, to some extent, the Image creators. For several years in the 1990s, their comics proved to be more-than-effective competition for the established franchises at Marvel and DC. Rob Liefeld's *Youngblood* #1 set a sales record for an independent comic-book company, moving just over one million units. Todd McFarlane's *Spawn* #1 broke Liefeld's record by selling 1,700,000 copies and settling into a long run as one of the industry's best-selling titles. With the comics-store market system entering its second decade, comic-book fans had refined their tastes in superhero escapism. Companies no longer had to spend years fashioning an identity for themselves. The 1990s comics aficionado was pickier, more discerning, and more willing to bank on his or her own assessment of the field over any editor's aggressive claims. Brand loyalty was history. In look and tone, the Image comics were a lot like the Marvel titles that the artists had left behind, and they sold in equal numbers.

As illustrators first and foremost, the Image founders placed great emphasis on splashy art, and a few titles distinguished themselves by attention to outside cultural influences that had developed long after Stan Lee first put words to the early Marvel characters.

Image comics, like the early Marvels, mixed touches of observed reality with the general fantasy of the superhero. The company's creators specialized in portraying the darker aspects of the real world: child molestation, the gaudy excess of celebrity, AIDS, and homelessness. Image made dour comics for a dour generation of male teens, and in so doing even briefly out-Marveled Marvel. Early Image titles regularly sold out impressive print runs. On a summer day in 1992, nearly 25,000 fans lined up in a Chicago hotel parking lot to meet the Image founders. In 1995 Image briefly eclipsed DC Comics as the number-two comic-book company, a feat that had taken Lee and the Marvel Bullpen nearly a decade to accomplish.

Stan Lee remained mostly silent about the Image effort. In a move reminiscent of Frank Sinatra hosting Elvis on television following the King's release from the U.S. army, Lee had conducted videotaped interviews with Leifeld, McFarlane, and Jim Lee that were sold in stores. For the Image founders, it was a nod of approval from one comic-book superstar to the newest generation. For Lee, it was a way to appear relevant and respected.

Image never matched the heights of its first few years in publishing. Under the nonreturnable system utilized by the comics-store market, owners had to pay for books before they shipped. If a comic book arrived later than promised, cash flow suffered. Shops were stuck with material that might have sold like hotcakes when originally scheduled, but less so at the later date. It was hard enough to sell a comic book in September at the numbers projected for it in June, but after an extended delay between issues, fans typically lost all interest in a book. Because of its initial sales successes, Image was in a unique position to expose retailers to big-money risk. Few shops could afford to order Image books modestly and risk being the one store in their area unable to meet demand for the next breakout hit. Image eventually improved its scheduling, and its distribution partners tightened lateness policies, but not before causing real damage to the comic-book retail landscape. Personality conflicts between founding members began to put a strain on the company. Liefeld left Image in 1996 to avoid being voted out by the other members. Priorities changed, and Jim Lee sold his studio and its portion of the Image Comics line to DC Comics in 1998.

McFarlane slipped slowly away from comic books and used his design savvy and business instincts to sell a Spawn movie to Hollywood and become a major toy mogul. As of 2003, the Larsen and Silvestri studios continued to produce comic books under the Image imprint, while Jim Valentino had stepped into an organizational role and recruited other creators to work under the Image umbrella.

Several other comic-book companies emerged in the 1980s and '90s, although none with the sudden sales impact of Image. Former Marvel editor in chief Jim Shooter attempted to repeat his success with a series of companies—Valiant, Defiant, Broadway, and Daring. Each company featured the straightforward editorial approach for which Shooter was known, and the kind of solid industry veterans with whom he had enjoyed success at Marvel ten years earlier. Unfortunately, the companies offered a creative foundation closer to Shooter's misfired New Universe than Stan's Marvel universe. Valiant was only briefly an industry presence, and each new company proved less successful than the one preceding it.

The most interesting mainstream company of the period, Dark Horse Comics, settled in the 1990s into a consistent fourth-place sales position behind Marvel, DC, and Image. Founded by Mike Richardson at the tail end of the independent company movement of the 1980s, Dark Horse played around with various publishing formulas—including an aborted superhero line—before developing into a two-way-street relationship with Hollywood. Dark Horse offered movie producers dozens of licensed properties that had already been through story testing in comic-book form, and the producers offered Dark Horse access to a few key licensed properties that the comic-book maker used to greatly expand its market share. Dark Horse became the home of the *Star Wars* license previously thought to have been depleted by Marvel, as well as various combinations of the latest in science-fiction movie monsters: the Terminators, Aliens, and Predators. By matching its properties to rising movie stars, Dark Horse was able to see movies made from *The Mask*, *Barb Wire*, and the Mystery Men characters from Bob Burden's strange *Flaming Carrot Comics*—none of which had been anywhere close to a hit in comic-book form.

Dark Horse chief Mike Richardson enjoyed the success that had eluded Stan Lee in years of Hollywood deal making. Even Denis was actually doing far more in front of the camera than behind it. He played versions of himself as a comic-book impresario in low-budget films *The Ambulance* (1990) and *Tequila Wine: A Vampire Odyssey* (1991). Also in 1994, Lee narrated *The Marvel Action Hour* animation show and introduced each cartoon in segments as a flesh-and-blood host in the manner of Walt Disney, greeting his True Believers and saying goodbye to the audience with a shouted "Excelsior!" Lee's best role, playing himself, came in Kevin Smith's 1995 box-office failure *Mallrats*. Smith, a devoted fan of Lee's writing who would later write comic-book scripts for Marvel's *Daredevil*, depicted Lee as an object of cultural devotion. Lee patiently answers the protagonist's bizarre questions about slightly crude Marvel ephemera, and counsels him on matters of the heart. In *Mallrats*, Lee emanates a daffy, highly romantic quality and comes off as a good-natured guy flattered by his status as a fount of comic-book wisdom. Few directors followed Smith's lead and wrote Lee into their movies. Stan's most notable appearances on film since *Mallrats* have been his Alfred Hitchcock–style cameos in *X-Men* (2000), *Spider-Man* (2002), and *The Hulk* (2003).

Stan's attempts to license Marvel characters for major film adaptations were so poorly received that they began to reflect badly on Marvel's publishing line. The Punisher, hugely popular in the comic books, could only muster a straight-to-video effort from second-tier action stars in a 1989 film that bore almost no resemblance to Marvel's original conception of the property. *Captain America* wasn't merely a bad film but a creatively desperate one, placing an odd pro-environment message over a pedestrian action plot that included a rubber-masked Italian fascist and a hero who faked illness in order to swipe someone's car. The unreleased *Fantastic Four* movie that would find its way onto the convention circuit via bootleg copies was the nadir of Marvel's movie efforts. Made by filmmaker Roger Corman's company in its famous cost-cutting mode at a time when fantasy and science-fiction movies were setting new standards for visual effects, the family that launched a comic-book empire looked ridiculous, cheap, and laughable.

But despite their failures on film and the setback caused by the departure of the Image artists, the early 1990s were a period of great hope for and belief in Marvel Comics, its characters, and its concepts. It was as if Stan Lee's giddy optimism and salesman's confidence had infused the company from its lowest production statter to its new owners. After financier Ron Perelman brought the company in early 1989, he brought in entertainment executives from outside comics in order to maximize what he perceived to be undervalued properties. As far as the new regime was concerned, Stan Lee remained a creative and public relations asset. To Lee's delight, Marvel immediately raised his salary. The new heads of the company encouraged Lee to continue with his schedule of light involvement in New York and the particulars of the comic-book business, and to spend the majority of his time pushing for Marvel animation projects and handling publicity.

The Perelman strategy for Marvel was to build an entertainment conglomerate based on the company's wealth of characters and concepts. Movies were an unlikely possibility, however. Marvel's track record in that area was execrable, and none of the characters seemed to have the built-in recognition level that made for successful film franchises like those featuring DC's Batman and Superman. Marvel's heroes had to be nurtured before movies were likely to bear box-office fruit. Television, with its lower investment costs, was considered a more effective tool for character development. Frustrating a movie strategy further, the rights for the Marvel character with the highest level of public recognition, Spider-Man, were hopelessly tangled among multiple holders after two decades of trying to get a film project off the ground.

Also, according to author Dan Raviv in his book *Comic Wars*, Perelman found the movie business distasteful. "Charity functions and Revlon events kept Ronald on a first-name basis with actors, directors, and studio owners," Raviv wrote. "But he scorned 'Hollywood accounting,' where a partner in a movie project never knew if he would get a dime. The notion of 'over-the-line' or 'under-the-line' profits was a foreign language to him. And having most of one's projects fail, while hoping to offset those losses with an occasional blockbuster, was not Perelman's idea of positive cash flow." Stan

Lee's dream since the 1960s of seeing Marvel characters in major motion pictures had been struck a sizable blow.

The Perelman brain trust wanted to emphasize Marvel as the cornerstone of a collectibles and licensing empire—a Disney Company built on pulp and superheroes rather than celluloid and funny animals. On a corporate level, this meant the rapid expansion of Marvel through the purchase of related companies. In summer 1992, Marvel bought trading-card giant Fleer Corporation for $286 million. In 1993, action-figure-maker Toy Biz exchanged a large portion of its stock to Perelman in return for a closer working relationship with the company and a reduction in Marvel's expensive licensing fees. In 1995 Marvel bought sports-card company SkyBox International for $150 million, and the Italian sticker manufacturer Panini Group for another $150 million. Unlike Marvel, for which Perelman had paid $82.5 million, none of these companies seemed undervalued, but at the top of their earning potential and asking prices. Further, each company came with substantial licensing fees for their biggest product lines. The marriage of these businesses with characters Stan Lee had spent years convincing fans were universally appealing fostered an irresistible publicity momentum. Marvel was offered as common stock at $2 a share in 1991, and by 1993, adjusting for splits, was worth $34.

When gimmick covers—published with different kinds of ink, or limited to a few copies, or featuring a number of different images—began to prove popular with fans, they fueled a trend of new comic-book sales as purchases based on their perceived future value as commodities. Some fans, realizing an unblemished copy held more value than one that was read, began to buy what they felt were potentially valuable comics and, without reading a page, sealed them in plastic. In the early 1990s, Marvel was able to sell a number of early issues of special relaunches of popular titles—*X-Force*, *X-Men*, *Spider-Man*—in part as future "rare" collectibles based on their event quality. Marvel and many comics buyers wilfully ignored the logic that anything with a print run of over a million copies could never be considered rare.

Marvel also pursued other tried-and-true strategies to increase the awareness of its core properties. Rather than introducing new characters, Marvel focused on developing multiple titles for each popular character or team. One memorable comic book, 1990's *Punisher Armory*, consisted entirely of pictures and descriptions of equipment used by the vigilante in his ongoing crusade to murder bad guys. Marvel even offered up numerous crossovers reminiscent of *Secret Wars* in a concerted effort to compel readers to buy a number of different books in order to follow a single, convoluted story. For a while, these efforts worked.

The decisive blow against Marvel came in 1995, when it hatched a plan to distribute its own product. Comics stores typically bought their comics from specialty distributors, companies that served as clearinghouses for multiple publishers. After years of building their business around this market, Marvel now felt that these distributors and the network of comic-book stores might not be up to the task of bringing Marvel's product to the widest possible audience. Marvel had been leaving its distribution and point-of-purchase salesmanship to a group of scruffy, barely solvent hobbyists. The shops varied widely in quality, many of them barely functioning as effective retail establishments. In the 1980s, Marvel sales representatives had gone so far as to institute a program whereby stores could more easily purchase cash registers rather than continue to dole change out of a cigar box. Marvel liked selling nonreturnable books to dedicated stores, but it wanted a greater commitment to Marvel than many comics-related businesses were willing to muster.

Rumors that Marvel would open its own stores ran rampant among comics retailers in 1994. Then, in 1995, Marvel announced that it would distribute its own comic books through a recently purchased regional distributor named Heroes World. In a series of retailer meetings held that spring, Marvel executives tried to allay fears that they would soon move into retailing themselves. They put the best face on the fact that, because of Marvel's move into distribution, many of the retailers had to change how they did business. Splitting orders between at least two distributors meant added paperwork and a reduction in the discount stores received on total orders from a single supplier. The reaction of some retailers bordered on hostility—in a Seattle meeting, many left the cramped suburban hotel meeting room after eating a free lunch. Some smaller retailers serving rural communities, who barely met the minimum order level for a single distributor when all the books they purchased were coming from the same place, suddenly found themselves unable to do business without purchasing extra product they almost certainly couldn't sell. Heroes World experienced huge growing pains moving to national distribution, and several stores complained of poor service. Worse, the loss of Marvel's business initiated a mad scramble among the remaining distributors for the other big publishers. By decade's end, only Diamond Distribution was still standing, and Marvel had abandoned the difficulties of self-distribution to return to the greatly reduced fold.

Comic-book stores, already fragile from the late-shipping practices inflicted by Image Comics and struggling to keep up with the explosion of new titles, began to blink out of existence with frightening regularity. The number of comic-book stores declined from over 10,000 in 1993 to just over 3,500 in 2001. Fans left in droves as well. Some lost their local retail outlet and a convenient way to purchase comic books. Others grew sick of the multiple titles, laborious crossovers, and manipulative sales gimmicks. Editors resorted to story hooks that were reminiscent of the moves that had been made in the late 1940s to goose interest in the Timely superheroes: characters were killed, costumes were changed, and supporting casts were revolved. Comic-book readers suffered burnout; comic-book speculators began to suspect their "investments" were largely worthless. They raced each other to the exit. By 2001 the best-selling Marvel comic books rarely exceeded 100,000 units in monthly sales, compared to ten times that at the start of the 1990s.

Marvel suffered on a corporate level as well. Collectible cards took a sharp downturn in sales in 1995, partly because of the collapse of baseball cards after the 1994 major league baseball strike. Sales of stickers through the Panini Group decreased, too. As comic-book sales deteriorated in 1994 and experienced a 7 percent drop in 1995, that meant that a third division of the proposed Perelman collectibles empire was now in trouble. The expected synergy between Marvel's characters and licenses for stickers and cards did not pan out. Only Toy Biz avoided the rapid decline, as action figures and toy licenses remained steady. In 1996 sales collapsed even further, particularly for Fleer/Skybox, bringing in some $150 million beneath divisional projections. By October 1996, Marvel was hemorrhaging money, its stock had collapsed by 85 percent, and the interest payment on the loans used to assemble its empire had driven money reserves down to a new low. Perelman's group took the company into Chapter 11 bankruptcy in December 1996, avoiding the bullet of Chapter 7 liquidation and the almost certain collapse of the American comic-book market.

In 1997 and 1998, the bankrupt company operated in a holding pattern, publishing fewer books and becoming a less vital market presence. The fight over Marvel's corporate future came down to two factions. On one side was a plan offered by Toy Biz executives Ike Perlmutter and Avi Arad. They wanted to merge the two companies, and use a combination of Toy Biz's value and bank loans to pay off the immediate debts. In the long run, they vowed to pursue the increased awareness of Marvel as a brand name through high-end movies and television deals that were anathema to Perelman. Perelman rival Carl Icahn offered an alternate system of relieving Marvel of its debt that decried interdivisional "sweetheart deals." He stressed that his was a better deal for the stockholders who had purchased into various bond schemes by which Perelman had created the Marvel conglomerate. A revised version of the Toy Biz plan was approved on July 31, 1998. Ron Perelman made between $250 and $300 million from Marvel through dividends, loans secured using Marvel as collateral, and tax breaks. Under his ownership, comic books had been exposed as a poor fulcrum for a collectibles empire. In the financial turmoil caused by the company's aggressive pursuit of power, hundreds of people who had made their living at Marvel, and in businesses for whom Marvel was the most important client, lost their jobs. The Marvel characters were not quite as popular as Stan Lee's enthusiasm had asserted. They could not keep people reading comic books that arrived late or looked sloppy. They could not keep them buying collectible cards or entice them into theme restaurants. The delicate framework by which Marvel had profited for years was now shredded by the company's overreaching ambition. Many towns now lacked a single place to buy comic books, once a part of American life as commonplace as Little League baseball and Saturday movie matinees.

Stan Lee had skirted the crumbling of the American comic book with considerable grace. He was firmly ensconced in his California lifestyle, with wife Joan a constant companion. They remained very much in love. Joan had written a book in 1987—*The Pleasure Palace*—and even dipped back into her acting days with some voice work for the Marvel cartoons. The family stayed close, and daughter Joan took up residence in a nearby home.

In 1994, when Marvel was seeking to consolidate the many facets of its empire, Lee accepted a contract that married his current salary to a limited number of promotional and executive engagements—in effect, a retirement package for a man who refused to retire. He had also dipped back into comic books. In 1988 he wrote a *Silver Surfer* graphic novel illustrated by the world-renowned French cartoonist Moebius. Lee helped Marvel extend its copyrights to future versions of its characters, writing issues of a book called *Ravage 2099*. Through most of the decade, Lee also tried to get a new comic-book line, "Excelsior!", off the ground at Marvel. Lee talked it up in several interviews, and at one point even announced the hiring of staff. The line was to consist of ten comics set in the near future and featuring as many top artistic and writing talents as Lee could muster. But in a decade of failed comic-book lines and massive financial worries, Marvel had little interest in investing in another series of books, even ones coordinated by Lee.

With efforts spearheaded by former Toy Biz executive Avi Arad, the new Marvel made a priority of getting its characters onto the big screen. The 1997 summer smash *Men in Black*, although not regarded as a Marvel Comics movie as much as films to come, hinted at the wealth of characters and concepts to be found in the obscure corners of Marvel's library. In 1998 a minor character from the 1970s horror title *Tomb of Dracula* became a late-summer hit in the movie *Blade*, starring Wesley Snipes. Snipes was a fan of Lee's comic books, and for years was attached to a Black Panther movie project. Finally, in 2000, *X-Men* rolled into theaters with an eye-popping $54 million opening weekend. The movie was largely derived from the Claremont era of the book rather than any of the comics Lee had scripted or even edited. A new Marvel Comics regime headed by well-connected industry veteran Joe Quesada and Fleer Corporation veteran Bill Jemas revived fan interest in the exhausted, stagnant Marvel heroes by hiring top creators from other companies and recruiting talent from other media. Adjusting the core titles to echo ideas from the better-received movies while paying close attention to forthcoming theatrical releases, by 2003 Quesada and Jemas had positioned Marvel to better capitalize on its movie successes. A fragile market watched every step.

Unlike *Blade* or *X-Men*, there was little doubt that *Spider-Man* would be a movie hit. Once again, Lee was made available for interviews and for promotion, billed as Spider-Man's creator and number-one fan. The project represented Lee's signature character, and it drew from elements found throughout his long run on the title. The poignant frustrations of a high schooler trying to assume adult responsibility that Steve Ditko had drawn so powerfully were evident in Sam Raimi's movie, but were frequently sublimated on screen by Peter Parker's unrequited longing for Mary Jane Watson, a character whose unforgettable visual stamp came from John Romita. For Stan Lee, the Spider-Man movie was a happy grace note after a long career, and a perfect capstone to a long decade in which the comic books from which he sprang had struggled to survive. Lee told reporters that this new Spider-Man was as recognizable as his own. Of course, by 2002, he had just learned how difficult ownership of one's own ideas could be.

MILLIONAIRE ON PAPER

Late one afternoon in June 2000, Stan Lee entered a conference room at the offices of Stan Lee Media, in Encino, California. At one end of the table sat Robert Diggs, also known as the RZA, leader of Wu-Tang Clan, a hard-core rap group whose music weaves together ghetto rhythms, kung fu movies, and comic-book mythology. At the other end sat Peter Paul and Ken Williams, the cofounder and CEO, respectively, of Stan Lee Media, an Internet start-up that was hoping to spin a new line of Web-based, Lee-created superheroes into profitable off-line products such as toys, movies, and television shows. The two sides were arranging a deal to transform Bobby Digital, the RZA's superhero persona, into an on-line cartoon character. Lee, grinning, had come to give his stamp of approval. He approached the RZA with hand extended. "Wait a minute," Lee said in his throaty New York accent. He contorted his body and threw the rapper a hip-hop style handshake. "Good to see you!"

They chatted for a while about Marvel Comics, the unlikeliest of duos to be found locked in conversation at a high-flying dot-com or anywhere else: the RZA, a gangsta rapper in baggy blue jeans, sporting gold-spiked knuckle rings, and the seventy-seven-year-old Lee, white-haired and clad in a gray silk shirt and black slacks. The RZA was a big fan. "I got my shit from you," he told Lee, citing his practice of tagging every Wu-Tang release with the line "RZA Presents."

The RZA rapped some of his Marvel-inspired lyrics: "Microphone gets cast to the floor. Shape-shifting. Heavy as the hammer of Thor."

Lee clapped his hands. "Oh, that's great! I like that! Hey, you're going to help me with the stories."

At an age when most wealthy people have shuffled off to golf course-accessible condos in Palm Springs, Stan Lee was riding a wave of stock-market hysteria back into the limelight. His characters—non-Marvel ones, this time—were in demand by theme-park operators and movie producers. He was the chairman and cofounder of a publicly traded company that was generating buzz on Wall Street. At one point, Stan Lee Media's market capitalization eclipsed that of Marvel, which was still clawing its way out of debt, and Lee mused aloud about the possibility of buying his old company. In June 2000, shares of Lee's Internet start-up were trading at $12, giving his 28-percent stake a paper value of more than $35 million and making him perhaps the oldest dot-com multimillionaire on active workaday duty.

In those heady days of overnight wealth creation, the business pages were awash with Internet boosterism, and Stan, the storied hypemeister, fit in perfectly. He spoke at technology conferences and appeared on financial-news networks to pump his venture. Newspaper and magazine reporters swooped in to chronicle this next exciting chapter in the life of the aging but still vibrant pop-culture icon. Lee had trouble navigating his way around Netscape, but he became a skilled new-media proselytizer. The reason for forming Stan Lee Media "wasn't so much a matter of money, although I'm sure there will eventually be a tremendous amount of money in the Internet," Lee said at the time. "I got into comics when they were just starting. I was lucky enough to be able to carve a niche and to make the company I work with the biggest company in the comic-book field. Here I have a chance to try and do the same thing again in a new field, which is much bigger, more powerful, and more comprehensive than comics could ever be. If it didn't pay anything, I would still want to do it."

When it all came crashing down six months later amid a mass of financial scams allegedly orchestrated by his business partner and confidant Peter Paul, Lee was decidedly less enthusiastic. Paul's machinations hastened the company's demise, which left Stan and thousands of shareholders with a pile of worthless stock. On a personal level, Lee felt wounded by the experience and betrayed by a close friend. It was a painful lesson for him to learn so late in life.

The story of Stan Lee Media is really the story of Stan Lee and Peter Paul, a relationship that dates back to the early 1990s. At the time, Paul was running the American Spirit Foundation, a nonprofit organization established by actor Jimmy Stewart to improve public education. The foundation sponsored mentoring programs and reading initiatives, hosted fundraising galas, and handed out annual Spirit of America awards to such luminaries as Bob Hope, Gene Autry, former President Ronald Reagan, *Star Trek* creator Gene Roddenberry, and Stan Lee. Paul eventually recruited Stan to become the organization's chairman and to head up its Entertainers for Education committee.

Over time, their association turned into friendship, and Paul began to take an interest in Lee's career. He felt that Stan's talents and brand name were being wasted at Marvel. By the time of the company's bankruptcy in 1996, Lee's role had been reduced to that of a figurehead. He still wrote the Spider-Man newspaper strip and acted as a promoter, but other executives had taken over the bulk of the Hollywood deal-making. Although Lee continued working on his own TV and movie pitches, his employment contract prevented him from competing with Marvel. "I was looking for ways to liberate him," Paul said in a June 2000 interview. "He was lying fallow at Marvel."

For his part, Lee valued Paul's connections, which brought the comic-book star into contact with celebrities from the worlds of entertainment and politics. In his autobiography, Lee credits Paul with introducing him to Al Gore, Muhammad Ali, Bill and Hillary Clinton, Tony Curtis, and many others. "I'm a guy who's impressed with someone who knows how to talk to headwaiters, so you can imagine how impressed I was with Peter Paul," Lee wrote.

What Stan didn't find out until later was that his new playmate had a checkered past. In the late 1970s, when he was a young lawyer in Miami, Paul was convicted of cocaine possession and of attempting to defraud the Cuban government out of $8.7 million. He served three years in federal prison and was suspended from legal practice.

Paul would later claim in press accounts and to Lee that his conviction arose out of top-secret work he had performed for the CIA involving a U.S.-sponsored plot to overthrow Fidel Castro. In one telling of this story, Paul said he had been framed by a rival government agency; in another, he laid the blame on communist sympathizers. No evidence has surfaced to confirm either version of events. After his release from prison, Paul moved to Los Angeles and spent the late 1980s rehabilitating his image through charity work. He cozied up to personalities such as Jimmy Stewart and former astronaut Buzz Aldrin, and for a time managed the career of romance-novel cover boy Fabio.

Paul's timing in hooking up with Stan was fortuitous. In the course of its Chapter 11 reorganization, Marvel had voided all of its contracts, including Lee's lifetime employment agreement. In fall 1998, the company's new managers offered him a two-year deal at a substantially reduced salary. Lee, sensing that he was being low-balled, brought in a lawyer to negotiate for more favorable terms. Given all of its then-recent turmoil, Marvel held a fairly weak bargaining position. Stan, on the other hand, had more leverage than he realized. Marvel was facing the prospect that terminating Lee's employment contract could also be construed as terminating a license that he had granted for the use of his characters. If that turned out to be the case, then the ownership rights to Spider-Man, the Fantastic Four, and the majority of the Marvel universe could possibly revert back to Stan, leaving the company bereft of its most valuable properties. That path would undoubtedly have led to years of litigation, which Lee might well have lost in the end. He was, after all, a Marvel employee in the 1960s, making his cocreations "work for hire." But a claim by Lee to his heroes would, at the very least, have cast a cloud on the copyrights of Marvel's primary assets at a time when it was struggling to regain its financial footing. To keep the stream of movie and licensing deals flowing, Marvel needed unencumbered title to its characters. In addition, the last thing the company wanted was another public-relations black eye, which it would have inevitably suffered by taking on its septuagenarian spokesman—the living symbol of Marvel Comics—in open court.

Marvel's corporate bosses quickly saw the wisdom of keeping Stan happy. His revised employment agreement, which he signed in

November 1998, was a considerable improvement over their initial offer. Under the terms of the contract, which once again covered his lifetime, Lee became the chairman emeritus of Marvel and his annual salary jumped to $810,000, increasing to a yearly maximum of $1 million as of November 1, 2002. Upon his death, Lee's wife, Joan, would continue to receive a pension of $500,000 per year for the rest of her life. The deal called for Lee to continue his promotional duties by attending comic-book conventions, giving speeches, and sitting for media interviews. He also stayed on as writer of the Spider-Man comic strip, for which he collected an additional $125,000 annually. Remarkably, given that Stan was no longer the point person in Hollywood, the agreement included a clause entitling him to 10 percent of the company's profits from movie and TV deals involving Marvel characters, as well as an "executive producer" credit on all productions. Back in 1998, when Marvel still had a horrendous track record on the big screen, that clause must have seemed insignificant. But later, once the millions of dollars started rolling in from *X-Men* and *Spider-Man*, it would cause a souring of Lee's relationship with his lifelong employer.

In exchange for all this cash and consideration, Stan signed over to Marvel complete and absolute rights to what was described in oppressive legalese as "any and all ideas, names, titles, characters, symbols, logos, designs, likenesses, visual representations, artwork, stories, plots, scripts, comic books or comic strips, episodes, [and] literary property" that he ever had a hand in, as well as "the conceptual universe related thereto." Marvel could rest easy: Stan's leverage was gone. Barring a contractual breach on the company's part, neither Lee nor his heirs could ever try to claim ownership of any of its properties. Lee didn't give up everything, though. He retained the rights to his own name and likeness, as well as the phrases "Stan Lee Presents" and "Excelsior!" More important, his new arrangement was nonexclusive, which meant that he could engage in activities that competed with Marvel's interests. He could even start his own company.

Peter Paul proposed a venture that suited the times—a dot-com built on the Stan Lee brand. As he had done at Marvel, Lee would create a legion of superheroes to appear in a series of short Flash-based animations called "Webisodes." The comic-book style storylines, blessed by Stan's touch, promised to revolutionize on-line entertainment and to pull in millions of eyeballs. Lee's main task was to build franchises; even if they stunk, licensees would come calling because of his good name and past accomplishments. Stan Lee Media's revenue model, as precarious as anything else in the Net economy, depended on advertising, sponsorship, and merchandising, with eventual plans for video games, cartoon shows, and movies. An early business plan projected a profit of $21.2 million on revenue of $119 million in 2004. Paul wasn't bashful: He predicted the company would displace Disney as a creator and marketer of kiddie brands.

Stan Lee Media opened its doors in January 1999 with three employees and $1 million in seed money. The company grew fast, numbering forty staffers by that summer. Lee was the creative head, directing the development of the first Web series, "The 7th Portal," about a multicultural group of software beta testers who battle an invading force of villains on the Internet. Paul handled the business end, although his felony conviction prohibited him from serving as an officer of the company. He ran the operation labeled as a consultant for strategic planning, business development, and new media.

Paul wanted to go public right away, but he encountered resistance from venture capitalists and investment bankers. "Raising money for a company that's built around a seventy-six-year-old man is a big challenge," Paul said. "I was advised and counseled that I could never take the company public because of that." Lacking strong backers to carry the firm through an IPO, Paul orchestrated a backdoor method of going public by merging with a publicly traded shell company named Boulder Capital Opportunities. This "reverse merger," which was carried out in August 1999, gave Stan Lee Media immediate access to stock-market capital, and gave day traders and comic-book aficionados a chance to own a piece of Stan Lee.

On its first day of trading, the share price rose 40 percent to $9. Lee proved as adept as ever at attracting publicity, with articles appearing everywhere from *USA Today* to *Time* magazine, the difference now being that every write-up gave a boost not only to his celebrity but also to his stock. Paul struck partnerships with a slew of companies, including IBM, software maker Macromedia, and Acme City, a Web site owned by Time Warner. Iwerks Entertainment signed on to turn "The 7th Portal" into an effects-laden theme-park ride. In February 2000, Stan Lee Media announced a deal to produce comic books and Webisodes starring pop-music stars Backstreet Boys; the company's stock zoomed up to $31, giving Stan, however briefly, a net worth on paper of $100 million.

As the projects multiplied, dozens of writers, Web designers, and animators were hired on. The firm swelled to 150 employees and took over the top floor and a portion of the ground level of an office building. Paul spared no expense promoting the Stan Lee brand and sustaining the illusion of a thriving company. To celebrate the launch of "The 7th Portal," he threw a 700-person party at Raleigh Studios, a Hollywood screening house, with performances by Jerry Lee Lewis, Chaka Khan, and Perry Farrell. Actors James Caan, George Hamilton, and Lou Ferrigno were in attendance to watch Larry King and director James Cameron pay tribute to Lee. President Clinton sent a letter of congratulations. Stan later traveled to East Asia with CEO Ken Williams to hammer out global licensing deals and to address a group of Chinese and Japanese cartoonists in the Great Hall of China.

But for all the glitz and publicity, Stan Lee Media was in terrible financial shape. Surviving from month to month, it was always desperate to secure more financing. The company burned through millions of dollars per month with little to show for its efforts. In the first quarter of 2000 it posted a net loss of $5.4 million on revenue of $296,000. As was typical of Internet start-ups, chaos reigned: the company seemed to be going in too many directions at once—on-line games, comic books, TV shows, even a Stan Lee line of clothing. An air of uncertainty and mild paranoia surrounded the enterprise. Visitors to the offices were required to sign a nondisclosure agreement. Paul, who owned 27 percent of the company through various trusts, kept tight control of Lee's "face time" with the media. There was also a general tendency to hype the operation with a confusing patter of new-media jargon. "We think out of the box here," Paul proclaimed. "Our role is to enable the utilization of a convergent team of multidisciplinary media talents to be focused on any appropriate activity that integrates the best aspects of the Internet with off-line activities to create a holistic approach to certain strategic objectives."

Stan played as big a part in the buildup as anyone else, and he put on a brave face for dot-com doubters. "I never worried when comic-book companies were going out of business," he said. "As long as what we're doing is entertaining, people will like it." Lee's Webisodes, with their herky-jerky animation, bizarrely named characters (Imitatia, Mongorr, Krog), and warmed-over plots, were a pale shadow of his previous works. They are unlikely to be remembered as anything more than a footnote in the tale of the brief, strange trip he took through the dot-com zeitgeist in his declining years. Even if they had been great, though, Stan Lee Media was on the wrong track; on-line animation companies were among the first to die when the Internet economy went south. But back in June 2000, sitting in his executive office decorated with a Spider-Man tapestry and a poster advertising his 1972 show at Carnegie Hall, Lee seemed genuinely excited to be back in the fray.

One day that month, he sat down with four staffers, ranging in age from twenty-seven to forty-four, to discuss an upcoming Webisode of "The Accuser." The Web animation series, another Lee creation, featured a wheelchair-bound lawyer who uses an armored battle suit, à la Iron Man, to fight crime. Reviewing a storyboard, Lee edited dialogue and reordered frames to make the show more vivid, more madcap—more Stan.

"On this picture here," Lee said, pointing to a page, "we've gotta change his expression. He looks like he's smiling there. He's gotta look like this." Lee pulled his arms to his chest and roared. As the plot thickened, he threw himself further into the scene. "We have them yelling, 'The Accuser, get 'im!'" Lee leaped to his feet, voice booming. "And he goes, 'Sorry guys, I'm the getter; you're the gettee!'"

In the corridors of Stan Lee Media, his enthusiasm was infectious. Many of his employees were longtime fans thrilled to be working with their childhood idol. "My whole reason for taking this job was because of Stan," said Tramm Wigzell, who was a production coordinator for "The Accuser." "You grow up in this country and you're a guy, it's kind of hard not to love Stan Lee."

That love didn't necessarily extend to the world at large. His critics questioned his Web credentials and dismissed him as a new-media carnival barker. "Stan Lee and the Internet economy are both creations of a superheated, overinflated, hyperbolic cultural environment," commented Gary Groth, editor of *The Comics Journal.* "It's a match made in heaven."

Some wondered if Lee's distinctive style of wisecracking, bombastic storytelling would strike a chord with a youthful audience accustomed to violent and sexually explicit entertainment. Stan, who didn't smoke or drink, had once named a character "Mary Jane" without realizing the drug-culture double entendre. By the standards of post-millenial pop culture, he was a square and kind of clueless. "I don't like too much violence," he said. "To me there's a great difference between an action-packed story and a violent story, and I don't like to do things that I don't feel I could say to any parent, honestly, 'Your child could read that.'" And yet, Stan Lee Media was planning an animated Web series for the RZA, who raps about shooting his rivals and kicking his "bitch to the curb." Did that concern Lee? Not at all, he said. "If they're popular with young people, I don't mind being associated with them. Maybe in our own way, we can turn them away from gangsta rapping."

The end for Stan Lee Media came swiftly and without public warning. By November 2000, the Internet economy had lost its luster. Dot-com issues were tanking on Nasdaq and venture capital was drying up. Stan Lee Media had run through most of its money and was struggling to stay afloat. Company executives reached an agreement for $2.2 million in short-term financing, but the deal came with a catch: the firm's share price had to stay above $1. Since the stock had been trading in the $7-to-$9 range, that stipulation appeared to pose no real threat.

Then, on November 27, for reasons that would become clear only later, Stan Lee Media's stock tumbled to $3 a share. The next day, it fell again to $1.75. Investors, alarmed by the sudden surge of activity, began a massive sell-off and the stock dropped below $1. By December 18, when Nasdaq officials halted trading of Stan Lee Media, it had nose-dived to 13 cents a share. Nearly $100 million of market capitalization had evaporated in less than three weeks.

Stan Lee's dot-com dream was over. Unable to claim its short-term financing, the company ceased production on December 15 and fired most of its staff. On the day of the layoffs, Lee was reportedly so distressed that he collapsed. His ex-employees, however, bore him no apparent ill will. As they were cleaning out their desks, a seven-foot-tall Spider-Man statue that they had ordered from Germany for Stan's birthday arrived at the office. Amid the desperate backing up of files and packing of desktop tchotchkes, they assembled the statue and passed around a card, filling it with good wishes for their former boss.

The story got worse. On January 2, 2001, Stan Lee Media, now reduced to Lee and a few executives, revealed that the Securities and Exchange Commission was investigating its stock transactions. It also disclosed that it had terminated Peter Paul's consulting agreement and that Stephen Gordon, the former executive vice president of operations, had been fired. The company suspected that its downfall had resulted from a financial deception perpetrated by Paul and Gordon. When the authorities moved in several months later, they arrested Gordon and several accomplices. Peter Paul, long gone, had relocated to Brazil.

According to federal indictments that were later filed against Paul and Gordon, the two men were at the center of a convoluted scheme involving stock manipulation, fraud, and check kiting that cost Stan Lee Media investors and financial institutions more than $35 million. Paul and Gordon, who had been business associates since 1997, allegedly inflated the price of the company's stock through a variety of methods that included making misleading statements to the press and hiring a Wall Street analyst named Jeffrey Pittsburg to plug the company in phony research reports. In one such report, issued April 28, 2000, when the stock was trading at $13 and the company had just posted a first-year net loss of $7.9 million, Pittsburg recommended Stan Lee Media as a "strong buy" and set a $75-per-share price target. In exchange for his "financial services," Pittsburg received a $20,000 retainer plus $8,000 per month, prosecutors said.

Paul and Gordon also opened accounts with Merrill Lynch and used them to borrow millions of dollars on margin, putting up Stan Lee Media shares as collateral. This effectively allowed them to convert their stock to cash without selling it outright, which, because the company was so thinly traded, would have significantly lowered the market price. Through sham companies, Paul and Gordon funneled more than $2 million of the borrowed money to Stan Lee Media, giving the appearance that the start-up had strong backing from outside investors when in reality it did not. "The financial arrangements for this company were built on quicksand," said Assistant U.S. Attorney David Seide. They spent the rest of the money on down payments for luxury homes and other personal items, according to court documents. Gordon's brother, Jonathan Gordon, who was then a broker at a Los Angeles branch of Merrill Lynch, helped clear many of the loan transactions. At the same time, he received $340,000 in under-the-table payments.

In October 2000, Merrill Lynch noticed that Paul and Gordon were over-leveraged and requested repayment on their loans, which by then totaled $5 million. Unable to come up with the money, the pair began writing hundreds of checks from empty bank accounts, creating the illusion that the loan balance was decreasing when in fact it was just being shifted around, according to the indictments. Eventually, they expanded the check-kiting operation to accounts at other banks. Over the course of a month, prosecutors said, they wrote more than $30 million worth of bad checks, causing an estimated $10 million in losses to three financial institutions.

Meanwhile, Paul and Gordon were selling large blocks of Stan Lee Media stock in order to demonstrate to Merrill Lynch that they were liquidating their shares for cash to repay their loans. In reality, though, Paul and Gordon were artificially propping up the market price by secretly buying back their own shares through Pittsburg and Charles Kusche, a Connecticut-based stock promoter, according to court documents and testimony. As Stan Lee executives, Paul and Gordon were limited by SEC regulations in how much of their company's stock they could sell. They sidestepped this restriction by using accounts in other names and paying Pittsburg and Kusche 55 percent of the share value to purchase and find other buyers for the stock, according to court documents. In this way, Paul and Gordon were able to conceal the fact that they were simultaneously buying and selling the shares. In late November, when they could no longer afford to buy back the stock they were selling, the share price declined, triggering a margin call by another brokerage firm from which Paul had secured a loan. The firm dumped more than 170,000

Paul-controlled shares, sparking the November 27 plunge. Stan Lee Media's stock price went into free fall and never recovered. The company filed for bankruptcy in February 2001.

Stephen Gordon was convicted in December 2002, along with his brother Jonathan, of fraud charges related to the check-kiting scheme. He faced additional charges in New York, with Pittsburg and Kusche, for stock manipulation. Peter Paul was arrested in Brazil in August 2001. He was extradited back to the United States in 2003 to stand trial.

Stan Lee had no apparent involvement in any of the financial wrongdoing surrounding his defunct company. Throughout his career, Lee has never shown a strong interest in business, and his Internet venture was no different. "He would sit in business meetings and occasionally say something," a friend of Lee's told *The Industry Standard*. "But mainly he'd sit there and doodle, or fall asleep." In the aftermath of Stan Lee Media's collapse, Lee uncharacteristically shied away from the press, issuing a steady stream of "no comment"s to reporters trying to reconstruct how it all went wrong. Stan has few equals when it comes to publicity on the upswing; damage control isn't really his thing. But he was clearly hurt by the incident and the disloyalty of his friend. Lee had treasured Paul's guidance and friendship. "He's the greatest partner a guy could have," Lee once declared. Now all of it—the big staff, the Hollywood parties, the multimillion-dollar stock wealth—was gone in a flash of duplicity. The Stan Lee brand had taken a beating. In his memoir, he remarked ruefully: "I'll never be so stupidly trusting again."

PART IX

"IF THIS BE MY DESTINY"

STAN THE MAN

It's difficult to divorce Stan Lee's legacy in the firmament of American pop culture from the bottom line. Marvel Enterprises is a film juggernaut. Movies based on the company's characters had grossed $722 million in domestic box-office receipts by the start of 2003, a year that brought three more major studio releases based on heroes cocreated by Lee. In the depleted but still active comic-book market, Marvel Comics dominates the sales charts. In January 2003, twenty-three of the thirty most ordered comic-book titles sold in North America were published by Marvel. Twenty of those comics featured characters cocreated by Stan Lee or fostered by Marvel during a period in which Lee still enjoyed a significant measure of editorial input. Licensing remains strong, too, fueled by the recent spate of Marvel movie hits. Such ancillary revenues have consistently hit eight-figure sums per quarter since mid-2000.

Stan Lee helped build a formidable entertainment empire. The settings and characters that he shepherded into existence are as significant and varied as the cross-media worlds offered up by the likes of George Lucas, Gene Roddenberry, or J. K. Rowling. Marvel Comics survives with no end in sight despite years of creative exhaustion, the rise of competing media, and Ron Perelman's aggressive leveraging of its properties. This, more than anything else, is a testament to the enduring appeal of the publishing style Lee brought to those books in the 1960s. Marvel will no doubt continue to exist, at least in its character-creation capacity, for as long as there are concepts to be mined for more popular media and audiences to be entertained with hero stories that seek to engage on both a fantastic and a human level. That movie audiences in 2002 connected with Spider-Man despite his being invented forty years earlier speaks promisingly of the longevity of the core Marvel characters and concepts. Stan Lee helped create something that will long outlive him, and in this way his legacy is assured.

Stan Lee's artistic legacy is more difficult to pin down. His weakest claim to significance comes in the area for which he is best known publicly—as a creator of lively and provocative characters and concepts. Because many of the artists whom he worked with are either dead or very old, and because it was years before the question was raised, the precise creative contribution that Lee made to each individual Marvel character will probably never be known. Despite public opinion and press-release hype, the overwhelming balance of existing testimony and textual analysis indicates that most of the popular Marvel characters were group efforts. According to testimony from John Romita and Gil Kane, two artists who worked with Lee in the 1960s, Stan's contribution to new characters was sometimes little more than a name on a piece of paper or an allusion to a popular movie actor. And Lee readily admits that the Silver Surfer and a few other key heroes weren't his in their original forms. Even those creations that Lee may have conceived wholly on paper before they saw realization in comic-book form, such as the Fantastic Four, changed greatly between Stan's conception and their eventual publication. Marvel's artists, by dint of their own skill and the nature of the collaborative Marvel Method, were not just interpreters of a singular vision, but active participants in creating characters and storylines. This is particularly true of Jack Kirby and Steve Ditko, whose unique contributions to story and character linger on in the Marvel line just as significantly as ideas that can be traced directly to Lee.

Stan Lee's primary artistic contribution was in the dialogue. Lee was a great believer in characterization, as were Kirby and Ditko. But what neither of those artists could do was improve on the flat, declarative writing style that comics had relied on since the medium's birth. The early Marvel comics featured loopy one-liners, combative verbal interplay between heroes and villains, and such bombastic look-at-me narrative tools as frequent alliteration and rough cribbing of familiar literary phrases. Lee was working years ahead of the boring conversations and stale captions to be found in the typical *Superman* or *Batman* comic book, and his writing style displayed a refreshing self-awareness that was extremely rare in the superhero genre. "That mock irreverence was just right for the period," Kane noted in 1994. Lee's gently conspiratorial way of speaking to his audience brought a new kind of reader into comic books—readers who got the joke, fans who appreciated the morality plays and fistfights for their theatricality rather than solely at face value. This helped Lee and Marvel to retain readers well into adulthood. One entertainment experience for the dedicated fan, one for the casual—it was a model for attracting audiences that would come to dominate popular entertainment over the next three decades. Some fans watch the *Star Wars* movies and dream of being Han Solo; others take in the films with thoughts of becoming the next George Lucas. Stan Lee's dialogue played to both groups of readers.

Although the issue of creative credit has clouded Lee's legacy among industry professionals, his initial choice to depend on Marvel's artists in the 1960s was one of the smartest moves he made in a vastly underappreciated editorial career. Lee was a magnificent comic-book editor. John Romita calls him "the best editor in comics history." In the days when comic books were true mainstream entertainment, derivative and puerile, Stan was as quick and productive on his own as some fully staffed editorial teams. He paid close attention to storytelling formula and very little to innovation. When Martin Goodman's 1957 distribution deal with DC raised the stakes on the value of each editorial move and provided more lead time to develop features, Lee took advantage of the opportunity and shaped two line revamps—monster-driven science fiction and "new" superheroes. These moves maximized sales of individual books through improved content and helped the devastated line survive long enough to make its comeback. By drawing on the creative contributions of his talented freelance artists through the Marvel Method, even if the motivation was to stabilize profit for less work, Lee helped move the American comic away from the drawn-story model that dominated several publishing-house styles and back into a love affair with its roots as a compelling visual medium, at once decorative and cinematic. When *The Fantastic Four* and the other early-Marvel titles began to post strong sales and to garner fervent fan support, Stan was able to grasp what Marvel was doing right and to replicate it across an entire line. Lee practically stumbled onto a formula for success, but once he did, he quickly charted its parameters and converted it into a house style. Motivating underappreciated illustrators such as Kirby and Ditko to produce groundbreaking work was a major accomplishment. But equally impressive was Lee's ability to get less distinctive artists such as Don Heck and Werner Roth to work in close approximations of those styles, while encouraging idiosyncratic visual stylists such as Jim Steranko and Neal Adams to build on them. Stan Lee helped create the content of the Marvel Comics empire, and then turned around and molded the franchising of that content in ways that sustained and even enhanced their popularity. Few entertainment figures have participated as fully in their own branding process.

But who wants to be known as the world's savviest comic-book editor? Even simply writing a comic book seems a somewhat dubious enterprise, no matter how important that writing may have been. The popular perception has long been that comic books are pictures with a few words added for effect—take away the words, and a page of comic-book art is still recognizable as such. There were uncomfortable moments in Lee's early promotional work when he acknowledged that he did not, in fact, draw the comic books in question. It's as if Lee was fully aware that he'd be unable to explain his contribution in a way that would make sense to a studio audience or a crestfallen host. Combined with Marvel's desire to give credit to whom was least likely to sue—by keeping it in the family—Stan Lee became more and more publicly known as the creative visionary behind Marvel's comic books rather than the man who gave them a voice. It was a betrayal of his collaborators by accretion of publicity, and thus hard to nail down to a single event when Stan might have gone too far. In fact, the inexact nature of ongoing public relations like Marvel's, and the perceived good that the glib, appealing Lee was doing on behalf of the company and the medium, are often cited by his defenders in a kind of shrugged-shoulder defense of his lack of generosity. Any move that Lee makes to publicly acknowledge his cocreators—correcting Larry King by mentioning Jack Kirby, dropping a name or two to *Time* magazine—is portrayed as his doing all he can to make things right for his fellow creators in the face of the pernicious laziness of media reporters. For some, this drives resentment even further. Although "Stan Lee Presents" neatly encapsulates Lee's numerous, general, and hard-to-quantify contributions to the original Marvel Comics, some artists remain indignant that the slogan was used in the 1970s, when Lee's creative input was largely absent. Since formally leaving Marvel's editorial operations in the late 1970s, Lee has spent a lot of TV and radio time stumping on behalf of characters he had absolutely no part in creating: Blade, Howard the Duck, Wolverine from the X-Men, even a homosexual re-imagining of the Rawhide Kid. In an era of diminished comic-book sales, Lee is paid more to talk about characters than Marvel pays most of the artists and writers who currently bring them to life. This may be a well-deserved reward for years of dutiful service, but it remains a bounty in which no other Marvel creator shares. It's no surprise, then, that where resentment for Lee exists, that resentment runs deep.

Lee has long played the victim when it comes to improving the industry on behalf of its creators. As a company man who also derived a significant portion of his income as a freelancer, and as a public figure benefiting from the success of Marvel's comic books, Stan was in a unique position to encourage improvement in the comics industry's deplorable track record concerning the treatment of its artists. Lee enjoyed a decent record as management dealing with talent. He was, by all accounts, a loyal editor, even hiring older artists who had done good work for him in the past and giving them assignments despite their diminished capacities. In the 1970s, Lee devoted one employee's time to returning original art pages from Marvel's vast storehouse, a hot-button issue at the time. But once he ascended to the management ranks in 1972, Lee seemed to side more and more with the businessmen who ran comics. Lee neither publicly supported those creators who objected to Editor in Chief Jim Shooter nor fought for Shooter to stay near the end of his editorial run. Stan's silence on the long and complicated struggle for Jack Kirby to see his art returned was massively disappointing to even Lee's biggest supporters. Despite Lee's protests—to Kirby and others—that there was little he could do, few who fought that particular battle of public relations and consumer pressure stepped up to support his position. Many of his peers and fellow professionals expected more from Lee than yet another suit in a war of neglect with the emerging comic-book artistic community. Lee failed them. By the end of the 1980s, Lee was so much a part of Marvel's larger public image that the feelings many had for him were dictated by whatever view they held of the company. A joyful, kindly uncle to millions of shy children in the 1960s and '70s, Stan Lee had become another corporate symbol of Marvel's marketplace dominance.

Stan Lee never wrote the Great American Novel. Worse, he seems to have fallen short of the qualities needed to write a fulfilling ending to his own improbable life story. After an eleven-year run managing a groundbreaking creative enterprise, in which he maximized the contributions of a varied team of artists and writers and turned them into a recognizable house style, Lee attempted to parlay his success into a solo act. His creative output since 1972 has been littered with failed efforts to become a Hollywood idea generator, both on behalf of Marvel and on his own. Yet Lee's writing on most of his scripts, cards, and treatments reads less like the savvy, sharp work of a writer simply denied his shot at screenwriting stardom than the naive and hopeful jottings of an eager wannabe, like entries in a diary kept by a schoolboy with big studio dreams. Even Lee's treatments of Marvel characters like Thor and the Silver Surfer lack an understanding of the potential of his own work that has since been reflected back at him by fans-turned-moviemakers such as *Spider-Man* scribe David Koepp and *X-Men* director Bryan Singer.

Marvel Comics were never noteworthy for the ideas on display, but for their glorious, clever execution: Lee's funny, distanced dialogue; Steve Ditko's evocative moral authority; Jack Kirby's sense of wonder and power. Working under Stan Lee's guidance and driven in large part by his hopes for financial success and cultural celebrity, the men and women working at Marvel in the 1960s built the kind of multifaceted quirky pop art that sustains entertainment enterprises. In lingering on for decades as the celebrity presence responsible for those efforts, Lee has managed to carve an unlikely career as creator emeritus for a body of work so broad it both exaggerates his public reputation and obscures his actual artistic contri-bution. Lee was briefly the most interesting creator in the comic-book art form. But the value of that legacy has faded, just as the American comic-book industry has faded. A story created from thirty-five years of press releases will always enjoy greater currency than one assembled from a nuanced understanding of an art form, more so when that art form is too far removed from the cultural mainstream for the public to appreciate the details.

Stan Lee's belief in Stan Lee gave him a life where a mansion's view of greater Los Angeles replaced a Bronx apartment's back-alley wall. But it also cost him any real chance of developing some-thing of his own, and it created an almost impenetrable block of half-truths and obfuscation that protects and inflates the reputation of the man doing the work at the cost of an honest consideration of the work itself. Stan Lee stands larger than life, lighter than air, and thinner than the pulp on which he made his name—a dispos-able product that better exists in our collective memories than under the yellowing light of serious examination. But, thanks in large part to Marvel Comics, we expect our heroes to have feet of clay.

EVER UPWARD

On a Wednesday morning in July 2002, five months before his eightieth birthday, Stan Lee sat in his office at MGM Plaza in Santa Monica. Clad in a checkered gray shirt, khaki pants, and white tennis shoes, Lee was worn out from weeks of media interviews for the *Spider-Man* movie, but he was doing his best to be agreeable. The conversation turned to a discussion of the ethnic roots of American comic books and the many Jewish artists, including Jack Kirby and Gil Kane, who signed their work with pseudonyms.

"I always loved the name Stanley Martin Lieber," Lee said. "I never thought of it as a Jewish name. I thought it was a very beautiful name. In fact, let me show you something. . . . " He stood up, retrieved a pad of paper and a pen from his desk, and installed himself next to a reporter on the office couch. "When I had nothing to do, I used to doodle by signing my name, over and over again. . . . I still remember the way I signed it. I signed it this way. . . . " He inscribed the name "Stanley Martin Lieber" in broad cursive script, and stared at it for a moment. "I always thought that was such a beautiful signature," he went on. "I would do it over and over again when I was listening to the radio, when the teacher was talking, whatever. I thought it looked so great. I was very proud of my name. I thought it was the greatest signature in the world. I was very unhappy when I changed it legally to Stan Lee, but I only did it because our lives were getting too confusing."

Recently, the life of Stan Lee, né Stanley Martin Lieber, had gone from confusing to downright hectic. The box-office success of *Spider-Man* had granted him another round of public visibility, neatly wiping away the embarrassing circumstances surrounding the downfall of his Internet venture. Lee's newly formed POW! Entertainment had signed a first-look agreement with MGM for movie and TV projects based on his non-Marvel concepts. An animated series called *Stripperella*, featuring the voice of Pamela Anderson, was in the works, as were several film deals with Bruce Willis's Cheyenne Enterprises. Stan's office, decorated with a life-size Spider-Man statue and littered with copies of the *Hollywood Reporter* and *Daily Variety*, shared a suite with the production companies run by director John Woo and actor Pierce Brosnan.

After more than twenty years of false starts and dead ends, Lee was still chasing his Hollywood dream. For all that he had accomplished as a comic-book writer and editor, all the artistic triumphs and fame, he felt incomplete. He had landed in comics by accident. He was young, hungry for work; it could have been anything else. Sometimes he wishes it *had* been something else. "I wish I had come to Hollywood and been a screenwriter," Lee said. "I wish I had the time to be a novelist. I think I could have done better. I mean, I would have loved to have written a great novel. I would have loved to have written a great bunch of screenplays. I would have loved to have written a Broadway show. I didn't have any big compulsion to write comics. It was a way of making a living." Would he trade in all of his achievements in comic books to have done those things? Lee paused, then responded, "It's a question that there is no answer to, because I'll never have a chance. God isn't coming and saying, 'Do you want to start again?' If he did, I don't know, I might . . . I might be interested in trying again."

Stan Lee is an old man, but he doesn't spend much time dwelling on his mortality. He's too busy for self-reflection. He's pitching movies, attending comics conventions, and punching the part-time clock at Marvel to earn his million-dollar-a-year salary. Even at this late stage in his career, Stan makes the news. In November 2002 he filed a $10-million lawsuit against Marvel, claiming the company had cheated him out of his cut of the profits from the *Spider-Man* film. According to the suit, Lee's 1998 employment contract entitled him to 10 percent of Marvel's profits from the use of its characters in movies and TV shows. Lee still hadn't received a penny from the billion-dollar-grossing *Spider-Man*, and he was concerned that he would also be shut out of the earnings from the 2003 films *Daredevil*, *The Hulk*, and *X2: X-Men United*. "It's like Colonel Sanders suing Kentucky Fried Chicken," quipped one observer.

Stan stayed out of the limelight when his lawsuit was filed, offering no media comments. He was reportedly too depressed about the imbroglio with his lifelong employer to talk about it in public. For its part, Marvel issued a prepared statement: "Mr. Lee has made contributions to Marvel and the comic-book industry in the past, for which he continues to be well compensated. Marvel believes it is in full compliance with, and current on all payments due under, the terms of Mr. Lee's employment agreement and will continue to be so in the future. However, Marvel does not comment on either pending litigation or threatened future actions." As of spring 2004, the case of *Stan Lee v. Marvel Enterprises, Inc. and Marvel Characters, Inc.*, was still pending.

Many years ago, when Stan was in his late fifties, he wrote a letter to his accountant regarding an ad he had seen in the paper for municipal bond issues that paid 7.4 percent tax free. "Does that sound like something to consider for my forthcoming 'pension fund?'" Lee asked. He needn't have worried. Pensions are for retirees, and he doesn't plan on retiring anytime soon. "I'm aware that there's got to be a time when I'm not going to be able to do this," he says. "But I hope that time is far off, because I'm really enjoying what I'm doing." He laughs. "Somewhere inside of this old body, there's a young guy trapped, trying to get out."

At some moments, Stan seems as youthful as ever, punctuating his statements with kinetic body movements, flicking his finger and thumb impatiently while he talks. But there are other times when Lee, with his white mustache and thinning gray-white hair, appears every bit the octogenarian. When he removes his trademark tinted glasses, the years are etched clearly in the wrinkles around his eyes. Pop culture has changed, too, abounding with violent and erotic fare that, at the end of the day, is beyond Stan's range as a writer.

Today's comic-book industry is virtually unrecognizable. Marvel bills itself as a "licensing-based entertainment company." DC is a subsidiary of AOL Time Warner. The comics themselves are disconnected from any sense of a larger readership. They're more stylishly illustrated, to be sure, but they indulge in recycled thrills made stale by years of repetition in service to their value as licensing properties. Gone forever is the feeling of open-ended possibility, of freeform fantasy willed onto a blank page, of giddy, self-aware, and slightly moralistic fun that Lee and his artistic collaborators brought to an art form lacking respect. Comic books are past the point of decline. The top titles struggle to sell 125,000 copies. Kids prefer to buy anything and everything else, and at $2.25 per issue, it's not certain they could afford to return.

Even Stan Lee doesn't read comic books anymore. He doesn't have the time.

SOURCE NOTES

Stan Lee cooperated in the reporting of this book by generously making himself available for several interviews, but he did not authorize its content. Coauthor Jordan Raphael interviewed Lee for newspaper and magazine articles prior to undertaking this project, and that material was used as well. Dozens of Lee's friends and former colleagues agreed to be interviewed, and they are identified below. Copies of Lee's personal and business correspondence were obtained from the Stan Lee Archives at the University of Wyoming's American Heritage Center.

Historical comic-book information, such as cover dates and circulation figures, came from the 2000 edition of *The Overstreet Comic Book Price Guide* and *The Standard Catalog of Comic Books*. Other books that were extremely helpful include Stan Lee and George Mair's *Excelsior! The Amazing Life of Stan Lee*, Les Daniels's *Marvel: Five Fabulous Decades of the World's Greatest Comics*, Mike Benton's *The Comic Book in America: An Illustrated History*, and Steve Duin and Mike Richardson's *Comics: Between the Panels*.

In the following list, sources are listed on a chapter-by-chapter basis. "AI" indicates material from interviews conducted by the authors.

CHAPTER 1: STANLEY LIEBER

AI: Stan Lee, Bob Wendlinger, Jean Goodman.

Daniels, Les. *Marvel: Five Fabulous Decades of the World's Greatest Comics.* New York: Harry N. Abrams, 1993.

Dewitt Clinton High School yearbook, 1939.

Faherty, Tim. "The Amazing Stan Lee Interview," *P.S.* December 14, 1977.

Kraft, David Anthony. "The *FOOM* Interview, Stan Lee," *FOOM*. March 1977.

Lee, Stan. Interview by Barbara Bogaev, *Fresh Air.* June 4, 2002.

Lee, Stan, and George Mair. *Excelsior! The Amazing Life of Stan Lee.* New York: Fireside, 2002.

New York Herald Tribune. March 1936–June 1938.

Raphael, Jordan. "The Invincible Stan Lee?" *Los Angeles Times Magazine.* July 16, 2000.

Thomas, Roy. "A Conversation with Artist-Writer Larry Lieber," *Alter Ego.* Fall 1999.

CHAPTER 2: MARTIN'S COUSIN-IN-LAW

Benton, Mike. *The Comic Book in America: An Illustrated History.* Dallas, TX: Taylor Publishing Company, 1989.

Benton, Mike. *Masters of Imagination: The Comic Book Artists Hall of Fame.* Dallas, TX: Taylor Publishing Company, 1994.

Daniels, Les. *Marvel: Five Fabulous Decades of the World's Greatest Comics.* New York: Harry N. Abrams, 1993.

Feiffer, Jules. *The Great Comic Book Heroes.* New York: The Dial Press, 1965.

Gifford, Denis. "Obituary: Martin Goodman," *The Independent* (London). June 15, 1992.

Harvey, Robert C. *The Art of the Comic Book: An Aesthetic History.* Jackson, MS: University Press of Mississippi, 1996.

Horn, Maurice (editor). *100 Years of American Newspaper Comics: An Illustrated Encyclopedia.* New York: Gramercy Books, 1996.

Simon, Joe, with Jim Simon. *The Comic Book Makers.* New York: Crestwood/II Publications, 1990.

Waugh, Coulton. *The Comics.* New York: The Macmillan Company, 1947.

CHAPTER 3: STAN LEE, PLAYWRIGHT

AI: Stan Lee.

Amash, Jim. " 'I Let People Do Their Jobs!': A Conversation with Vince Fago," *Alter Ego.* November 2001.

Amash, Jim. "A Long Glance at Dave Gantz," *Alter Ego.* March 2002.

Bell, Blake. *"I Have to Live with This Guy!"* Raleigh, NC: TwoMorrows Publishing, 2002.

Benton, Mike. *The Comic Book in America: An Illustrated History.* Dallas, TX: Taylor Publishing Company, 1989.

Daniels, Les. *Marvel: Five Fabulous Decades of the World's Greatest Comics.* New York: Harry N. Abrams, 1993.

Duin, Steve, and Mike Richardson. *Comics: Between the Panels.* Milwaukie, OR: Dark Horse Comics, 1998.

Harvey, Robert C. *The Art of the Comic Book: An Aesthetic History.* Jackson, MS: University Press of Mississippi, 1996.

Hewetson, Al. "Syd Shores, a Biography and Interview," *Alter Ego.* November 2001.

Lee, Stan. *Secrets Behind the Comics.* New York: Famous Enterprises, 1947.

Lee, Stan, and Jim Mooney. "The Ginch and Claude Pennygrabber," *Terry-Toons* #11. August 1943.

Pitts, Leonard Jr. Stan Lee interview. Unpublished, early 1980s.

Rattazzi, Delfina. "The Marvelous Stan Lee," *Andy Warhol's Interview.* March 1973.

Rowes, Barbara. Stan Lee profile, *People.* January 29, 1979.

Simon, Joe, with Jim Simon. *The Comic Book Makers.* New York: Crestwood/II Publications, 1990.

Vassallo, Dr. Michael J. "Vince Fago & The Timely/Marvel Funny Animal Dept. (1942–1945)," *Alter Ego.* March 2002.

Waugh, Coulton. *The Comics.* New York: The Macmillan Company, 1947.

CHAPTER 4: BRING ON THE BAD GUY

AI: Stan Lee, Dick Ayers, Gene Colan, Iden Goodman.

Bell, Blake. *"I Have to Live with This Guy!"* Raleigh, NC: TwoMorrows Publishing, 2002.

Comics Magazine Association of America. *Comics Code.* 1955.

Comics Magazine Association of America. *Comics Code* (Revised). 1971.

Decker, Dwight. "Fredric Wertham—Anti-Comics Crusader Who Turned Advocate." http://art-bin.com/art/awertham.html.

Feiffer, Jules. *The Great Comic Book Heroes.* New York: The Dial Press, 1965.

Groth, Gary. "Gil Kane Interview, Part I," *The Comics Journal.* October 1995.

"The Hewletts: A Four-Part Segment of the Five Towns," *Long Island Historical Journal.* www.lihistory.com.

Lee, Stan, and George Mair. *Excelsior! The Amazing Life of Stan Lee.* New York: Fireside, 2002.

"A Letter to Our Readers and Their Parents!" *Amazing Mysteries* #32. May 1949.

North, Sterling. "A National Disgrace," *Childhood Education.* May 8, 1940.

Nyberg, Amy Kiste. *Seal of Approval: A History of the Comics Code.* Jackson, MS: University Press of Mississippi, 1998.

Vassallo, Dr. Michael J. Original research, 2002.

Wertham, Fredric. *Seduction of the Innocent.* New York: Rinehart, 1954.

Wertham, Fredric. *A Sign for Cain: An Exploration of Human Violence.* New York: Macmillan, 1966.

CHAPTER 5: THE BIGGEST COMIC-BOOK COMPANY IN NORTH AMERICA

AI: Stan Lee, Gene Colan, John Romita, Bruce Jay Friedman, David Markson.

Brevoort, Tom (editor). *The Golden Age of Marvel Comics.* New York: Marvel Comics, 1997.

Daniels, Les. *Marvel: Five Fabulous Decades of the World's Greatest Comics.* New York: Harry N. Abrams, 1993.

Hollifield, Scott. *Marvel Comics Title Chronology.* www.samcci.comics.org/marvel.html.

Jaffee, Al. "Stan the Man," *The Comics Journal.* October 1995.

Lee, Stan, Jack Kirby, Steve Ditko, Dick Ayers, and Bill Everett. *Monster Masterworks.* New York: Marvel Comics, 1989.

Lee, Stan, and Stan Goldberg. "Kathy's Sensational Slacks!" *Kathy* #20. December 1962.

Lupoff, Dick, and Don Thompson. *All in Color for a Dime.* New Rochelle, NY: Arlington House, 1970.

Robbins, Trina. *A History of Women's Comics From Teens to Zines.* San Francisco, CA: Chronicle Books, 1999.

Sadowski, Greg. *B. Krigstein Volume I.* Seattle, WA: Fantagraphics Books, 2002.

Vassallo, Dr. Michael J. Original research, 2002.

Von Busack, Richard. "What Keeps Comic Books Alive Today," *San Jose Metro*, October 1999.

CHAPTER 6: JOLLY JACK AND STURDY STEVE

AI: Stan Lee, Gene Colan, Robert Katz.

Duin, Steve, and Mike Richardson. *Comics: Between the Panels.* Milwaukie, OR: Dark Horse Comics, 1998.

Groth, Gary. "Gil Kane Interview, Part I," *The Comics Journal.* October 1995.

Groth, Gary, Jack Kirby, and Roz Kirby, " 'I've Never Done Anything Halfheartedly,' " *The Comics Journal.* February 1990.

Harvey, Robert C. *The Art of the Comic Book: An Aesthetic History.* Jackson, MS: University Press of Mississippi, 1996.

Raphael, Jordan. "Spider-Man's Long-Lost Parent," *Los Angeles Times.* April 29, 2002.

Vassallo, Dr. Michael J. Original research, 2002.

CHAPTER 7: THE ESCAPIST

AI: Stan Lee, Gene Colan, Bruce Jay Friedman.

Daniels, Les. *Marvel: Five Fabulous Decades of the World's Greatest Comics.* New York: Harry N. Abrams, 1993.

Jones, Gerard, and Will Jacobs. *The Comic Book Heroes.* Rocklin, CA: Prima, 1996.

Lee, Stan. *Blushing Blurbs.* New York: Madison Publications, 1961.

Lee, Stan. *Golfers Anonymous.* New York: Madison Publications, 1961.

Lee, Stan. *More You Don't Say!* New York: Non-Pareil Publishing, 1963.

Lee, Stan. *Origins of Marvel Comics.* New York: Simon and Schuster, 1974.

Lee, Stan. "Twenty-Five Years? I Don't Believe It!" *The Comic Book Price Guide*, 16th edition. Cleveland, TN: Overstreet Publications, 1986.

Lee, Stan, and George Mair. *Excelsior! The Amazing Life of Stan Lee.* New York: Fireside, 2002.

CHAPTER 8: THE WORLD'S GREATEST COMIC MAGAZINE

Lee, Stan, and Jack Kirby. *The Fantastic Four* #1. November 1961.

CHAPTER 9: SECRET ORIGINS

AI: Stan Lee, John Romita, Dan Adkins.

Daniels, Les. *Comix: A History of Comic Books in America.* New York: Bonanza, 1971.

Daniels, Les. *Marvel: Five Fabulous Decades of the World's Greatest Comics.* New York: Harry N. Abrams, 1993.

Ditko, Steve. "Art!?," *Avenging World.* Robin Snyder and Steve Ditko, 2002.

Ditko, Steve. "An Insider's Part of Comics History, Jack Kirby's Spider-Man," *Avenging World.* Robin Snyder and Steve Ditko, 2002.

Duin, Steve, and Mike Richardson. *Comics: Between the Panels.* Milwaukie, OR: Dark Horse Comics, 1998.

Jones, Gerard, and Will Jacobs. *The Comic Book Heroes.* Rocklin, CA: Prima, 1996.

Lee, Stan. "How to Create a Cultural Legend in Your Spare Time," *Impact Magazine.* 1977.

Lee, Stan. Interview on *60 Minutes II*, "The Superheroes." October 30, 2002.

Lee, Stan. *Origins of Marvel Comics.* New York: Simon and Schuster, 1974.

Thomas, Roy. "A Fantastic First!" *Alter Ego Volume Two* #2. Reprinted in *Alter Ego—The Comic Book Artist Collection.* Raleigh, NC: TwoMorrows Publishing, 2001.

Vassallo, Dr. Michael J. Original research, 2002.

CHAPTER 10: WHAT MARVEL DID

Catron, Mike. "The Bob Haney Interview." Unpublished.

Dean, Mike. "Stan Lee and the Rebirth of the Superhero," *Origin Stories 2.* Doctoral Dissertation, University of Wisconsin, 2000.

Lee, Stan. *Origins of Marvel Comics.* New York: Simon and Schuster, 1974.

Lee, Stan, and Steve Ditko. *The Amazing Spider-Man.* 1962–65.

Lee, Stan, and Steve Ditko. "The Origin of Dr. Strange," *Strange Tales* #115. December 1963.

Lee, Stan, and Steve Ditko. "Spider-Man!," *Amazing Fantasy* #15. August 1962.

Lee, Stan, and Jack Kirby. *The Fantastic Four.* 1961–66.

Lee, Stan, and Jack Kirby. *The Incredible Hulk.* 1962–63.

CHAPTER 11: LIVE AND ON CAMPUS

AI: Stan Lee, Bill Schelly, Gary Groth.

Cooke, Jon B. "Flo Steinberg Interview, Absolutely Fabulous," *Comic Book Artist.* March 2002.

Finston, Mark N. "Comic Editor Climbs Princeton's Ivy," *Princeton Star-Ledger.* March 18, 1966.

Freedland, Nat. *New York.* January 9, 1966.

Hahn, Joel. "Comic Book Awards Almanac." www.enteract.com/~aardy/comics/awards.

Kamishlian, Isabelle, and J. Geoffrey Magnus. Letters to Stan Lee. Stan Lee Archives. March–May 1964.

Kempton, Sally. "The Super Anti-Hero in Forest Hills," *The Village Voice.* April 1, 1965.

Lee, Stan. Biographical Profile. Stan Lee Archives. Undated.

Lee, Stan. Letter in *The Comic Reader* #16. February 23, 1963.

Lee, Stan. Letter to Stewart Baker. May 15, 1969.

Lee, Stan. No-Prize Envelope. Stan Lee Archives.

Schelly, Bill. *The Golden Age of Comic Fandom.* Seattle, WA: Hamster Press, 1995.

Schelly, Bill. *Sense of Wonder.* Raleigh, NC: TwoMorrows Publishing, 2001.

Tulenko, Tim. Letter to Stan Lee. December 1965.

Wells, Earl. "Once and for All, Who Was the Author of Marvel?" *The Comics Journal Library: Jack Kirby.* Seattle, WA: Fantagraphics Books, 2002.

CHAPTER 12: STAN LEE, EDITOR

AI: Stan Lee, Scott Shaw, John Romita, Dan Adkins.

Amash, Jim. "Stan Goldberg on John Buscema," *Alter Ego Volume Three* #15. June 2002.

Gustaveson, Rob. "Fifteen Years at Marvel: An Interview with Roy Thomas," *The Comics Journal*. December 1980.

Jones, Gerard, and Will Jacobs. *The Comic Book Heroes*. Rocklin, CA: Prima, 1996.

Lee, Stan. "Bullpen Bulletin," printed in various Marvel Comics. November 2000.

Lee, Stan, and John Buscema. *The Essential Silver Surfer* (Reprint of 1968's *The Silver Surfer* comic book). New York: Marvel Comics, 1998.

Lee, Stan, and Steve Ditko. *The Amazing Spider-Man*. 1964–66.

Lee, Stan, and Jack Kirby. *The Fantastic Four*. 1965–68.

Raphael, Jordan. "Spider-Man's Long-Lost Parent," *Los Angeles Times*. April 29, 2002.

White, Ted. "A Conversation With the Man Behind Marvel Comics: Stan Lee," *Castle of Frankenstein* #12. 1968.

CHAPTER 13: MOVING ON UP

AI: Stan Lee, Gerry Conway, Steve Lemberg, Barbara Gittler Lemberg.

Comics Magazine Association of America. *Comics Code* (Revised). 1971.

Friedman, Bruce Jay. *Even the Rhinos Were Nymphos*. Chicago: University of Chicago Press, 2000.

Helper, Stefan. Letter to Stan Lee, regarding efforts to coordinate the presentation of anti-drug materials in comic books. Special Action Office for Drug Abuse Prevention, September 12, 1972.

Jones, Gerard, and Will Jacobs. *The Comic Book Heroes*. Rocklin, CA: Prima, 1996.

Lee, Stan, and George Mair. *Excelsior! The Amazing Life of Stan Lee*. New York: Fireside, 2002.

O'Neil, Dennis, and Neal Adams. *Green Lantern/Green Arrow* #76. April 1970.

Shooter, Jim. "Marvel and Me," *The Comic Book Price Guide*, 16th edition. Rocklin, CA: Overstreet Publications, 1986.

"Stan Lee at Carnegie Hall," advertisement, *New York Times*. December 12, 1971.

CHAPTER 14: FRIENDS OF NEW MARVEL

AI: Stan Lee, Steve Lemberg, Gerry Conway, Carla Conway, Marv Wolfman, Len Wein, Denis Kitchen, Joe Brancatelli, Tony Isabella.

Benton, Mike. *The Comic Book in America: An Illustrated History.* Dallas, TX: Taylor Publishing Company, 1989.

"Charles Goodman, A Publisher, 55," obituary, *New York Times.* March 3, 1996.

Cooke, Jon B. "Vengeance, Incorporated," *Comic Book Artist.* December 2001.

Daniels, Les. *Marvel: Five Fabulous Decades of the World's Greatest Comics.* New York: Harry N. Abrams, 1993.

Lee, Stan. "'Hello, Culture Lovers!' Stan Lee at James Madison University." Recorded by Jim Dawson. *The Comics Journal.* October 1978.

Lee, Stan, and George Mair. *Excelsior! The Amazing Life of Stan Lee.* New York: Fireside, 2002.

Rovin, Jeff. "How Not to Run a Comic Book Company," *The Comics Journal.* February 1987.

Thomas, Roy. "A Conversation with Artist-Writer Larry Lieber," *Alter Ego.* Fall 1999.

Thomas, Roy. "Roy Thomas on Stan Lee" (letter), *The Comics Journal.* February 1978.

von Hoffman, Nicholas. "Marvel Comics, Astounding!!! Fantastic!!!" *The Washington Post.* December 23, 1971.

CHAPTER 15: BUILDING THE BRAND

AI: Stan Lee, Len Wein.

Beatts, Anne. "Conversation with Stan Lee," *Oui.* March 1977.

Faherty, Tim. "The Amazing Stan Lee Interview," *P.S.* December 14, 1977.

Ferris, Tim. "Spider-Man Meets Pusher-Man," *Rolling Stone.* April 1, 1971.

Green, Robin. "Face Front! Clap Your Hands, You're on the Winning Team!" *Rolling Stone.* September 16, 1971.

Lee, Stan. "How I Invented Spider-Man," *Quest.* July/August 1977.

Millard, Max. "Eastsider Stan Lee," *The East Side TV Shopper and Restaurant Guide.* January 13, 1979.

Penfold, Phil. "Extra Man," *Newcastle Evening Chronicle.* 1976.

Quinn, Katha, and Peter McGowan. "Interview with Stan Lee," *Celebrate Magazine.* December 1976.

CHAPTER 16: STAN LEE, AUTHOR

AI: Stan Lee, Marv Wolfman, Gerry Conway.

Brayshaw, Christopher. "The Monument Carver's Store," *The Comics Journal Library: Jack Kirby.* Seattle, WA: Fantagraphics Books, 2002.

Cooke, Jon B. "John Byrne's Early Marvel Years," *Comic Book Artist.* February 2000.

Gartland, Mike, and John Morrow. "You Can't Go Home Again, Kirby's 1970s return to the 'Snake Pit' of Marvel Comics," *The Jack Kirby Collector.* August 2000.

Lee, Stan, and Jack Kirby. *The Silver Surfer.* New York: Simon and Schuster, 1978.

Millard, Max. "Eastsider Stan Lee," *The East Side TV Shopper and Restaurant Guide.* January 13, 1979.

Wolfman, Ira. "Stan Lee's New Marvels," *Circus.* July 20, 1978.

Zoglin, Richard. "Who Has More Energy than the Hulk? Stan Lee," *Us.* July 11, 1978.

CHAPTER 17: STAN IN HOLLYWOOD

AI: Stan Lee, Will Eisner, Steve Krantz, Lloyd Kaufman, Steve Lemberg, Gerry Conway, Jason Squire, Don Kopaloff.

Beatts, Anne. "Conversation with Stan Lee," *Oui.* March 1977.

Brown, Scott. "Insider-Man," *Entertainment Weekly.* July 12, 2002.

Collins, Thomas. "Comics-to-listen-to Coming on Radio," *Newsday.* November 11, 1971.

Cunningham, Barry. "Pow! Zap! Comics Convene," *New York Post.* July 1, 1971.

Eden, David. "CBS Weaves Its Spider-Man Into Another Schlock TV Hero," *The Detroit News.* April 12, 1978.

Forbes, Victor. "Presenting, the Man Behind Spider-Man, Stan Lee!" *SunStorm Magazine.* February 1978.

Fryxell, David A. "Stan Lee, 24 Hours in the Life of Spider-Man's Creator," *The Ambassador.* November 1979.

Galton, Jim. Cadence Internal Correspondence to Stan Lee. Subject: Universal Deal. December 15, 1976.

Hiltzik, Michael A. "Untangling the Web," *Los Angeles Times Magazine.* March 24, 2002.

Jankiewicz, Pat. "An Interview with Stan Lee," Conducted at Chaffey College. 1985.

Kleinfield, N. R. "Superheroes' Creators Wrangle," *New York Times.* October 13, 1979.

Kramer, Lee. Letter to Ned Tannen. Re: The Silver Surfer. March 10, 1980.

Lee, Stan. Letter to Alain Resnais. May 23, 1979.

Lee, Stan. Letter to Alain Resnais. April 9, 1980.

Lee, Stan. *The Monster Maker* (screenplay). 1971.

Lee, Stan. Speech to the Comic-Book Symposium at the Vanderbilt Forum. Vanderbilt University. April 29, 1972.

Lee, Stan. *Spider-Man: The Motion Picture* (outline). May 1982.

Lee, Stan, and George Mair. *Excelsior! The Amazing Life of Stan Lee.* New York: Fireside, 2002.

Marvel Comics Group, Marketing Objectives. 1973.

Marvel Comics Group, Marketing Objectives. 1974.

Monaco, James. *Alain Resnais.* Oxford, UK: Oxford University Press, 1979.

Plume, Kenneth. "Interview with Stan Lee," Filmforce.ign.com. June 28, 2000.

CHAPTER 18: THE EVIL EMPIRE

AI: Stan Lee.

Benton, Mike. *The Comic Book in America: An Illustrated History.* Dallas, TX: Taylor Publishing Company, 1989.

Bierbaum, Tom. "Stan Lee's Imperfect Heroes Lifted Marvel to Top of Heap," *Variety.* September 17, 1986.

Clemmons, Nelda. "Stan Lee Isn't Too Amused by What's Happening to Comics," *Tampa Times.* August 19, 1978.

Daniels, Les. *Marvel: Five Fabulous Decades of the World's Greatest Comics.* New York: Harry N. Abrams, 1993.

Duin, Steve, and Mike Richardson. *Comics: Between the Panels.* Milwaukie, OR: Dark Horse Comics, 1998.

Groth, Gary. "Pushing Marvel into the '80s: An Interview with Jim Shooter," *The Comics Journal.* November 1980.

Hagen, Dan. "Stan Lee," *Comics Interview.* July 1983.

Kleinfield, N. R. "Superheroes' Creators Wrangle," *New York Times.* October 13, 1979.

Kraft, David Anthony. "Jim Galton, Marvel's Top Man Talks," *Comics Interview.* February 1983.

Masters, Kim. "New World to Buy Marvel Comic Firm," *Los Angeles Daily News.* November 21, 1986.

Thomas, Michael David. "Straight Shooter, an Interview with Jim Shooter," *Comic Book Resources.* www.comicbookresources.com. October 6, 2000.

Thomas, Roy. Letter to Mr. James Galton. April 10, 1980.

Zotti, Ed. "Egad! Marvel Trying for Wham Bam Video Act," *Advertising Age.* October 19, 1981.

CHAPTER 19: STEP RIGHT UP!

AI: Stan Lee, Gary Groth, John Romita, Mark Evanier, Neal Adams, Robert Katz.

Borax, Mark. "Jack Kirby," *Comics Interview* #41. 1986.

Clowes, Dan. *Pussey!* Seattle, WA: Fantagraphics Books, 1995.

Cwiklik, Greg. "The Ringmaster's Importance," *The Comics Journal.* October 1995.

Dean, Mike. "The Fight for Jack Kirby's Marvel Artwork: An Overview," *The Comics Journal Library: Jack Kirby.* Seattle, WA: Fantagraphics Books, 2002.

Ditko, Steve. "An Insider's Part of Comics History, Jack Kirby's Spider-Man," *Avenging World.* Robin Snyder and Steve Ditko, 2002.

Ditko, Steve. "Who Owns Original Art," *Avenging World.* Robin Snyder and Steve Ditko, 2002.

Eisner, Will. "Jack Kirby," reprint of an interview from 1982, *Shop Talk.* Milwaukee, OR: Dark Horse, 2001.

Eisner, Will. "An Open Letter to Marvel Comics," *The Comics Journal.* August 1986.

Groth, Gary. "House of No Shame," *The Comics Journal.* February 1986.

Groth, Gary, Jack Kirby, and Roz Kirby. "'I've Never Done Anything Halfheartedly,'" interview, *The Comics Journal.* February 1990.

Heintjes, Tom, Jack Kirby, and Roz Kirby. "'I'm a Guy Who Never Gave Anybody Trouble,'" interview, *The Comics Journal*. February 1986.

Horrocks, Dylan. *Hicksville*. Montreal: Drawn and Quarterly, 2002.

Kahn, Jenette, Dick Giordano, and Paul Levitz. Letter dated November 19, 1985, *The Comics Journal*. February 1986.

Kirby, Jack. *Mister Miracle* #6. February 1972.

Lafler, Steve. "Stan the Man," *The Comics Journal*. October 1995.

Lee, Stan. *Origins of Marvel Comics*. New York: Simon and Schuster, 1974.

Lee, Stan. *Son of Origins of Marvel Comics*. New York: Simon and Schuster, 1975.

Morrow, John. "Art vs. Commerce," *The Jack Kirby Collector*. April 1999.

Sadowski, Greg. *B. Krigstein Volume I*. Seattle, WA: Fantagraphics Books, 2002.

Salicrup, Jim, and David Anthony Kraft. "Stan Lee," *Comics Interview*. July 1983.

Wardle, Paul. "The Two Faces of Stan Lee," *The Comics Journal*. October 1995.

Wells, Earl. "Once and for All, Who Was the Author of Marvel?" *The Comics Journal Library: Jack Kirby*. Seattle, WA: Fantagraphics Books, 2002.

CHAPTER 20: IN STAN'S IMAGE

AI: Stan Lee.

"Bye Bye Marvel; Here Comes Image: Portacio, Claremont, Liefeld, Jim Lee Join McFarlane's New Imprint at Malibu," *The Comics Journal*. February 1992.

Daniels, Les. *Marvel: Five Fabulous Decades of the World's Greatest Comics*. New York: Harry N. Abrams, 1993.

Dean, Mike. "The Image Story, a Four-Part Series," www.tcj.com. October 2000.

Dean, Mike. "Wolfman Loses Blade Lawsuit Against Marvel," *The Comics Journal*. December 2000.

Gray, Brandon. "X-Men Weekend Breakdown 2000," www.boxofficemojo.com. 2000.

Groth, Gary. "Tarnished Image," *The Comics Journal*. March 1992.

Lee, Stan. *History of Marvel Comics*, Chapters 1–3. Unpublished.

Marvel Entertainment Group, Inc., Appellant v. Brad Elliott, Respondent, New York County Supreme Court. June 7, 1990.

Mougin, Lou. "Larry Marder Interview," *Comics Interview* #142. 1995.

Norris, Floyd. "Two Financiers Cross Swords Over Marvel," *New York Times*. December 28, 1996.

Raviv, Dan. *Comic Wars*. New York: Broadway Books, 2002.

Reynolds, Eric. "CBRI/Other Worlds Confront Image, Comic Shop Owner Takes Image to Task for Aloof Attitude and Breaches of Professionalism," *The Comics Journal*. August 1993.

Reynolds, Eric. "Image Cuts Back," *The Comics Journal*. August 1993.

Reynolds, Eric. "Image Cancels Two Issues of *Spawn*," *The Comics Journal*. July 1994.

Reynolds, Eric. "Industry Sales Records in 1993 Shadowed by Collapse of Speculator Boom, Image Receives Brunt of Criticism for Their Role in Market Crash," *The Comics Journal*. February 1994.

Spurgeon, Tom. "Perelman/Bondholder Battle Heats Up," *The Comics Journal*. March 1997.

Stump, Greg. "Image Adds More Non-Superhero Titles to Its Roster," *The Comics Journal*. February 1997.

CHAPTER 21: MILLIONAIRE ON PAPER

AI: Stan Lee, Peter Paul, Tramm Wigzell, Gary Groth, David Seide.

Berkowitz, Ben. "Stan Lee Holder Peter Paul Flees to South America, According to Cohort's Affidavit," www.Inside.com. March 5, 2001.

Christie, James. "China Rolls Out Red Carpet for Stan Lee," *Red Herring*. August 24, 2000.

De La Cruz, Donna. "Paul Indicted for Stock Manipulation," Associated Press. June 12, 2001.

Dean, Mike. "If This Be My Destiny," *The Comics Journal*. April 2001.

Debaise, Colleen. "Spider-Man Creator Launches Comics on the Internet and the Big Board," *The Wall Street Journal Interactive Edition*. August 23, 1999.

Form 10Q for Stan Lee Media, Inc. Filed May 15, 2000.

Grove, Lloyd. "The Reliable Source," *The Washington Post*. August 17, 2000.

Indictment against Peter Paul, Stephen M. Gordon, Jeffrey Pittsburg, and Charles Kusche. Filed in the United States District Court Eastern District of New York, June 12, 2001.

Lee, Stan, and George Mair. *Excelsior! The Amazing Life of Stan Lee.* New York: Fireside, 2002.

Leeds, Jeff. "Comic Book Site's Co-Founder Indicted," *Los Angeles Times.* June 13, 2001.

Raphael, Jordan. "The Invincible Stan Lee?" *Los Angeles Times Magazine.* July 16, 2000.

Rich, Laura. "The Trials of a Comic Book Hero," *The Industry Standard.* March 9, 2001.

Rosenzweig, David. "3 Indicted by Federal Grand Jury in Check-Kiting Scheme," *Los Angeles Times.* October 26, 2001.

Stan Lee's Employment Agreement with Marvel. November 1, 1998.

Stroud, Michael. "New Superheroes on Wall Street," *New York Times.* August 15, 1999.

CHAPTER 22: STAN THE MAN

AI: Stan Lee, John Romita.

"Diamond Top 50 Sales Report," www.icv2.com. January 2003.

"Top Movie Franchises," www.boxofficemojo.com. December 2002.

CHAPTER 23: EVER UPWARD

AI: Stan Lee.

Dean, Mike. "Stan Lee Sues Marvel for $10 Million," *The Comics Journal.* December 2002.

Diop, Julie Claire. "Comics Legend Stan Lee Sues Marvel," *Newsday.* November 13, 2002.

Lehmann, John, and Dareh Gregorian. "Bitten by 'Spider,'" *New York Post.* November 17, 2002.

INDEX